Comparative
Foreign Relations:
Framework and
Methods

Comparative Foreign Relations Series
Edited by David O. Wilkinson, University of California, Los Angeles
Lawrence Scheinman, University of Michigan

Comparative Foreign Relations: Framework and Methods
David O. Wilkinson, University of California, Los Angeles

The Foreign Relations of the United States
Michael H. Armacost, Pomona College

The Foreign Relations of China
Robert C. North, Stanford University

The Foreign Relations of France
Lawrence Scheinman, University of Michigan

forthcoming:

The Foreign Relations of the United Kingdom
Michael R. Gordon, University of California, Santa Barbara

The Foreign Relations of the Soviet Union
Morton Schwartz, University of California, Riverside

The Foreign Relations of Germany
Peter H. Merkl, University of California, Santa Barbara

The Foreign Relations of Japan
Hans H. Baerwald, University of California, Los Angeles

The Foreign Relations of India
Sudershan Chawla, California State College at Long Beach

The Foreign Relations of the U.A.R. and the Arab Middle East
Jivan Tabibian, University of California, Los Angeles

Comparative Foreign Relations: Framework and Methods

David O. Wilkinson
University of California,
Los Angeles

Dickenson Publishing Company, Inc.
Belmont, California

Library of Congress Catalog Card No.: 78–81340
Printed in the United States of America

Contents

Contents

Acknowledgements

This book owes much to the inspiration provided the author at various times by Stanley Hoffmann and James Rosenau. It could not have assumed its present form had the author not been able to draw upon the work of the Institute for Strategic Studies, of Arthur S. Banks and Robert B. Textor, of Bruce M. Russett and his colleagues, and, in lesser degree, of many others. It would not have been finished before 1975 had it not been for Joe Dana, Dickenson political science editor.

Foreword

The COMPARATIVE FOREIGN RELATIONS SERIES is designed for foreign policy courses that employ a comparative approach, as well as for courses in comparative politics and international relations that survey the foreign relations of key states. Because the basic literature is lacking, few courses today are able to make a genuinely comparative examination of national actors in the international system, in the manner increasingly adopted for the study of domestic politics. This series has been prepared to fill the need for such a basic literature.

The series presents an analytical model and case materials for beginning a comparative study of foreign relations. As a method of studying foreign relations phenomena, comparison allows us to investigate the differences and similarities among states in relation to the international system, and thereby generate or test propositions about the external relations of states.

In order to compare cases, an analytical model or framework should be used—that is, the same set of subjects and questions should be used to arrange and present information about each case. The analytical model of the series is presented in the core volume, *Comparative Foreign Relations: Framework and Methods*, which outlines a framework for describing the international situation and foreign policy of a state, explaining its current policy, analyzing its current problems, and projecting its future problems and policy alternatives. The case materials are presented in the various country volumes, which, following the analytical model, describe and explain the foreign relations of specific important states since 1945 and sketch their main current and anticipated problems.

The books in the series make comparison possible by presenting material of the same nature about each case; however, the actual comparisons must be made by the reader. Some ways in which the series might be used to further the comparative study of foreign relations are presented in the preface to the core volume.

David O. Wilkinson
Lawrence Scheinman

Preface

This book contains the proposal that those who intend to examine the recent and current foreign relations of any state or group of states should go about that examination in a certain way, employing a certain sequence of topics. It therefore presents a framework and some methods for analyzing foreign relations. Such intellectual equipment is sometimes called an *analytical model* and sometimes termed a *theory as a set of questions.*[1]

To give a full analysis of any state's foreign relations, one must *describe, explain,* and *project* its situation and its policy in the near past, the present, and the near future. One must answer the three broad questions: What are its foreign relations like? Why are they as they are? How are they likely to develop? To be able to answer these broad questions, the analyst needs to have them specified further: he needs more and narrower questions. Most chapters of this book consist of just such selected and detailed sets of questions. In addition, some chapters suggest methods of organizing and carrying out the research of individuals and groups who are attempting to find the answers to these broad questions about a given state.

---

[1] See Stanley H. Hoffmann, *Contemporary Theory in International Relations* (Englewood Cliffs, N.J.: Prentice-Hall, 1960), p. 40 for this label; pp. 174–75 for the kind of research program that such a question-theory entails; and pp. 180–81 for sets of questions which have served as starting points for this volume.

Several chapters go so far as to present some hypotheses about the kind of answers that such researchers and research groups will actually find. Thus, this whole book should be read as a proposal—proposed questions and methods, possible answers—that is appropriately dealt with by trying the researches it suggests.

In *describing* the foreign relations of a state, one must investigate its near past and present *situation* and *policy*. Policy is to be viewed as a response to a situation that presents a *challenge* (raises a problem—a threat or an opportunity) for the goals of a state. The key elements of a state's international situation are its *status* (relative "power") and its ongoing *conflicts* with other states.[2] Aside from examining the mere *content* of policy (its goals and means), the analyst is normally called upon to make broad judgments about its *quality* (its coherence, stability, efficiency, realism, farsightedness, and success). Therefore, Chapter 1, "Describing the foreign relations of a state," presents a standardized list of questions on the situation, content, and quality of policy, along with suggestions of how and by what criteria they might be answered.

After the description and judgment of foreign relations comes the task of *explaining* the state's policy: Why is it what it is? This implies that a researcher is going to ask causal questions about his subject: What influences, what main factors must be called to account for the substance of this foreign policy at this time? What in the present and in the past explains why a country does what it does instead of something else? The largest portion of this core volume, six chapters, consists of material for the explanation of policy, and this is not an accident; it is the explanatory portion of the discipline of foreign policy analysis, as it has grown until this time, that is the best developed.

In explaining foreign policy, one must first analyze the effects of (1) *power* or *capability*, and (2) the conscious planning, decision, and *will* of leaders, and its interplay with the inertia of *prescription*, of historical tradition and bureaucratic routine. Residual but important factors include (3) *political culture*, (4) *political institutions*, and (5) *political processes*. Each of these main factors is discussed in a separate chapter; each chapter contains a further set of detailed questions to be asked in explaining the foreign policy of any state, and some chapters also include proposals for the organization of research into such explanation or hypotheses about what the results of such research will be.

After the description and explanation of the foreign policy of a state, queries will naturally arise relating to the state's future foreign relations. The projecting of foreign policy is a subject difficult to grasp, for we must discuss the possible and the probable, not the actual and the historical; we must treat choices yet to be made and developments yet to occur. This book suggests that, even in so insub-

[2] Since to describe a situation is in part to explain policy, extensive examination of the relative "power" of a state is reserved to the section of the book on explanation.

stantial an area, some methodological apparatus can put order into disorderly speculation. There already exists a simple schematic technique of clarifying present policy problems and alternative future policies. This volume examines and amplifies that approach, and suggests how it might be applied to any state's current problems of policy. There also exist various methods of speculating about the course of events in the future history of states and of the world system: this volume presents them as research methods, as techniques that research groups might well employ in projecting policy into the future.

The best use of the COMPARATIVE FOREIGN RELATIONS SERIES is as a stimulus and guide to research. Beginning students should probably employ it in a *problem analysis* or for a policy *description;* those more familiar with the facts of world politics may work into the *comparison* and *explanation* of policy; more sophisticated students may take off into *forecasting* and *theoretical debate.*

1. An analysis of a major problem of U.S. foreign policy (for example, adjusting the general line of U.S. policy toward China) can be done using the background provided by the U.S. country volume (and, in this instance, the China volume), and employing the techniques outlined in Chapter 8 of the core volume. Such an analysis could readily be coupled to two simulations of statecraft: in the first, a single research group would inquire into the problem in a systematic manner, as if the researchers represented a group of statesmen concerned with solving the problem; in the second, alternative policies selected by the researchers would be "gamed" or tested in practice by becoming the instructions for one team of players in a diplomatic game.

2. The very description of some nations' foreign relations is a highly controversial matter: today, this is true for America, France, Russia, and China, among others. Furthermore, time often works a rapid change in the character of a nation's foreign affairs, as new men take office, new crises are weathered, new decisions are made. Finally, many middle and small powers' external relations cannot be described in this relatively small series. Thus, the descriptions presented in this series may be confuted, updated, or extended. The chapters on description in the country volumes provide answers, and that in the core volume provides questions, by which students organized (or self-organized) into a research group that aims to describe the foreign relations of some particular state may be guided; the bibliography of this volume is designed as a research guide, to be of further aid to such students.

3. The comparisons which are required to provide more and better generalizations about the foreign relations of states remain to be drawn. The explanatory sections of the core volume contain several hypotheses; the explanatory sections of the country volumes contain material to which these hypotheses apply. The hypotheses can be "tested" by reading core and country volumes together: where they

fit poorly or not at all, similarities among the country volumes may suggest alternate and superior hypotheses.

4. To debate or update an explanation, or to construct an explanation for the foreign relations of a state not covered in this series, will be both more laborious and more rewarding than to construct a new description. The country volumes contain substantial explanatory material; the core volume has six chapters on the method of explanation, and a research guide and bibliography to provide aid in finding sources.

5. Students of world politics, interested in the anticipation of alternative future worlds (consisting of states' capabilities, conflicts, problems, and policies) might draw on the future-oriented chapter of the core and country volumes to do a projection of the future of the world system. Separate groups might separately project the future situations, problems, and policies of individual states. These projections might then be combined by analysis or by a simulation to provide one probable or several possible futures for the entire international system. Such a "futurible" might then in turn become material for a problem analysis of the policy of some state whose goals are threatened by it.

6. To the theoretically minded, the core volume model will invite appraisal, revision, overhaul, or replacement. It may then stand as a target, a first term in a dialectic: an object to work from, against, and past—to negate, to incorporate, and to transcend.

David O. Wilkinson
University of California,
Los Angeles

Comparative
Foreign Relations:
Framework and
Methods

part one

Describing foreign relations

1

Describing the foreign relations of a state

The description of the foreign relations of a state requires us to inspect both its international *situation* and its foreign *policy*, as they relate to one another. A state's situation conditions its policy; the outcomes of its policies may affect its situation. Broadly speaking, the elements of a state's situation include its international *status* (relative *capabilities* and *influence*), its *conflicts* with other states, and the *problems* which its status and conflicts pose for its goals. But since status is also a portion of the explanation of policy, and since current problems are central to the anticipation of future policy, the main treatment of these features of a state's situation is reserved for Chapters 3 and 8, respectively. This chapter is therefore mainly concerned with presenting a standardized list of questions that will permit the making of orderly judgments about the *content* and *quality* of policy, while recording major elements of the state's situation as well. Situational features are also discussed in the first section of the chapter, which presents a set of types of state *roles* in world affairs, for a state's world role is its general line of policy defined with regard to its status and to its involvement in conflicts.

Some ideal types of role

This section contains a typology of foreign policies, or rather of world roles, that a state might conceivably play in its international environment. Each role is logically associated with certain techniques of foreign policy, certain methods of creating and using capabilities. No state is as likely to be found pursuing one pure role as it is to be vacillating among several, or displaying several tendencies simultaneously; concrete (actual) types of policy are more complex than ideal (abstract) types; the observer of any state's behavior will often have to note the existence of evidence for more than one alternative role. With this warning, a typology such as the following may prove useful for descriptions; if it does, it may also have comparative use.

Certain roles are ordinarily confined to strong states deeply engaged in international conflicts of the moment; others are generally pursued by strong states with no immediate interests in the chief tensions of the day; still others generally are acted by states of lesser rank in the power hierarchy. The international system contains world powers, that is, states with an interest (and with the capabilities that are needed to make that interest felt) in the general world structure and a distribution of values (prestige, status, territory, product, a voice in general settlements, and so forth). It also contains states that, unable to play more than a minor role at the world level, can still take a major part in the drama on one continent or in one of the vaguely defined regions or geographic subsystems of the international system—Southeast Asia, the Middle East, Africa, and so on.[1]

The role typology distinguishes among the roles of *first, second,* and *third parties* in international relations. These positions are defined by the relationship of their holders to the main international struggles of the time, and by the ability of the states in question to pursue independent and self-determined policies. *First parties* are independent powers, of the first rank or below, whose activities produce and sustain the major conflicts (and alignments) of the day. Their roles are defined by their goals and the resistance to them. *Second parties* are lesser powers who act as allies, and whose world role is defined by the kind of relationship which they have to their principal ally. *Third parties* are major and minor powers which stand outside the supreme conflicts of the time, but whose world role is defined by the relation which they have to such conflicts.

This role typology does not distinguish between world roles and subsystem roles, because these are fundamentally of the same types, once it is understood that world powers are *de facto* members of virtually all subsystems, while lesser powers generally have a minor role in the world system, a major role in their own regional subsystems, and perhaps a small part in one or two other geographically contiguous or distant subsystems.

The typology of first-party roles is based upon four further general, ideal-typical distinctions: militant versus reactive policies;

[1] And we should note that, like regional great powers that are world middle powers, world powers normally play roles in their own localities quite different from and even more imposing than those they have in other subsystems of which their great resources and not their geographic nearness make them members.

real policies versus policies of prestige; policies of extension versus policies of defense and policies of counterattack; objectives of political power versus objectives of political order. A *reactive* policy is responsive, and generally hostile, to the initiatives of other states; thus, a state whose policy orientation is basically reactive will appear, when it detects no significant threat to its interests, to have a posture rather than a policy, to pursue "readiness" and "preparedness" without being ready or prepared for anything in particular; it leaves the first move up to others. A *militant* policy, by contrast, is the property of a state with some definite plans for changing the world; it has fixed its goals, analyzed the world situation and the opportunities it presents, counted its resources, and set about doing what it can to get what it wants.[2] The distinction between *real* policies (such as the pair above), and policies of image or *prestige* that mimic them is the difference between substance and shadow. The rhetoric of a policy of prestige is vastly out of balance with the resources behind that policy; great objects are proclaimed, but nothing material is sacrificed for their attainment; politicians and diplomats strike poses and mouth warnings; threats are made without preparations, and alliances without armies; the object of such policies is to provide masses with drama, leaders with attention, and foreign offices with employment. Policies of *extension* and of *defense* need little explanation; they mark the respective responses of the dissatisfied and of the satiated to the discovery that the external environment is full of opportunity, or full of threat. Policies of *counterattack* respond aggressively to a perceived threat abroad, and to a perceived opportunity to reach out to it and destroy it. A state may seek to extend or to defend simply its *power* (status, capabilities, influence, and therefore security) or its realized or idealized political *order*: the gross objectives are easy to attribute, hard to prove, and yet of the highest importance to judge.[3]

Roles of first parties with militant policies

Real, militant, extensive policies directed at objectives of order aim at the creation abroad, normally by export, of an order which is seen as just or useful. When such policies are directed at objectives of power, they seek to increase capabilities, annex territory, extend influence. When pushed to their limit, the first type becomes an

[2] This distinction is likely to be confusing when applied to a pair of states long engaged in bitter conflict. Two states with reactive policies that, through one momentary deviation or misperception, enter a conflict can keep at it as long and vigorously, each reacting to the reactions of the other, as two hostile states with militant policies or one militant and one reactive state. It is probably best in such cases to say that an initially reactive policy has, by gaining momentum, become a militant policy, but this is still not fully satisfactory.

[3] Compare the ideal-type policies of status quo, imperialism, and prestige in Hans J. Morgenthau, *Politics Among Nations*, 4th ed. (New York: Knopf, 1967), Part II.

agitation for world revolution, and the second turns into a challenge for world empire or world hegemony.

Real and militant first-party roles

	Order	Power
Extension of	(Revolutionary and reformist roles) Export revolution Export ideals	(Challenger and imperialist roles) Increase capabilities and/or influence Enlarge sphere-of-influence Annex territory
Defense of	(Conservative and status quo roles)	(Dominant and defensist roles)
Counterattack Against	(Counterrevolutionary and disruptive roles)	(Balancer and anti-Imperialist roles)

Exporting revolution. States that have undergone a great transformation in their political or social constitution, and particularly those states whose transformation was recently achieved through a conscious application of force against prolonged bloody resistance in which foreign states were involved, often evolve a coherent, operational, deeply felt notion of an ideal political order. Active idealism, an angry resentment born of class war and transferred to the foreign friends of the old regime, a comparison of the overthrown old order with that prevalent abroad, fear of a foreign plundering expedition or a foreign-aided restoration all combine and impel the new regime to see if revolutions parallel to its own cannot be predicted, provoked, or aided abroad. The revolutionary leaders, of course, see justice incarnated in themselves and their regime; to replicate it abroad is right, to weaken its enemies is useful. If their idealism fades, inertia, bureaucracy, routine, material interests, or the real *élan* of the foreign proselytes may sustain the policy even so. A policy of exporting revolution needs at minimum one of two instruments: an inspired propaganda and a doctrine of subversion, or a revolutionary army. The first aims at converting some nucleus of intelligent and vigorous men to the resolution to seize power for the new doctrine of justice; the second intends to use the revolutionary state as a base and safe haven, and to exploit weakness or chaos abroad to conquer some foreign state and reorder its politics by force in the interests of the movement. A really devoted revolutionary state will realign all the traditional arms and means of foreign policy—diplomacy, war, probing, intervention, investment, subsidy, occupation, colonial government, subversion, espionage, trade—and the newer ones—mass communication, international

7

and transnational organization, education, and cultural exchange—to foster its political exports.[4]

Exporting ideals and reforms. Revolutionary states grown older, and states undergoing sizable but fairly peaceful political-social transformation, often display a milder version of the policy of extension and export of their own political order. Reformist states are characteristically tolerant of the governments of the foreign states whose politics they are interfering with, and those governments themselves tolerate or welcome the intrusion. The reformist state "pays" the target government with protection, praise, goods, or services, and often trains the native priests, bureaucrats, technicians, agitators, or soldiers who are expected to carry out the foreign ideal. Reformist propaganda appeals for "order and progress," "peaceful transformation," or, in short, nonviolent change gradual enough not to scare off any substantial segments of the old ruling groups.[5]

Acquisition of capabilities; extension of influence. These directly power-seeking policies are usually concealed under slogans of prestige ("rightful place," "place in the sun") and idealism ("national equality," "independence"). Capabilities are increased in order to increase influence and success. The state builds its armed forces, forces its economic development, seeks the newest weapons, imitates the diplomacy of older great powers, and otherwise mobilizes its internal resources to give it greater respect and a louder voice in international affairs. The most substantial means of acquiring lasting influence abroad seems to be rapid, sustained, and independent internal economic growth.[6]

Expansion of a sphere of influence; world dominance. These are extensions of a power-seeking policy. A desire for security, for the prestige of empire, for exploitable economic territory, or for "markets" to which revolutionary doctrine may be "exported," often finds issue in a policy that stakes out a limited foreign area as the sphere within which the expanding power demands exclusive hegemony. The demand of a great state for permanent peace, complete security, total order, or ideal justice may lead it to act as if the entire international system were its legitimate sphere of influence, and to assault other great powers singly or en masse in the interest of its

[4] This is probably a fair description of some part of the external policy of Russia and China—and, despite its capability status, Cuba—in certain periods since their Communist revolutions. How large a part, and at what periods, are specific questions that country-students will try to answer, in order to permit comparativists to generalize about the conditions under which policies of revolution-exporting seem to arise (and to succeed).

[5] Parts and periods of policy of the United States, Russia, and perhaps China, may be described in these terms.

[6] See postwar policies of Russia, China, and Gaullist France.

own paramountcy. States and statesmen following an objectively expansive or world-imperial policy may ignore or repress that fact, and permit idealistic or security-defending intentions to combine with a peculiar situation to steer them onto an unwilled but not unwelcome imperial course. The techniques of expanding power are hardly different from those of conserving it, and employ every instrument from the most subtle diplomacy to the bloodiest warfare: but a state that is involved in more wars, quarrels, menaces, and coalitions than most others of its power rank at a given time usually becomes an expansive rather than a defensive power, whatever its desires; the quantity of conflict transactions, rather than the type, and the quantity of successful conflict transactions are probably the best indicators of an objective drive toward power. Those expansive great states that are involved in all the main conflicts of the day, and that line up most other great states with or against them in serious power struggles, would seem to be objectively on a course toward world dominance, whether they desire it or not.[7]

Irredentism. This policy sometimes takes the more general name of "revisionism," since it is normally associated with an attempt to revise an old treaty of peace, in which the irredentist state agreed under force to disclaim a piece of territory it had formerly claimed or ruled. At any rate, irredentist policies demand the accession of certain "lost" or "national" or "natural" territories (*irredenta*) now possessed by someone else. Irredentist techniques begin with gentle and persistent raising of the diplomatic question, and progress through appeals to international courts and councils for justice, intense agitation and subversive political penetration of the population of the irredentum, military maneuvers and threats, forceful probes and incursions, reaching their climax in guerrilla warfare and open invasion.[8] Irredentism commonly arises when a nationality begins to acquire political consciousness and state organization, only to discover some of its bordering members under alien sovereignty, as well as when the losers of recent wars begin to recover their independence and nerve, or when the losers of ancient settlements begin to grow in capabilities and to read their more sentimental books of national history.

Defensive and counteractive policies. Militant defense or counterattack implies that a state has perceived and has reacted to a long-term challenge to the position it holds. That position may be a sphere of influence that some waxing state threatens to penetrate or

[7] Russia and, some would argue, the United States.

[8] Many modern states have irredenta great and small. Red China has Taiwan (among others, most of the rest being under Russian control); the Republic of China has the mainland. West Germany has East Germany, and East Germany has West Berlin. North and South Korea, and North and South Vietnam, each have each other. Pakistan has Kashmir, the Arab states collectively have Palestine. Japan has claims against the United States and Russia, neither of whom claim any irredenta at this moment.

partition, in which case an active defense means a long plan of consolidation, containing the opponent within the prior limits of his effective hegemony or at least excluding him from one's own. That position may be a political status quo (world, regional, foreign, or domestic), a form of government that seems just and right, or it may be a substantive distribution of territory, wealth, and prestige that represents (to this state) the essence of law and order; "just" government may be under challenge from foreign-based or internationally rootless revolutionary elites or the "lawful" distribution of goods under challenge from an ambitious revisionist state. Or the position under attack may be one of hegemonic or at least great-power status in an international hierarchy, which the revolutionary vigor or the nationalistic power drive of some dissatisfied state threatens to upset. Active defense in all cases implies consolidation, exclusion, and containment. Alliances, military budgets, political attention, mobilized capabilities, all are partially redirected to convince the opponent of the value of self-restraint, or to restrain him coercively if that is needed. With these policies often go certain substantive concessions designed to reward the challenger for limiting his demands, and certain psychological concessions designed to divert his demands into the realm of prestige and status.[9]

Counteractive policies simply move from the orientation of preserving a value to that of destroying a threat. They involve attempts to overthrow or disrupt existing order (rather than to replace it with a new one), or to degrade the capabilities, puncture the influence, or break up the territories of an opponent. Any deliberate nuclear attack today would presumably represent a policy of defense through counterattack. Less extreme counteractive policies include attempts to undermine the influence and neutralize the capabilities of a menacing state by organizing a coalition to put it down by force (the "balancer" role) or by subverting and fragmenting its external or internal structure of authority.

Other roles of first parties: masquerades and reactive defense

Every ideal type of active policy has an ideal fraud that mimics it. Revolutionary export is aped by revolutionary rhetoric, policies of active defense of the status quo by postures. These rhetorics and postures are true policies; they are simply not the policies they pretend to be. They are policies of *prestige*, of image. They are designed to procure psychological gratification cheaply, to satisfy some elite or mass public that wants effortless satisfaction. The pseudorevolutionary statesman shows that he is a man of the revolution by proclaiming its ideals, and reduces the risks of exporting revolution by cutting off funds, arms, troops, inspiration, and other supplies. Masquerade policies are normally to be detected by the

[9] This is the main theme of America's post-1945 world policy, as it is for most NATO allies. It is also, arguably, one key note in Russian and Chinese policy.

disproportion between words and deeds, words and funds, words and force.[10]

Reactive policies of defense of a sphere of influence, of an international power structure, of a foreign political status quo, and especially of the current territory, political structure, political independence, or mere existence of one's own state, are distinguished from active policies by their residual and occasional nature. Most states will take steps to hold on to whatever they have that they value, when such values are openly threatened; most states have frequently to take just such steps; but normally such steps have a short-term character, are immediate responses to immediate and transient threats.[11]

Second-party roles

States that lack the capabilities, tradition, or leadership needed for playing main roles are nevertheless often to be found actively participating in the chief world conflicts of the day as more or less

Second and third party roles	
Second-Party Roles	**Third-Party Roles**
Mediator	Mediator
Provocateur	Provocateur
"Independent"	Neutral
	Isolate

temporary allies of some larger state. As such they too have regular and distinct roles. Three are marked by specific divergence between their goals and the demands of alliance, inner conflicts reflected by ambiguous, vacillating, or complex policies and/or internal struggles.

1. The *mediator* ally is marked by a tension in policy objectives. Its goals in a conflict are to maintain its reputation as a loyal ally and at the same time to reduce and compose the conflict in which its partner is a principal by promoting discussions, suggesting compromises, carrying messages, and opposing precipitate or adventurous operations.[12]

2. The *provocateur* ally is marked by another tension. It seeks to maintain its status while at the same time urging or provoking

[10] French policies of power acquisition, Chinese policies of exporting revolution, and United States policies of exporting reforms all appear to contain large amounts both of reality and of prestige-seeking masquerade.

[11] The same states to be scrutinized for real and active policies of one sort or another ought to be examined for the corresponding masquerades and reactive policies.

[12] Britain and Japan to the United States versus Russia and China; Yugoslavia to the Soviet Union versus the United States, to some degree, during the Khrushchev era.

firmer or more belligerent moves by its larger partner against the mutual opponent.[13]

3. The *independent* ally, again, has ambiguous and conflicting desires. Its status as ally (and therefore the military protection or the economic ties that its partner can supply) and as a weaker partner contradicts its desire to maintain complete national political independence.[14]

Other types are less easily instanced, and may be pure ideal types. The *perfect* ally finds its interest so well protected by its coalition that its full foreign-policy attention abroad can be given to mediating and composing differences within the coalition. The *insecure* ally is confronted by clear and immediate internal or external threats too large to be met with its own resources. Its principal diplomatic effort is devoted to milking its allies, to get those resources or promises that are so vital. The *jackal* state is an ally of the moment in a violent conflict that it joins for immediate material gain. The *nil* ally is too small, distant, weak, or backward to have any but *pro forma* interests or utilities.

States or factions within them may display a succession or a complex of these alliance-attitudes, and the state whose world or regional role is confined to an ally posture can act as a main power in a smaller regional or local subsystem.

A comparative study of many states playing the same role will surely show that there is a logical set of problems and techniques to go with each, and that there is a definable way in which each role can be played very well or very badly; it is this inner logic and rational strategy of each role that will be of special interest to students of foreign policies who look at states in terms of the ideal roles that their actual behavior best approximates.

Third-party roles

States that do not happen or choose to be engaged in the major conflicts of some period as active participants nevertheless have distinctive possible roles. In respect to any particular war or dispute, states may be *mediators*, whose interest and policy are to pacify, compose, placate, and restrain the extreme opponents and to promote compromises and surrenders.[15] In respect to such a dispute, they may be *nonaligned* or *neutral* (actually, not rhetorically) and interested in keeping out of the conflict and maintaining normal relations with all parties,[16] or they may play the role of *provocateur*, promoting

[13] The partitioned states (China, Germany, Korea, Vietnam) to their great-power allies versus their other halves or *their* great-power allies, from time to time.

[14] Periods in the policy of China and France, and even Britain.

[15] Some parts of the policy of India and Yugoslavia regarding the cold war, and of the United States regarding anticolonial struggles.

[16] Many small and underdeveloped states regarding the cold war.

(even instigating) the dispute in order to profit by the mutual preoccupation and weakening of the disputants by undermining the influence of both.[17] A successful policy of neutrality toward and noninvolvement in all international disputes makes a state an *isolate*, a role pleasant to weak states who have little to gain and much to lose from foreign entanglements, or to strong and growing states who do not care to seem threatening to the old established powers they intend to surpass. A consistent policy of mediation of all international disputes is appropriate to weak and idealistic states with no sense of a stake in any given quarrel, and to strong and growing states that seek to appear benevolent rather than threatening to those affected by their growth.

* * *

This abstract, ideal role-typology is a preliminary classification system. It will be useful only in porportion as it helps classify empirical instances or tendencies of state behavior. The more actual cases there are of states behaving in one or another role, the more material there will be for answering questions: What are the characteristic signs that a given role is being played? What sorts of problems, alternatives, decisions, and outcomes are associated with this or that role? What aspects of the international and national systems explain the assumption of a given role by one or another state?

A full test of this role typology would require an extended inquiry. All we need to ask is whether it can be used to describe, summarize, understand, and compare the recent foreign activities of various states, and whether it does these jobs better than they would otherwise be done. If so, it will be useful; if not, it should be replaced, and the progressive discipline of political science will surely replace it.

Requisites of a comparable description

The preceding typology is intended to be tried and used. Its proper trial is as a prod to the kind of research and analysis in which students of comparative foreign relations must necessarily engage: writing, arguing, and defending *comparable* descriptions of several states at a time. Such studies may begin with alternative possible characterizations of the general line of policy of any state, and should hope to end with one complex and defensible characterization. These ideal types may be used in preparing the initial alternatives, and might combine in the complex result. But some further mechanical and procedural guidance is probably in order for those who propose to follow out the program of this chapter by actually going to work and describing some state's foreign policy. There are many fashions in which a descriptive account of the foreign relations

[17] China regarding the United States–Russian controversy; the United States regarding the Sino-Soviet dispute; Russia and China regarding anticolonial and postcolonial controversies.

of a state—its active response to its world situation—can be given, but if the account is given to permit comparison and generalization, it should observe two constraints.

First, the report should appear as a narrative of fairly standard form. This implies that, in making up and structuring each such narrative, the same list of questions, employing the same set of concepts, will have been answered. This chapter, therefore, continues by providing a list of eight sets of questions, whose answers would constitute a uniform picture of the recent foreign relations of any state.

Second, the descriptions must be at a high enough level of abstraction to reveal similarities, induce comparisons, and suggest generalizations. Now, any normal answer to such a standard list of queries will be full of proper nouns, of references to unique persons and events: the Truman Doctrine, the containment policy, Secretary Dulles, the Berlin blockade, the decision to intervene in Korea, the NATO alliance. But for comparative purposes, it is necessary to work with common nouns, and to refer to individual persons and things as if they were instances of a class of items. The problem of moving from a journalist's world of unique people doing incomparable things into a scientific world where every individual is an instance of one or several classes (so that comparison is reasonable and generalizations theoretically possible) is the *typological* problem. No really satisfying typology now exists for the classification of lines of policy. This chapter has already presented a scheme of classification that is intended to have certain comparative use, but it will help in supplying answers to only two of the following eight sets of queries. For generalizations to be made from the answers to the rest of the sets, the students of policy must exert themselves to develop more typologies in the very act of answering the other six sets of questions.

Elements of a standardized historical description

What is the system?
> What are the time-boundaries of the period?
> What is the organizational form of the world system?
> What is the power structure of the world system?
> What is the structure of world conflict?
> What is the durability of the organization, power-structure, and conflict-structure?

What are the state's foreign relations like?
> How important is foreign policy?
> How autonomous is foreign policy?
> What are the objectives of policy?
> What are the rank and the world role of the state?
> What are the main conflicts (and alignments) of the state?
> What have been the key crises and decisions?
> How successful is policy?
> What is the quality of policy?

Time boundaries and main events

The replies to the following pattern of queries about the foreign policy of any state in the post-1945 international arena will provide a report that has the necessary prime quality of *standardization*. Two alterations would be necessary to adapt the question list to apply to foreign policies in some different period. First, evidently, one would need a definition of the time boundaries of the period,[18] along with some good rational grounds for treating this period as representing one coherent phase in the history of the international political system, and the periods immediately adjacent to it in time as representing other distinct phases. Because it represents the end of a general war that radically altered and shrank the membership of the topmost rank of the hierarchy of powers, 1945 seems a reasonable time-boundary marker. A number of events, none of which has yet occurred, could bring to a close a period thus opened: a full settlement, reconciliation, and *de facto* world condominium of the two remaining powers of the first rank, America and Russia; an indubitable achievement and exercise of a position of dominance by either; an equally indubitable achievement of power equality by China, or more remotely by some West European confederation; a new general war with a consequent radical alteration of power relationships.[19]

Second, one would have to extract and picture those key phenomena, at the level of the international system, to which all state members of the system were in that period forced to make some adaptation. To make the separate accounts of state policy economical, these unique systemic phenomena can often be concentrated and labeled. Abstractly, the significant features of any given period in the history of the international system will be (1) the form of organization of the world political system;[20] (2) the world power structure;[21] (3) the structure of world conflict;[22] (4) the durability of each of these structures (and of history, as represented by their sum), durability being the degree of tendency of each such structure (and of the historical period that they mark) to retain or to change its special character. In the absence of a full theory of international politics that describes these typological variables of the international system in detail, the key features of a given period can be concretely and briefly

[18] For example, 1919–39, which is the most commonly accepted dating of the interval between the two world wars, at least among Europeans.

[19] Of course, the application of other criteria than those of power, opposition, and violence—phenomena so preeminent in the study of international politics —would create alternative periodizations, by no means necessarily arbitrary.

[20] With universal empires and collections of independent territorial states forming the clearest organization-types.

[21] With such major types as one-power-dominant or two-great-power worlds.

[22] With such varied types as the single, two-sided, world-polarizing conflict, the conflict with three mutually hostile camps, the struggle of *A* versus *B* and of the *AB* alliance versus *C*, the consistently shifting pattern in which the majority of a collection of states successively opposes one and then another of the collection because it is at the moment the strongest or the weakest.

dealt with. In our epoch, the labels of *cold war, decolonization,* and *dealignment* limn the whole changing systemic order: the collection of territorial states, the bipolar structure, the long but restrained conflict between two military-economic-ideological camps, the almost incidental breakdown of the West European empires, the greater or lesser withdrawal of large areas from the main conflict and the two camps, the rise of China as a secondary principal in the main conflict parallel with its rejection of Soviet leadership and strategy. These are the key systemic phenomena of the post-1945 period, to which all states with foreign policies have adapted. Even if we cannot yet describe the current world political system in the abstract as one of a set of systemic types, we can reasonably require that an account of any state's post-1945 foreign relations describe its response to these key, concrete, world-level phenomena.

Questions for describing foreign relations

Aside from these historical specifics—period and main events—the following question list is constructed around concepts that apply to every state with external relations. Each of these analytical concepts is vital to the notion of foreign policy. Hence, each is examined in some detail to show the usual problems that confront the observer who tries to answer such questions.

   1. External orientation. In the overall national policy of this state, how important is foreign policy (the attempt to deal with and to control the external world) by comparison with domestic policy?

This question contrasts states with different types of priorities, as reflected in the amount of money, number of personnel, and share of leadership time and attention allotted to managing their internal and external environments. The size of the budgets and of the organizations of a state's diplomatic and external defense establishments in proportion to the size of domestic expenditure and bureaucracies provides one measurement; the relative prominence of externally oriented men in the highest councils of state and of foreign-policy themes in public addresses provides another. This aspect of politics has a causal significance; we wonder about its effects because there is a common-sense hypothesis that connects high preoccupation with manipulating the international environment with success abroad, and another hypothesis that foreign preoccupations characteristically cause leaders to lose touch with domestic needs, whose neglect erodes the domestic political support the leaders require to stay in office. In order to discuss such hypotheses in a sensible way, we must have some idea of the cases to which they apply; systematic historical description is one way to identify these cases.

   As phrased above, question 1 could be answered for a very limited period—say a year, since American budgets and other statistics are largely tabulated on an annual basis—or as a quantitative average for the entire chunk of history since World War II. But when we begin dealing with 5-year, 10-year, or 20-year periods, we also want to know (for any variable, not just this one) how its value has changed over time. Did United States foreign policy consistently occupy the same proportion of government time, manpower, and money over this entire period? Or was there a single trend toward more and more (or less and less) attention to foreign policy, or a cyclical rhythm of more, then less, then more? Or a pattern of foreign crisis—suddenly increased attention abroad—then slowly decreasing external attention—then new crisis? Or some other pattern? And why? Any pattern in events that can be found and plausibly explained is possibly of profound, even though perhaps of unpredictable, significance.

2. *Foreign policy autonomy. In the making of overall foreign policy, how much autonomy is there for external considerations?*

In other words, how much control of public opinion, or how much readily available public acquiescence, does the regime have in foreign policy? How fast can policy be changed in response to changes in external parameters, with the confident assumptions that domestic opinion will easily tolerate policy changes? And on the other side, how much delay in effecting major policy shifts is caused by a divided and fractious domestic constituency that is slow to be led and unable or unwilling to shed weak leaders? One looks here for "great debates" on foreign policy that lead to paralysis rather than decision; for shifts in policy persistently attempted and persistently undercut; for abortive regime attempts to mobilize support and resources for a given policy. One looks, on the other hand, for tours de force, changes of front or of allies, startling reversals, military involvements and extrications, and all sorts of maneuvers conceived and performed without effective and substantial internal protest or resistance. A significant hypothesis connects a regime's capacity to act and react swiftly and freely abroad without home difficulties with the chance of its foreign policies for success; again, to verify this piece of political wisdom one must identify the cases to which it should apply.

3. *Objectives. What have been the main goals of foreign policy since World War II? What are they now? What major changes in these goals have there been? When, and why?*

The substance of a country's foreign policy at any moment can best be analyzed as a set of *goals* or *strategic objectives* supplemented by a less apparent set of *tactical objectives,* a set of *policies* or a coherent *general line of policy,* and a set of *commitments.*[23] *Objec-*

23 A deeper and more extended analysis of the policy of a given state will also seek to detect *objects of behavior, long-term goals,* and *fractional interests* governing policy. *Objects of behavior* may be conceived of as the social

17

tives are the particular, limited, fairly stable, conscious and deliberate ends or targets sought by policy at a given moment. Policies and commitments are more concrete. A *policy* is a specific, deliberate course of action for achieving some objective; a *commitment* is a specific employment of resources in support of a given policy. The *general line of policy,* where it exists, is the unifying and overriding strategic imperative that connects area policies (for example, Far Eastern, European) and functional policies (for example, military, economic), and subordinates them to objectives of higher and lower priority, of shorter and longer run.

A state's actual commitments (actual undertakings with troops, money, goods, and materially supported words, whether threats or promises) are one main source for the analyst seeking to specify its policies. Other analytical sources are prior analyses (by academicians and others) and official and unofficial apologies and denunciations (by propagandists, journalists, academicians, and others). Among these sources, actual commitments are of particular value in distinguishing merely verbal rituals from real policies, in revealing policies that are "secret," that is, publicly unacknowledged, and in clarifying just what the priorities among a nation's policies are. And as commitments reveal policies, so specific policies, the general line of policy, the consequences and tendencies of prior policies, and the mass of verbal sources are the materials weighed by analysts trying to define the strategic objectives of a state.

But there is so much argument, concealment, and deceit in the market of world opinion about state policy that an analyst is often justified in presenting two or more conflicting alternative answers to the question "What is the general line of state *X*'s foreign policy?" Observers, apparently competent and without emotional,

---

equivalents to unconscious motives or instinctive drives. An object of behavior is disclosed by an analyst, not conceived by a policymaker; it is the predictable or logical long-run outcome of behavior that is consciously directed at other, short-term objectives. It is the discernible but unintended consequence of activity without much forethought or foresight. It is easier to put together a collective list of objectives and objects of behavior than to discriminate between them, since such discrimination usually involves attempts to read the secret thoughts of men who do their best to conceal them.

Those states with stable governments, bureaucracies, and party systems usually have self-defined "national interests," "permanent interests," "historic objectives," or long-run values, which the changing objectives of successive moments and years are designed to secure. These *long-term goals* may or may not add up to a coherent vision of "the good life" or good world order. Though long-run values may be vaguely conceived, they are of interest to the foreign policy analyst so long as they are operational, that is, so long as they are strategic objectives that seem to have some rank in an actual set of priorities, some place among the often conflicting objectives that are constantly reconciled in decisionmaking, some role in the adjustment of strategies. But they are often so hard for the analyst to discern, clarify, and map in their relation to one another and to daily decisions that he may have to settle for the partial picture of policy that he can infer from a state's actual use of force and threats, and its delivery of money and materiel.

Policy is frequently deflected by the *fractional interests* of influential persons and groups. Special private interests (personal, sectional, economic, religious, partisan, ideological) that divert public policy are sometimes evanescent, sometimes deeply embedded in political institutions and processes.

official, or ideological commitments, have disagreed radically about the answers to such questions. Foreign-policy students without governmental duties are not under intense pressure to provide one definitive answer to such deep questions. When evidence equally supports or equally fails to support conflicting answers, or when any answer can be given only on the basis of some empirically weak or unverifiable assumption, an analysis that presents several contrasting pictures of X's real objectives and general line, along with the strengths and weaknesses of each picture, is a reasonable one.

4. *Status and role. What is the position of this state in the world power structure? What is its world and local capability and influence rank? Does it act as a first party, a second party, or a third party in the world system and in the subsystems of which it is a member?*

The description of a state's role has already been treated. The description and analysis of its status is discussed in Chapter 3, under the rubric of "rank," which is employed primarily as an explanation of policy. Generalized descriptions should at least sketch the ranks and roles of the states described, without which the other aspects of their situations will have little significance.

5. *Conflict and cohesion. What have been and are now this state's major conflicts and tensions; with whom; over what? What relations have its special objectives and conflicts had to the main systemic conflicts of this period? What blocs, alliances, and alignments has it joined, avoided, or left? Why, for what goals, and with what effect?*

The international system can be pictured as a set of actors with policy objectives and lines. But the objectives of some states cannot be achieved without frustrating other states, so the system can also be depicted as a set of tensions among mutually incompatible goals. The policies of all states therefore contain a persuasive-and-coercive element that strives to resolve tension by transforming other recalcitrant, hesitant, reluctant, slow, or hostile states into objects that perform properly in the eyes of the subject state. Every relation between two states contains two opposed manipulations. Generally, for any state at any time, a few of these manipulative relations occupy most of its time and resources and constitute its major conflicts of the moment. A state's major conflicts are often easier to discern at any moment (because they involve commitments of verbal, material, and psychic resources) than the exact underlying tension of objectives; hence, visible conflicts provide a clue to the character of less visible objectives. Relations of conflict must be specified in any account of a state's policy, because they have characteristically been the relations most significant in terms of consequences for the power and values of states and for the structure of the international system.

To construct a coherent sketch of the role of a given state in the world system, one must display the fit of the particular objectives and struggles of that state into the most important systemic conflicts of the time. No post-1945 foreign policy can be described without reference to the state's alignments (or nonalignments) over time with respect to the cold war, the colonial question, and the struggles to break up the cold-war blocs. A state's position on these issues, and on others of global concern, largely accounts for (and is partly described by) its associations, transitory or lasting, with other states for the achievement, through conflict, of common goals. These associations should therefore be described with respect not only to a state's objectives in entering and maintaining them and to a state's losses and gains realized in them, but also as if the coalitions had lives of their own largely subordinate to the conflicts that they engender, sustain, or reflect.

6. *Crises and decisions. How have this state's conflicts and tensions expressed themselves in major foreign policy crises and decisions? What values have been at stake in each crisis, what goals gained and costs incurred by each key decision? Which such decisions have been controversial? Doubtful? Notably successful or unsuccessful?*

Just as a line of policy breaks down over time into a succession of concrete commitments, so a relation of conflict appears in historical action as a succession of concrete crises embedded in the general tension. One model of the stages of development of a crisis—and probably the model most often applicable—begins the crisis with one state's decision to use new means to force a favorable resolution of a conflict, continues through a volley of decisions and counterdecisions in which all parties make new commitments of material and nonmaterial resources to assure a favorable outcome, and ends with one state's decisions to postpone or abandon most of its designs, cut its losses, and pull back its resource commitments. A specific descriptive account of a state's foreign relations in a given period therefore properly moves from the general to the specific by breaking down conflicts into crises. Crises in turn can be broken down into goals at issue, decisions to act, decision-forcing consequences of these decisions, and outcomes obtained in the crisis. The inner clashes that take place over great decisions and the outcomes of such decisions are major clues to the *quality* of foreign policy, a judgmental and controversial matter intimately related to the question of *content*.

7. *Outcomes. Which overall policy goals have been secured or retained, which missed or lost? Why were the latter lost? Bad judgment, bad luck, impossible circumstances?*

Decisions succeed or fail; goals are reached or missed. Or so we might like to believe; history is ambiguous. There are degrees of success and failure, more and less, clear and obscure. But where the observer sees (or thinks he sees) a signal gain, and even more when he notes a patent loss, he is under a rational obligation to describe what he sees and to account for it. The state that has suffered the loss may have done so because its targets were beyond what its powers and resources gave it any reasonable hope of reaching; because its leaders and political organization disposed of that power, those resources, inefficiently; or because resources that would normally have been adequate, managed by a policy that should normally have been sufficient to its aim, encountered an unforeseen and rationally unpredictable and irreversible check, a strategic surprise. The first two cases constitute bad policy; the third excuses it. If and when the observer finds instances that he believes to fit clearly, even neatly, into one or another of these slots, he can contribute best to the descriptive debate on policy by providing reasons (containing empirical evidence and purged of rhetoric, emotive judgments, and logical or semantic frauds) that elucidate the general character of this specific surprise or impolicy and that illustrate the general character of surprise and impolicy *per se*.

8. Quality. What, in the broadest terms, is and has been the quality of national policy? Can we call it broadly efficient *or inefficient? How* coherent *and orderly or confused and inconsistent is it? How* stable *or transient is it in stable circumstances, how* adaptable *or rigid in change? How far is it* realistic—*has it sought to secure, and has it secured, power adequate to the pursuit of its goals, or has it prudently restricted its goals to the compass of the available capabilities? How far is it* long-sighted *in its anticipation of future threats and opportunities, and of the remote consequences of current acts?*

If we judge a policy to be efficient, we mean to say that its authors have shaped, directed, and ordered their capabilities in the service of their goals, rather than ignoring, wasting, or squandering their resources or misdirecting them towards ends of lesser priority. If we judge a policy to be coherent, we mean to say that its well-known objects and priorities are conscious and clearly related, generally consistent, and ranked or balanced when not consistent. A stable and adaptable policy changes for good and real reasons rather than as a result of internal power struggles. Policy is rigid when its failures do not lead to the application of new capabilities, to patience based on a reasonable projection of opportunities ahead, or to an attempt to seek new and more attainable goals; it is adaptable when new and real threats and opportunities are promptly met and swiftly seized.[24]

---

[24] The analysis of quality ought to be, though judgmental, both factual and rational rather than emotive. To judge without evidence, without criteria, without reference to a notion of quality and rationality of universal scope, or without an attempt to assess what was controllable, what was impervious to control, and what was purely contingent in the situation of the actor under study, is to imitate bad politics, even to enter it, and not to understand it.

At this point in the argument, we had better pause and take thought. The analytical questions here proposed—the last three in particular—must themselves be questioned. They are of direct political significance; they are judgmental, controversial, resistant to empirical and consensual replies, liable to be answered according to the observer's personal bias. They venture into realms that political scientists have been inclined to abandon to political journalists. But if no rational answer can in principle be given to the questions "Was this policy a failure? Was it a failure because it was a bad policy?" then the study of policy and of politics has value only as an entertainment. The method and standards for arguing these matters well and with discrimination are but poorly known. But still, as I believe that the study of politics has a practical use, I judge that such notions as "failure" and "bad policy" have some meaning and some determinability. Only in the asking and answering of these questions will an explicit method be developed for asking and answering them well. The first such answers (and questions) are therefore foredoomed to obsolescence, if they evoke better analytical modes: a trivial cost.

Conclusion

The initial sources for an inquiry beginning from nowhere are, properly, polemical and journalistic, as well as scholarly and journalistic. The scholarly books on a nation's policy, the articles in the journals of world affairs and of academic political science or area studies, will contain their share of assessments and of evidence. They should be supplemented with a full ration of what the government (in its leaders' speeches and official documents and press), its various opposition parties and factions (in speeches and interviews), and journalistic commentators (in the national and foreign press) claim and judge to be the case. These sources will never substitute for careful reflection, but they may provoke it.[25]

Joint research into the description of a state's policy has its usual advantage here. When researchers discover that there is seldom a shortage and usually a tremendous surplus of opinions and evidence about the content and quality of any state's policy, they may usefully organize themselves around the differences of opinion that appear within their group (rather than the many more differences that will appear in their sources), to argue, according to jointly understood concepts of evidence, toward a single conclusion about content and quality, or toward explicitly defended alternative conclusions with some agreement on the significance of accepting each and on the evidence (if any) that would be decisive for the acceptance or rejection of each. It may be that an individual will understand daily events and acts of state better if he has several alternative notions of what each great state is or may be doing than if he is willfully confined to one notion or ignorant of all others.

[25] For a list of sources, see the Research Guide and Bibliography to this book.

part two

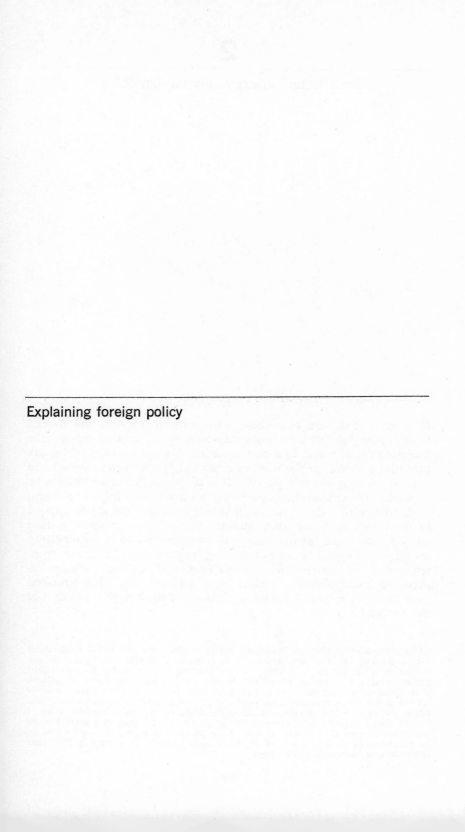

Explaining foreign policy

2

Main factors in explaining foreign policy

It is suggested here that those who want to explain the overall foreign policy of any state, once they have described that policy, take a certain set of steps, in a certain order. A large number of factors potentially useful for the work of explaining have been collected and grouped as chapters in Part Two. It is proposed that these factors be applied to the explanatory task in the groups those chapters present, and, further, that the chapters (that is, the factor groups) be applied in the *order* in which they appear there. The suggestion is that inquiry into some factors will yield more results than inquiry into others, that *capability* (or power) factors rank first, *"will"* (or "consciousness" or "leadership") factors next, and *residuals*, stabler aspects of sociopolitical structure and history, last. This proposal embodies a hypothesis—really, a guess—and the hypothesis is that of the author.[1]

---

[1] The Comparative Foreign Relations Series model does not itself rank these factors in any order of importance. It is eclectic; it allows each country-book author to select for analysis those factors that he sees as especially significant for explaining the foreign policy of his own subject country. But I do believe that there is a certain rank-ordering among these factors; that *generally speaking* the world role and state behavior of any country is accounted for best when we look at the general list of explanatory factors in a certain order. I believe that a hypothesis can reasonably be presented, alleging that some factors account for more of national behavior than others and therefore belong first in an examination of such behavior. My hypothesis weights the factors in the order of explanatory strength given above.

Power/weakness

The hypothesis is that any country's world role over any period is first and best accounted for[2] in terms of its *capabilities*.[3] Relative to the rest of the world of states, these capabilities determine its stature in the systemic hierarchy of powers of the time. Strength in capability-resources (whether of material goods or of prestige) makes ambitious projects feasible and increases their chance of success; weakness constrains, restrains, and limits choice and independence. If the hypothesis is correct, the contrasts between the behavior of great and small powers should be, on the whole, more significant than any other kind of contrasts in state behavior. A state's position in the international power structure, according to this hypothesis, is the strongest environmental or international-systemic influence on state behavior. (See Chapter 3 for further details.)

Will and prescription

The hypothesis continues: The next best explanation of why a country's world role is as it is at any time lies in the nature of its *political leadership*. Vast differences will be found *between* and great similarities *within* two ideal classes of states.[4] One such class will be distinguished by the presence of a conscious, policy-controlling will,[5] the other by its absence. The hypothesis is that the more one finds of this kind of hostile, dynamic leadership, the more its nature and peculiarities explain policy, while the less one finds of such "will," the more one will be able to explain policy by referring to traditions, history, and stable bureaucratic habit. Conversely, abrupt shifts of policy should more often than not coincide with the presence or appearance of a leadership of this kind.[6] (See Chapter 4.)

[2] But see below (pp. 28–29) for the question of the impact of the international system as an environment.

[3] Capabilities are, of course, not merely material. Material resources are, however, easiest to measure, and over a long period of time provide the best index of which powers are "great" and "greatest." The hierarchy of material power may be grossly constructed by comparison of military budgets, population, arable national territory, national income, gross national product, energy production, steel production, military personnel, trade, and such statistics as *per capita* energy production and energy production times population. Once such a hierarchy of material power has been provided for any period, it can be corrected for nonmaterial influences by examining the behavior of any high-ranking set of states to see which other states these materially strong actors treated as equals.

[4] These two ideal classes represent poles of a real continuum.

[5] *Will* implies dissatisfaction, innovation, negative affect (hostility), strong motivation, and high activity. It could be measured in part by the relative amount of conflict behavior initiated and carried out against opposition, in part by the contents of leaders' communications about foreign policy.

[6] "Ideologies" and "principles" of policy are often *constructed* by dissatisfied leadership, which controls and manipulates them; the tools of a conscious leadership often become the traditions and habits of a routinized leadership as time passes.

Residuals

This category includes such elements as *political institutions, political culture,* and the style of the domestic *political process.* The hypothesis is that, after the capability-explanation is employed, and if the will-explanation is weak,[7] these factors adequately explain the remaining individual policies and resemblances of policy among states—and that there is no special order of primacy in explanatory power among these elements. (See Chapters 5, 6, and 7.)

This hypothesis can be subjected to a preliminary test by readers of the Comparative Foreign Relations Series and to a more developed test by students of foreign policy who use the series as a research tool—the core volume as a proposal to apply certain questions to certain sources, the country volumes as illustrations of how previous workers have used this proposal.

The preliminary test is as follows. If the formula that explains policy first by state power, then by the condition of the independent will of the political leadership, and then by other residuals is a sound one, then certain states' foreign policies ought to be most obviously comparable. Those states that at a given moment in time are closest to one another in capability ranking *and* most similar in terms of leadership will and routine ought to have policies that are more like one another, on the whole, than like other states' policies. The similarities and differences of policy[8] should be largely attributable to similarities and differences in these two factors.

The more extended test is of a different form. It requires the formation of a working research group of students of foreign policy, the selection of a single state for study, the description of its foreign policies since 1945 (see Chapter 1 for methods, and the relevant chapters of other volumes in the series for illustrations of such description), and finally an attempt to explain these policies.[9] According to the hypothesis presented above, the most direct and easily understood causal relationships will emerge if research workers begin by trying to explain policy by capability, turn next to the character of leadership, and turn last to those institutional, processual, cultural, and historical factors here called *residual.*

The international system

One might argue, and it has been argued, that the explanatory factor most powerful in accounting for any state's policy is really the

---

[7] That is, if goals are heavily influenced by tradition and history, rather than by decisionmakers largely free in mind from the restraints of the past.

[8] See Chapter 1 for the kinds of similarities and differences that are being talked of.

[9] Preferable for such a test would be a state whose capabilities, leaders, *and* foreign policies have all changed markedly several times since 1945: in any case, the point is not to select a state that is stable in all three respects, since that would permit no striking internal contrasts.

condition of its environment—the international system. To look at the capability of a state is, however, to look at its status as a power among powers, and thus to look at the international system from a certain perspective. This hypothesis and the Comparative Foreign Relations Series model thus escape the accusation that they read foreign policy exclusively as a product of internal factors. Nonetheless, it is true that we might directly and systematically have discussed the differential impact on state policy of power status in a global or regional power structure of many equals, as contrasted to the impact of power status in a structure where there are one or two inordinately powerful states. Perhaps only limits on time, space, and ingenuity prevent it; but it seems probable that extended empirical analysis of systemic impact on state policy within one systemic phase (as that since 1945) should await much further elaboration of abstract and comparative studies of the international system.

This partial neglect of the influence of the system is only admissible so long as we are explaining the policy of one state, or comparing the policies of several states, within what can reasonably be called the same phase or structure of the international system. If we were to attempt the vastly more ambitious task of constructing some general theory of foreign policy or of comparative foreign relations, then the character of the international system (its unification, polarity, uniformity, power stability, war-proneness, characteristic violence, and systemic stability) would probably have to come first on the list of explanatory factor groups; correspondingly, future researchers will probably find very large simultaneous alterations in the roles and policies of many states at a time of phase-change in the international system. But since World War II we have seen more than 20 years of a multistate, bipolar, heterogenenous[10] system, with no general war and a constant real possibility of one, with the same two key powers, with recurrent regional crises and limited wars, and with a broad spectrum of plausible interstate violence whose most destructive levels are most carefully prepared for and whose lower levels are most frequently used. Despite fluctuations in alliance and bloc patterns (not so radical as has been supposed), it is reasonable to count this period as a single phase in the history or development of the world political system. When we deal with the policies of states in this period, it becomes reasonable to assume that some systemic influences are held constant within a single phase of the system, and that others are represented by the differentiation of states according to their power status in the system.

Chapters 3–7 are organized in order to be useful for individual and group research purposes. Every effort has been made to give these chapters a research-promoting approach, where questions are presented instead of answers, hypotheses instead of conclusions,

[10] Aron's term, implying that the actors in the system "are organized according to different principles and appeal to contradictory values." Raymond Aron, *Peace and War*, trans. Richard Howard and Annette Baker Fox (Garden City, N.Y.: Doubleday, 1966), p. 100.

schemes rather than results of inquiry. It is perhaps normal practice to present a topic, weigh diverse opinions thereon, and arrive at some balanced judgment of these opinions. But the attempt here has been to present a topic, break it into segments for analysis, ask the questions that researchers must ask, and suggest some possible answers that are neither endorsed nor rejected. This book is intended to be incomplete; its reader will gain nothing from it unless he completes it for himself by applying it, in comparative reading of the country volumes or in his own research.

These chapters have therefore been roughly shaped to the following plan.

1. A list of factors—capability, institutional, cultural, and so forth, as appropriate to each chapter—that are generally of importance in explaining the content of the foreign policy of any state, or its qualities of stability, adaptability, coherence, efficiency, and power-adequacy.
2. Explication of the meaning of each such factor, and a set of questions to be asked in analyzing each country for each factor.
3. General hypotheses about the importance of each such factor in any country.[11]

The more typological the factors in any chapter, the easier it is to proceed from factors to questions to hypotheses, and the more schematically they can be treated. This is the case with Chapter 6, "Political institutions," in particular.

Certain overlaps between these chapters have been inescapable; two of the most important will be noted at this point.

1. High V phenomenon (Chapter 4), a homogeneous political culture (Chapter 5), high executive dominance of foreign-policy decisions and bureaucracy, supercontrol of the foreign-policy bureaucracies, totalitarian regime, high stability of leadership tenure, low *personalismo,* and high charisma (Chapter 6), speedy decisional style, efficient political communication, high social homogeneity, high social modernization and political mobilization, and low external penetration (Chapter 7), all other things equal, would appear to add to the *capacity for collective action;* therefore, they affect capabilities (Chapter 3), as well as directly influencing the content and quality of policy.
2. A strong degree of the V phenomenon (Chapter 4) very frequently involves an elite and homogeneous relevant political culture (Chapter 5), a strong-to-totalitarian executive, a ruler-

[11] These are not intended to form a coherent theory, but rather to display many possible generalizations, not excluding theories, guesses, prejudices, and gross fallacies; they may number more than one—all perhaps mutually inconsistent —on each factor. The general null hypothesis (to the effect that some factor is in general of no importance in explaining the contents or quality of foreign policies) will be liberally employed, with the intention of stimulating argument and deliberate formulation of contrary generalizations by readers.

dominated or supercontrolled bureaucracy, an authoritarian or totalitarian regime, elitist leadership recruitment, high leadership charisma (Chapter 6), speedy decisional style, and interest articulation primarily by individual members of the elite (Chapter 7).

It should also be remarked that certain topics that might have been treated separately and explicitly are instead divided or dealt with only by implication. *Nationalism* in the sense of a population's concept of itself as a community is dealt with as cultural (Chapter 5) and social (Chapter 7) homogeneity; in the sense of a population's spirited unity it is handled under the head of capacity for collective action (Chapter 3); in the sense of conscious or routinized objectives and dispositions to act of the ruling groups, it is an aspect of will and prescription (Chapter 4). *Ideology* in general is similarly handled under what seemed to the author the apter rubrics of will and prescription (Chapter 4) for rulers, and political culture (Chapter 5) for the larger political class. The impact of the *external environment* is, as already stated, considered as focused in the area of capabilities (Chapter 3), although it is also represented by the structured perceptions of that environment by the political class (Chapter 5) and the ruling groups (Chapter 4). Finally, *political leadership* factors are divided between those to be studied as personality characteristics of a few leaders (Chapter 4) and those that are statistically modal characteristics of the occupants of a large number of less significant bureaucratic roles (Chapter 6).

3

Capability

The issue in this chapter is how, and how far, it is possible to explain the foreign policy of a state by its capabilities.[1] Explaining policy in terms of capabilities means accounting for policy objectives by referring to a state's own consciousness of those capabilities, attributing tactical lines of policy to the specific capabilities that the state does and does not have, and explaining the outcome of a "power struggle"[2] or "control contest" as a result of the relative capabilities of several states involved in the conflict.[3] The chapter begins with an analysis of the main factors of power: the geo-demographic resource base; the military, economic, and political means (capabilities) of taking action to influence others; and the political and socio-psychological capacity of a state's population for collective action. Special attention is given to the types of military means required for high influence in the contemporary world system, and to the meaning of *war* as a condition in which a new "balance of power," grounded upon a

[1] The more traditional term is *power*. The use of the term *capabilities* is here correlated with a focus on *relatively* material, changeable, measurable, and manipulable forms or factors of state power—military and economic means, in particular.

[2] This phrase, more familiar than the next, unfortunately connotes a struggle for capabilities rather than for the achievement of resisted objectives in general.

[3] Employing such explanations does *not* imply that all foreign policy objectives and lines and outcomes are determined exclusively by the amount and distribution of material power.

multiplication of the kinds of capabilities that may be used to attain influence, comes into being. Economic means are analyzed in terms of their flexibility of use.

The general relationship of capability to policy is then examined at some length. The contemporary world "power structure" is sketched, along with the connections between a state's capabilities and its world influence; the specific effects of several states' capabilities upon their policies is then analyzed. Some broad hypotheses about the impact of capability upon policy are suggested and lead to proposals for needed research on the topic of power and policy. The chapter concludes with an outline explaining how it may be used to research the relation of capability to policy in any state.

Factors of state power (base, means, capacity): a checklist

The following categories may be taken to constitute the elements or determinants of power, largely reassembled and organized from other such classifications.[4] They are therefore conventional, if not traditional, for the most part. They constitute a filing system, or rather a checklist. Anyone examining the strengths and weaknesses of one state, or comparing the relative power of two states, can use such a list to structure his assay or comparison.

1. Geo-demographic base

a. Spatial. Surface and dimension of the territory, location and strategic position of the state, types of frontiers, power and attitudes of neighbors, and geo-technological distance from other powers' military reach

b. Material. Dimension and fertility of arable land, natural resources of energy and raw materials

c. Populational. Size, density, ethnic homogeneity, cultural and educational level, and distribution of technical and organizational skills

2. Military-economic-political means

a. Economic. Total production (Gross National Product), **per capita** production (**per capita** GNP), industrial production, heavy industrial production; total revenue and expenditure of central government, government spending as a percentage of GNP, defense expenditure as a percentage of GNP, private consumption

---

[4] See Raymond Aron, *Peace and War*, trans. Richard Howard and Annette Baker Fox (Garden City, N.Y.: Doubleday, 1966), pp. 52–55.

as a percentage of GNP; gross domestic capital formation, value of accumulated national capital, annual growth of GNP and **per capita** GNP; level of development of the whole economy, of the financial, commercial, industrial, and technological sectors, and of international trading and technological relationships of dominance, subordination, independence, and interdependence

b. Military. Total defense expenditure; independence or dependence of military structure on foreign trade and aid; number and quality of soldiers; quantity, quality, and type of weapons and systems of combat; quality of military organization and discipline

c. Political. Government expenditure for foreign aid, foreign service, foreign information, foreign intelligence, foreign political penetration and support of factions, forces, and movements; quality of operational organizations and of systems of political strategy

3. Capacity for collective action

a. Social. Degree of social integration, national cohesion, popular unity, social organization, institutional flexibility, solidarity, and social discipline

b. Moral or psychological. National character, morale, spirit, inventiveness, flexibility, perseverance, and adaptability

c. Moral and political. Quality of command, diplomacy, bureaucracy, policy, and rule

The policy impacts of base and capacity factors

Not all of these factors of power are to be studied in the same way, and only some of them will receive much further examination here. This chapter will concentrate on military and economic means, with some references to the less visible political capabilities of states. It will be difficult to go at all deeply into the question of the effects (or the study) of geo-demographic base, and of capacity for collective action. The results of the first express themselves indirectly, the second can hardly be judged except qualitatively, broadly, *ad hoc*, and ex post facto.

This does not imply that the geo-demographic base or the capacity for collective action are unimportant: in China, for instance, grave fluctuations in the capacity for collective action have recently accounted in part for many policy failures, while China's geo-demographic base is vital in understanding why the long-term fear of China so apparent in certain states' Far Eastern objectives exists even among very prudent or sympathetic statesmen. But except for very long-run considerations (such as bulk large in all China policies), the influence of the geo-demographic base on policy is mostly indirect and expressed through the military-economic material complex, and the fluctuations in this complex are more immediately significant than the slower fluctuations of geodemography.

Base

There is one basic generalization that links the base complex of geographic and demographic factors with the means complex of military and economic capabilities: the larger the material and populational base, the greater the long-term potential economic capability of the state.[5] Thus, a brief examination of the crudest statistics will soon convince us that the low levels of development of the large base complexes of China, India, Brazil, perhaps Indonesia and Pakistan, and even of the Soviet Union make their long-term economic-capability potential much greater than their current actual economic capability. This in turn leads one to consider them as having a very long-run power status much higher than their current high or low rank.[6] The sense that this is so could influence, and in some cases has influenced, the long-term objectives of their policy; the desire to entertain ambitious objectives in the future in some cases has occasioned the postponement of immediate attempts to secure long-run goals, so as to permit concentration on the growth that may secure those goals in the distant future. Thus, a very large base complex, and a potential of military and economic capabilities much larger than those actually now possessed, may promote long-term planning and a shift in foreign policy concerns away from immediate gratification.[7]

Capacity

The capacity for collective action undergoes certain radical and evident transformations. China, for example, has swung from extreme incapacity to extreme capacity on more than one occasion since 1945; France showed a steadily decreasing capacity in the 1950s until the Gaullist regime strongly reversed the deterioration; the United States has had some rather notable drifts, with its limit of

[5] By contrast, the higher the levels of economic development and output, the higher the middle-term potential military capability; the higher the current military and political capabilities and the capacity for collective action, the higher the general short-term status of the state is likely to be. (Other things, in turn, become probable and possible results of status; see below).

[6] The Canadian economic potential might be similarly enormous, if Canada's population matched its material base.

[7] Many Westerners are quite unable to sympathize with, to visualize, or even to conceive of very long-term goals and planning. Consider, though, the recent history and the scope of economic planning in the Soviet Union, China (at some times), and perhaps India.

incapacity perhaps reached in 1951–52, and of capacity perhaps in 1947–48, 1962, or 1965; Britain has declined significantly, unsteadily, and slowly in capacity since 1945; Russia has generally maintained a high capacity, with lows during severe collective-leadership crises or power struggles and highs during periods of near-monarchy.

Since these transformations have explanatory value, they cannot be overlooked, but this capacity segment of power is difficult to examine in detail for any country except from the inside and long after the fact; and, being nonmaterial, its more delicate changes are difficult to sense, let alone to measure and compare. We must be content with saying that there are some gross and apparent changes over time in the collective capacity of any state to act. If such change exists, it has causes; perhaps it can then be controlled. And it would be significant it if could be controlled, for a high capacity for collective action permits the rapid mobilization of the geo-demographic base to increase economic capabilities; it permits heavy appropriation from economic capabilities for the maintenance, improvement, and application of military and political means; and it makes the effective application of those means more possible and more likely.[8]

Means or capability factors, 1:
contemporary military capabilities and their
impact on policy

Conflict and the use of coercive force to deter, contain, and win conflict and implement policy are characteristic features of politics as we know it. In modern world politics, where there exists nothing approaching a world state, world law, a monopoly of coercive force, a consensus on justice, or a political order generally recognized as legitimate, military means are central to the attainment of goals by most states. Their presence or absence, level, and quality directly affect policies, whether those policies seek to attain, use, maintain, or restrict military means. They are of prime importance in any calculus of relative state power. It is no accident that the most influential states today are the greatest military powers, rather than the greatest moral powers; nor is it a coincidence that such centers of moral influence as France and China are also great military powers, and seek to become greater. And it is not by mistake that charismatic leaders of weak states (for example, Castro and Ho Chi Minh) with foreign ambitions have sought to develop means of military action

---

[8] For further material in other chapters relevant to the capacity of a state for collective action, see page 30. The size, scope, functional differentiation, cultural secularization, rationalistic mentality, technical competence, instrumental good-functioning, organizational coordination, and central control of a modern bureaucracy are perhaps the prime factors in the capacity for collective action of states today.

that will turn their physical weaknesses to strength and the strength of the great powers to weakness. In the detailed scrutiny of the consequences of capabilities for policy, the consequences of military capabilities should be studied first of all.

But today there are at least three radically different kinds of military capabilities that states may have, capabilities that draw on different kinds of technology and have vastly different costs. They are useful for very different purposes, and states that are very weak in one of the three areas are at times very strong in another. The new dimensions of warfare in the post-World War II period therefore require that these three levels of military capabilities be considered at some separate length: nuclear forces, "conventional" forces, and "people's war" (insurgency, guerrilla warfare, counterinsurgency) forces.

Nuclear force capability

The hardware of nuclear capability has shifted in 20 years from aircraft with atomic bombs to missiles with warheads; the facility necessary to qualify as a first-class nuclear power can now be termed "a (first and) second-strike countervalue deterrent." Two states, America and Russia, now qualify as first-class nuclear powers. Three (Britain, France, and China) have dependent, inadequate, or primitive nuclear capabilities, and at least France and China aspire to the first rank. But first nuclear rank today does little enough good for those who have it. The fact of nuclear stalemate, plus a still general and prudent unwillingness to accustom the world to the use of nuclear weapons, makes the positive utility of these "ultimate" weapons extremely limited.

It is less important to detail the particulars of modern weaponry than to note that central-war (nuclear) forces now cost the United States about $7 or $8 billion a year to maintain; that such an expense is less than 10 percent of the GNP of Germany, Britain, France, Japan, and, probably, China, and that estimated defense expenditures in the vicinity of 10 percent of GNP are not unknown for the United States and the Soviet Union, among others.[9] Serious as well as token nuclear proliferation is therefore a real possibility.

A "serious" nuclear capability is a system of combat that will permit any state to destroy or thoroughly disrupt and degrade the political, economic, and social structure of one or two very large and populous areas (areas the size of the United States, Russia, China, or Western or Eastern Europe as units) on one occasion, swiftly and at

[9] See, for example, Bruce M. Russett, Hayward R. Alker, Jr., Karl W. Deutsch, and Harold D. Lasswell, *World Handbook of Political and Social Indicators* (New Haven, Conn.: Yale University Press, 1964), p. 79. Also, *The Military Balance 1968–1969* (London: Institute for Strategic Studies), which puts the defense expenditures of six Middle Eastern countries at 10–14 percent of GNP, China's at 9.2 percent, America's at 9.8 percent, and the Soviet Union's at 9.6 percent in 1967.

one blow, despite any military assault or defense these areas may muster. It must be a second-strike[10] as well as a first-strike force; it need be devastating only countervalue, not counterforce.[11] Such force is generally known as a *deterrent,* a term implying that the cost of using such an instrument against an enemy who has a similar facility is so high as to outweigh the possible gain in all but the most extreme situations. Consequently, the main intention of having such a force is not to use it but to threaten its use so credibly as to leave the ego-state's opponents unready to create situations that the ego-state defines as *extreme.*

The problem of credibility and the terror of uncertainty in such nuclear systems is created by the enormous loss that would be involved in using them against an enemy similarly equipped. Such forces can destroy the people of an enemy, but they cannot prevent the enemy from destroying one's own people in return, or perhaps first. This limitation makes their use for purposes other than the second blow in a mutual murder inherently and permanently dubious. Consequently, the threat of nuclear escalation into central war, with which the United States defends Western Europe against the fear of a Soviet "conventional" land invasion, regularly shows strain. It is very hard for the Western Europeans (and for the Russians) to believe that the United States would, knowing the cost, be the first to use nuclear weapons against the USSR. American deterrence in Western Europe therefore has perpetually to be shored up by expressions of determination, and even more by immense investments of men and resources in nuclear-linked conventional combat systems, which are too small to prevent Soviet conquest of Europe but so large that to write them off would be dreadfully damaging to the United States and political suicide for the government responsible—all this merely to make the nuclear threat believable. To ensure the credibility of nuclear deterrence of anything but an enemy nuclear attack on one's homeland requires enormous expenditures in order to make clear to all that the honor of the nation, the prestige of the state, and the life of the government have really been committed. This expense cannot be sustained in many places through the world; where it is not sustained, nuclear commitments (rocket-rattling) tend to be unbelievable and not believed, and therefore, if not meant, useless bluffs, or, if meant, dangerous stupidities.

[10] *Second-strike* ability means that this violent damage can be done even if the full weight of a maximal attack directed at the strategic nuclear forces is first received by the ego-state; obviously, a state that can strike second can also strike first.

[11] *Counterforce* capability could, if it struck first, destroy enemy strategic nuclear forces and prevent a return blow; but United States and Soviet strategic forces are now so numerous, dispersed, hardened, concealed, mobile, and sophisticated that neither can be said to have a counterforce capability against the other. United States and Soviet *values* are cities, population, and productive facilities. Both states are thoroughly vulnerable to a *countervalue* nuclear attack from the other, and each possesses countervalue capabilities sufficient to inflict great damage on the other's values.

This is the prime nuclear stalemate: for a great power, nuclear weapons are mandatory, costly, and worthless. These expensive systems of combat are necessary, as long as others have them, for states that do not choose to depend upon the generosity of a nuclear power for their security; they are also almost useless in the majority of international transactions. One cannot seriously threaten to use them (without suffering immense and constant costs to keep the threat credible) against a full nuclear state; and the fact that developed states are better targets for limited or covert nuclear war than underdeveloped states, combined with the immense danger of entering a world in which limited nuclear war is an acceptable and legitimate daily transaction, has thus far been obvious enough to keep the serious threats of nuclear against nonnuclear powers minimal. The first inspired maniac who has a bomb to deliver and who is able to perceive his own suffering at the nonimplementation of his grand dream for universal human virtue as world-shattering in its intensity will perhaps bring about that new world: until then, nuclear power permits and assures only a certain limited independence from the influence of other nuclear states, and not much more of that than most economically powerful states have in any case. But its cost restrains nuclear powers from spending as heavily as they otherwise might on the conventional and subconventional forces that, ironically, are far more serviceable in the nuclear age.

Conventional force capability

The nuclear stalemate makes conventional forces as relevant as ever in principle; the cost of being a party to the nuclear stalemate has limited their actual relevance severely. The conventional forces of Britain (regular armed forces, 427,000; army, 210,000) are retreating from the world to Europe, following France (505,000; 328,000) in part because of the decision of both states to spend military funds on keeping up something of a nuclear force; German forces (456,000; 326,000) are confined to NATO, and Japanese (250,000; 174,000) to obscurity, by imposed peace settlements that have left these governments concerned mainly with economic capabilities. The great conventional forces of our day are those of the United States (with world mobility), the Soviet Union (with hemispheric mobility), and China (with limited subcontinental mobility).[12] But one may not omit the large and locally significant armies of the Republic of China (armed forces 528,000; army, 372,000); South Korea

---

[12] *The Military Balance 1968–1969* gives estimated sizes of armed forces at approximately 3.5 million men for the USA, 3.2 million for the USSR, 2.7 million for China. Armies alone alter the picture: 2.5 million for China, 2 million for the USSR, 1.5 million for the US. The relative weakness of China's air and naval forces accounts in part for her limited mobility; the relative weakness of America's army (though these figures do *not* reflect the weapons or quality of forces) restricts the significance of the global mobility provided by her air and naval forces.

(620,000 and 550,000), and North Korea (384,000; 345,000); North Vietnam (447,000; 440,000), and South Vietnam (410,000; 370,000); India (1,033,000; 950,000), and Pakistan (324,000 and 300,000); nor the locally significant forces of Israel, Jordan, and the UAR, of Turkey and East Europe, and of South Africa.

The commitment of most of these forces to specific locales and to specific enemies is notable. The United States is tied to Western Europe and to China's eastern periphery; the Soviet Union is bound to Eastern Europe (against Germany and the East Europeans as much as against America) and to China's northern periphery; China is largely held down on its frontiers with Soviet and American power. Similarly, the forces of the Republic of China are locked to those of the mainland, and the Koreas and the Vietnams are chained to one another, like Israel and the Arabs. South Africa is committed against Black Africa without and within her borders, Turkey against Greece and Cyprus as well as the USSR, Eastern Europe against Germany and NATO as well as its own population. The relatively greater mobility that sea power, sea access, airlift, and foreign military bases provided the United States formerly gave her (until the Vietnam war tied down all her truly ready reserves) a major edge in conventional power not entirely reflected by the numerical strength of American forces.

The committed forces have also served largely as deterrents. But America, Russia, China, North Vietnam, and South Korea, especially, have been able to detach varying contingents at varying times for several purposes—intervention or counterintervention in foreign revolutions; "showing the flag," symbolic violence, and the routine work of broadening or sustaining spheres of influence; mutual support to allies in return for their previous or pledged aid; probes of weak spots at the frontiers of enemy power; support and escalation of external insurgencies or counterinsurgencies. These and, of course, direct assault on foreign territory or on enemy states and regimes are the main active functions of modern conventional forces. Their main passive functions include defense by deterrence, occupation of an "imperial" sphere, and actual defense from foreign invasion or penetration. All these characteristic uses of force are to be found in the recent history of the heavily armed states. Large conventional capabilities therefore remain necessary for states with world interests, large ambitions, or large and specific local enemies, if they intend to be capable of maintaining those interests, advancing those ambitions, and achieving a sense of security against those enemies.

Subconventional force capability

The same goals, in a more restricted range of situations, call for the capabilities of subconventional or *people's war;* at least the conditions of the contemporary world seem to reward those who have such capabilities. *People's war* generally involves the use of a population (or segments of a nation) against its own government, under the leadership of an indigenous local elite with obscure and complex foreign connections. Historically, this form of war originated as a "spontaneous" technique of insurgency against a native government or a foreign or semiforeign occupation or colonial regime. But its effectiveness and cheapness (from an outside actor's point of view, *not* from that of the people in question) have made it also into one technique of a foreign policy that aims at exporting revolution—or, rather, at homogenizing a state's environment (by installation of regimes similar in nature to one's own)—or at expanding an imperium (by installing subordinate regimes abroad). Subconventional techniques are usually effective only in states already disturbed by profound internal alienation and distance between elites and masses, by partition, or by a large foreign political penetration or economic or military presence.

The current tactics of insurgency depend upon substituting large and politically militant human masses for advanced military technology and materiel, part-time for full-time soldiers,[13] moral for material superiority, and extreme if primitive mobility through difficult terrain for advanced logistics and large semimobile numbers of troops. The state that is able to foment foreign insurgency can hope thereby to serve objectives of homogenization (and, perhaps, territorial expansion) that a conventional-force stalemate (or the certainty of great power intervention) would otherwise leave frustrated. The state that wishes to foment foreign insurgency requires a complex of key exportable political commodities: this complex must include a military doctrine; it may also include appropriate weapons, instructors, leaders, a political or politico-religious faith, and trained soldiers.

Guerrilla insurgency can normally be put down or contained by government (and sometimes foreign) forces, if they can reach and keep a very large numerical superiority over the insurgents[14] or if they are prepared to employ a temporary superiority to uproot, purge, or annihilate the insurgent population-base. The second method is still unacceptable to the main non-Communist states and the first is at times unfeasible and at other times too much of a strain on already stretched conventional forces. Consequently, those whose world or regional interests call for permitting no hostile alterations of the status quo in areas suitable for and targeted for insurgency must either give up and depart (for example, France and Britain), develop the capability for early and effective aid for suppression of insurgency (for example, the United States in Latin America), or be prepared to pay the costs and take the risks attendant on attempts to saturate insurgency with conventional force (for example, the USSR in Eastern Europe, the United States in Vietnam, and possibly China

[13] Thus eliminating the distinction between combatants and noncombatants.

[14] *Very large* means on the scale attained by the British in Malaya, not on the much lesser scale achieved by the United States in Vietnam.

in Tibet). Counterinsurgent aid capability is as yet poorly developed[15] and still an American property, with all that implies about overemphasis on crisis policy and emergency response, the lack of long-term planning and adequate preparation, and the contrast of military might with peacetime paralysis. The record of recent counterinsurgency is consequently uneven.

Summary

The current nuclear systems are necessary for those who seek the prestige of being first-class powers. The systems involve a swiftly evolving technology that compels ceaseless competition for superiority. They are too costly and dangerous to use. If fully maintained by lesser powers, their cost is likely to cripple the conventional establishments of those powers.

Conventional forces are still necessary (if not always sufficient) to guarantee regional stalemates and the status quo against other conventional forces and against insurgency. Large and highly mobile conventional forces are still the most useful tools of states concerned with world stability, and among the more useful resources of those concerned with containing global or hemispheric imperialism or revolution. Conventional forces are particularly useful for deterrence of conventional or insurgent assault, for intervention in internal violence, and for the escalation of insurgency and counterinsurgency situations that are out of control at lower levels of violence.

Insurgency is an export commodity whose costs are low and prospects rather dubious. It is useful for states with rather specific nationalist-territorial and revolutionary-political objectives in a large segment of the globe. Counterinsurgency would be an appropriate technique for their opponents, if these opponents knew how to make it work and were prepared to sustain its costs.

The spectrum of techniques; the distinction between power in peace and power in war

The various techniques of foreign policy can be placed on a spectrum, ranging from the most violent and coercive forms of action to nonviolent verbal modes of dealing and bargaining. Such a spectrum is significant only because of an ancient convention of international relations, the distinction between "war" and "peace," and because of a modern convention, the distinction among war, "cold war," and peace. For in "wartime" virtually all means and techniques for getting one's way are admitted to be legitimate and are employed by

---

[15] It appears to involve a military package (weapons, training, financing, military doctrine, leaders) with some political-economic ribbons (ideologies of political development and reform or of economic development and equalization; aid for economic and social development). In all probability the package should be the ribbons, and vice versa.

states; in a "cold war" some of the most violent methods are deliberately not employed by the combatants; in "peacetime" the international customs of a period admit the use of only the least violent techniques.[16] But this means that there is a theoretical distinction among the war capabilities, cold-war capabilities, and peacetime capabilities of any state. Its peacetime power may be much greater than its wartime power, or much less, and this imbalance must affect its policy. If a state is weak in peace, it will be tempted to follow a violent policy. If it is weak in war, it will be tempted to follow a pacific policy. If it is weak in peace and in war but has a high cold-war potential, it must incline to wage cold war; if it is weak in cold war but strong in peace or in war, it may waver between nonviolence and extreme violence.

The spectrum of interactions today includes nuclear war, conventional war, subconventional (insurgency) warfare, symbolic violence (nuclear deterrence and gunboat diplomacy), economic constraint, political penetration, propaganda, diplomatic persuasion, and corruptive, trading, or benevolent economic side-payments. The resources required to pursue these techniques vary, obviously. Pure diplomacy or negotiation is cheapest; subconventional warfare, political penetration, and propaganda are relatively inexpensive, like economic side-payments intended to corrupt agents rather than to convince principals. A minimum of material technology is required for subconventional warfare, penetration, propaganda, and diplomacy, and a minimum of political technology is required for corruptive economic side-payments.

The most "normal" or "peaceable" techniques involve diplomatic persuasion and benevolent or trading economic side-payments. Peaceful relations are relations of debate, gifts, and bargaining: talk, aid, and trade. Few pairs of states enjoy fully peaceable relations in the contemporary system; usually, those that do are old friends and good allies or states that have no terribly significant relationships. The most "warlike" techniques are unlimited nuclear or conventional war. Few pairs of states are at war for long in the current international system. The most significant relations today are those of limited and indirect warfare, symbolic violence, propaganda and political penetration, and economic constraint and corruption. The most widespread sort of relations between states ranges from armed peace through permanent crisis or permanent emergency, to protracted conflict and a balance of terror. It is the condition of cold war. This condition characterizes the relations of America and Russia, America and China, and America and the most aggressive minor Communist states and movements. But Russia and China are also at cold war; so are the divided Germanies, Chinas, Koreas, and Vietnams; so are India and China, India and Pakistan, Greece and Turkey, Israel and the Arabs, South Africa and Black Africa, Cuba and Latin America, and others.

[16] Cf. Aron, *Peace and War*, p. 57, for the distinction between peace and war.

Cold warfare

In a cold-war relationship, it is normal—and it is normal around the world today—for some states to be the standing objects of penetration, propaganda, and corruptive side-payments from others. The relationship may become scandalous at times, but it is accepted. It is normal—and all concerned come to accept it as lasting and regular —for some states to become the objects of economic constraint, subconventional warfare, and symbolic violence (including the threat of nuclear war) from others, and to reciprocate. Today the long-term semiwar relationship is easy for states to enter and hard for them to leave.

Vietnam may or may not add limited conventional war to those stable relations of accepted mutual violence. In any case, only the relations of mass conventional warfare and limited nuclear war have not been put to the practical test in this period. Nuclear and mass conventional warfare probably still fall under the head of true warfare, that all-legitimizing relation in which all the latent national energies are released and concentrated upon one violent embrace.

Aside from nuclear and mass conventional warfare, we have today a number of lasting relationships that are possible between two states, each relationship having a certain autonomy and stability, all created by decision and sustained by routine, each sanctioning the use of certain capabilities and techniques. These relationships are fairly stable, but not entirely so. The failure of the technique in question to gain the intended results, a deep and general sense of frustration, and the possession of the means necessary to act often combine to induce a state to escalate such a relation; long-continued failure and the want of any alternative means for escalation may tempt a state to normalize its relations with another. In the decision to enter such a relationship, the belief that one possesses the capabilities to profit from it is a proper and frequent contributing factor; in the decision to terminate or abandon such a relationship, the sense that one's state lacks the capabilities to exploit it is often a major factor, as rationally it should be.

War, cold war, and peace

Even today, the decision to perceive one's state as "at war" appears to be of a special character, however obscured by cold-war techniques and their frequent use. The decision to enter war tends to increase radically (if sometimes only temporarily) a country's capacity for collective action, thus making more of the accessible geo-demographic base subject to mobilization for political uses and more of the economic means subject to political appropriation. At the same time it obviously increases the relevance of military capability to success in attaining foreign policy objectives.

Therefore, states whose objectives are large, whose capacity for collective action in peacetime is low, and whose military means are notably better than their nonmilitary capabilities are subject to a strong pressure to militarize their foreign policies, and are likely to swing rather sharply from ineffective to effective but violent diplomatic practice. This is particularly true of states that ignore or mismanage large segments of the gradation of intermediate means between persuasive diplomacy and full-scale war, whether through necessity, ignorance, moral principle, deficient planning, or inadequate politico-strategic doctrine. Such states, relatively weak in cold-war time, are under constant pressure to move up the spectrum of violence toward war. America is one such state.

On the other hand, the absence of significant wartime capabilities, and the absence of an ally or a concert of great powers that can be relied on to provide wartime capabilities in moments of need, limit the scale of objectives that may be pursued with a large chance of success to those for which peaceable capabilities are adequate, thereby rendering a state dependent upon the indulgent or at least cooperative mood of other well-armed states. This cooperation is so unreliable in world affairs as to leave states that are stronger (or more capable of sustaining their own independence and security) in peace than in war quite insecure.

States weaker in war potential than in peacetime capability are therefore under constant pressure as well, but in this case the pressure produces a variety of responses. The same pressures that operate on all war-weak states have combined with very different ambitions, fears, and hatreds to produce extreme alignment with one great state (for example, the cases of Poland and South Korea), defensive-armed neutrality and noninvolvement (Sweden and Switzerland), extreme withdrawal and isolation (Burma), aloof and independent but definite alignment (many South American states), the deliberate attempt to play off one major state against another (France and India), or the attempt to combine multiple weaknesses into united strength and to settle weak-state affairs mutually and to the maximum exclusion of the great states (the Organization of African Unity, and several less enduring Third-World blocs).

Some imbalances in the spectrum of capability

In the current world, the peaceful and warlike power of the states probably would not appear radically different in rank order in too many cases, but there are changes enough when the gradations from persuasion to nuclear force are considered to be worth an examination. The absolute conventional and lesser capabilities of the United States would probably be increased more than those of any other state as a result of the decision to go to war. America's peacetime standing military capabilities are kept down by the dual, persistent pressures of moralistic auto-limitation and the anti-government-spending ideology of private consumption. These restrictive pressures have permitted peacetime (or cold-war time) preparedness of forces sufficient to go to nuclear war or to undertake a short, fast, distant military intervention; they permit the maintenance of an organization that, if fully utilized, could become ready in a year or so to fight a major conventional war, and that can as it stands sustain the fighting of a minor one indefinitely. But the restrictive operations of one or the other or both of these pressures preclude, divert, sabotage, weaken, corrupt, or straitjacket peacetime capabilities other than (and perhaps including) the diplomatic. The capabilities of the United States give it a greater chance of success in conventional war than in counterinsurgency, political warfare, or propaganda, and thus tempt it to militarism. They give it a greater chance in economic purchasing than in these other areas, and thus tempt it to wasteful spending.

The relative change in capabilities of the Soviet Union or China from peace to war would depend upon the nature and location of the war as much as upon the opponent. The Soviet Union is best able to apply its conventional capabilities against Germany and the East European states, China's northwest and northeast frontiers, and along the axis from Moscow to Suez. China, when she can act militarily at all, can do so abroad most effectively in Korea and the Soviet Far East, and less readily in northern and eastern Indochina and against Formosa. But even her most imposing frontiers, most distant from Peking, need not be points of weakness. If all nuclear forces and the conventional capabilities of the United States were nullified and the conventional forces of China and Russia were combined and employed in a simultaneous and general conventional war of expansion with their border states, it seems probable that a line of occupation could be drawn rather rapidly at the Rhine and the Mediterranean on the one hand, and the Sea of Japan, Malacca Strait, and Bay of Bengal on the other. This particular excess of wartime over peacetime capability at the borders is balanced by a deficit of conventional capability (typical of non-sea-mobile powers) in areas much more distant, and it is negated currently not only by the opposition between these states but also by the American presence and nuclear threat. So the USSR and China are not under strong pressure to militarize their foreign operations.

But the excess of Soviet and Chinese wartime over peacetime power vis-à-vis *some* of their foreign opponents, and the negation of this excess, are important because they reveal the active or dynamic nature of the stalemate in recent and contemporary world politics. A sudden weakening in the nuclear deterrent posture of the United States could and probably would produce, as the period of a single and fairly logical sequence, a great increase in the peacetime influence of the Soviet Union in Western Europe and the Middle East, and in that of China in East and South Asia; probably also an attempt by the West Europeans jointly or the Germans alone to acquire or underwrite a credible second-strike anti-Russian nuclear capability, and a try by India and Japan to protect themselves against China by becoming nuclear powers. Thus the change in the military capability of one state may lead to a whole sequence of adjustments abroad, which are to be understood not in the simplistic terms of an "arms race," but in the complex terms of relative capabilities, the neutralization of influence by opposed capabilities, and the temptation to violence provided by peacetime weakness combined with large war potential.

Means or capability factors, 2: economic capability and its relation to policy

Turning next to the economic means of policy, we shall find that their direct utility as tools of action is strictly limited. But the level of a country's economic development, its rate of economic growth, and the proportion of its population that can be supported while not directly engaged in production are nonetheless strikingly important characteristics. Economic means are most important for their convertibility, their flexibility. It is that flexibility which therefore warrants attention, as it relates to the flexibility of other factors of power. When the convertibility of economic means becomes clear, the significance of the very uneven world distribution of economic capabilities will become plain: there is an oligopoly of capability, a very unequal and stratified world society. This creates a narrow oligarchy of world influence, and the specific qualities of political influence make this oligarchy even narrower and therefore more frustrating for the policy of *all* the states that are its members than one would expect from a mere examination of the world economic hierarchy.

Flexibility

Flexibility is an important quality, possessed in different measure by different brands of capability. The quality is that of breadth, in application and in *use*. The United States nuclear deterrent is useless for fighting a war in Vietnam, for amusing or soothing De Gaulle, for bringing Israel and the Arabs to the reasoning point, for turning Castro's attention inward, for pleasing everyone concerned with Rhodesia, for diverting Indian and Pakistani attention from one another to China, for settling the German problem, and so forth. It is not merely that it has been tried and failed; no trial seems reasonable in principle, because a threat of massive destruction (and suicide) is neither credible nor sufficiently delicate to make such fine adjustments. Persuasive diplomacy is applicable, in principle, to these situations and to many others; in that sense diplomatic capabilities are more flexible than nuclear-strike forces. (They may be no more effective in fact.) A high-quality diplomatic corps is capable of doing more, and more varied (if not always more important), things than a high-quality second-strike force. Similarly, it seems probable that ready funds are capable of being applied to more foreign problems than are gunboats, a conventional mass army, or even a good political penetrative apparatus, though these may in turn have a wider breadth of application than a nuclear deterrent; and an air-sea-mobile ready conventional force is probably good for more things than a land army with a large semitrained reserve.

The criterion of flexibility ought to be applied in the evaluation of any state's total capabilities, along with the more conventional criteria of effectiveness, cost-effectiveness, and orientation to actual problems. Thus we want to know whether a state is prepared to meet its actual challenges, whether it is adequately prepared to meet them, and whether its level of preparedness is attained at the lowest possible cost—but also whether it is ready to meet a very broad spectrum of probable and possible challenges (threats and opportunities) of strikingly differing types.

There is another sense in which power factors may be flexible: breadth in *conversion*. The most broadly convertible power factor is economic capability; but the capacity for collective action, and (indirectly) the geo-demographic base, are also potential sources of capabilities directly applicable to foreign policy, even though they may not themselves be directly applicable. Thus a very large surplus economic production above subsistence and maintenance needs, regularly devoted to private consumption, may be taxed to support foreign aid, covert operations, or conventional forces. The larger a state's GNP and *per capita* GNP, the more of this highly flexible economic capability it has and the more variety it can introduce into its actual means of action.

Similarly, a united, organized, literate, skillful, obedient, and dedicated population would provide a state with a large general capacity for collective action, useful to increase its economic means or to enlarge its conventional forces. But it is more normal for private ties, political dissidence and disaffection, personal independence and political education and skepticism, or general ignorance to limit economic productivity and the will to conform politically. All states perpetually struggle against the tendency of citizens to see themselves as the ends to which the political order ought to be the instrument: there is often some grave difficulty in persuading them to take the contrary view, as the frequent need of statesmen to reiterate their appeals for dedication, self-sacrifice, and subordination of individual desires to the collective will indicates. But the prize is so desirously pursued because it is so rewarding: the collective volition of an organized mass renders hostile subversion, propaganda, threats, bribes, boycotts, and violence ineffective; it can even liberate emotional and physical energies otherwise untapped. An astute leadership can mobilize these energies, materialize them through economic work, organize them for mass war. This collective militancy, if long sustained, may be as flexible as a heavily industrialized and diversified economy: it can supply the motivation for long-trained and highly organized political penetration, propaganda cadres, and subconventional forces (which are especially difficult to support without self-sustained morale and motivation).

Thus, economic capabilities and collective capacity represent highly flexible but potential capabilities, while other actual capabilities have a varying breadth of application. And economic capabilities are perhaps at any moment the more worth discussing: more material, more measurable, steadier, more subject to control, and easier to turn to a wide range of services.

The oligopoly of economic capability

There is a radically uneven distribution of economic, as of military, capabilities in the world. This is clearly shown by the 1957 GNP table,[17] whose figures are out of date but whose rankings and scalar characteristics are still significant. At that time the GNPs of 122 states or units ranged from $443 billion to $30 million; the average GNP (mean) was $9 billion; half the states had GNPs below $1 billion. When the $443 billion range of state GNPs is divided into tenths, one state (the United States) alone occupied seven of these tenths alone (*i.e.*, the whole range from $133 to $443 billion had but one tenant); one state, the USSR (with an estimated GNP of $122 billion), occupied the eighth tenth (the range from $88 to $133 billion) alone; three states (Britain, Germany, and China, with GNPs of $61 billion, $50 billion, and, estimated, $46 billion, respectively) occupied the ninth tenth (the range from $44 to $88 billion); and in the last tenth (the $44 billion and below range) were found 116 of the 122 cases. The GNP of the United States was more than three times as large as that of the second state, Russia, which was in turn almost twice the size of the third contender, Britain. The United States' GNP was larger than that of the next nine nations combined, and larger than that of the following 112 nations combined. Thus the United States had more than one-third of the gross world product, and nine states (the USSR, the United Kingdom, West Germany, China, France, Canada, India, Japan, and Italy) had nearly another third collectively. There then existed in the world an international oligopoly of economic capabilities—and it was an oligopoly of unequals.

The oligopoly exists now, as it did then. Several sets of GNP statistics (for 1965 and 1967)[18] shows the United States' GNP consistently more than twice as large as the Soviet Union's; this in turn is more than twice as large as the GNP of any of four clustered third-rankers (Germany, Japan, Britain, and France). China may belong in this group, or (want of data forces us to say) it may belong to the next cluster of states, again with GNPs roughly half the size of

[17] In Bruce M. Russett *et al.*, *World Handbook*, pp. 152–54. Recollect that these statistics are only roughly correct and only roughly meaningful.

[18] 1965 statistics: A. F. K. Organski, *World Politics*, second ed. (New York: Knopf, 1968) pp. 210–12; Herman Kahn and Anthony J. Wiener, *The Year 2000* (New York: Macmillan, 1967), pp. 159–64. 1967 statistics: *The Military Balance, 1968–1969.*

the third level's: Italy, Canada, and India. There is another gap, and then, fairly close together, in the fifth rank, Poland, East Germany, Australia, Czechoslovakia, Mexico, and Sweden;[19] another gap, and Brazil, Argentina, Pakistan, and South Africa;[20] another gap, and then Turkey, Venezuela, and Colombia;[21] then Nigeria, the Philippines, Chile, the UAR (Egypt), Thailand, and Indonesia;[22] then Israel, Morocco, Algeria, Saudi Arabia, and Iraq.[23] The first five or six ranks, at least, suggest both the membership and the hierarchy in this oligopoly of economic production.

These, then, are eight ranks in an oligopoly of economic production. In order to convert this hierarchy into a pattern of economic potential for political influence, some account must be taken of elementary geography. We have already done so by striking out those states who live in the penumbra of two much wealthier states: this has already somewhat understated the influence of Rumania, Yugoslavia, and Cuba. Pressing our logic onward, however, let us construct potential constellations-of-influence, without regard to any actual relations among states, by assuming that a state's influence in any locale varies with its economic production, but has a rapidly diminishing effect as its distance from the locale increases.

The oligarchy of influence

This abstract rule of inference suggests the following influence-and-conflict constellations. The United States dominates the Western Hemisphere north of the equator: within its quarter-sphere, Mexico has residual dominance in Central America, with a competition of Venezuela and Colombia for residual influence in the Caribbean; farther South, Brazil, Argentina, Chile (west of the Andes only), and the much attenuated influence of the United States compete. The Soviet Union is first in Europe, Asia, and the Middle East, but dominates only East Europe: a quadrangular competition of America, Russia, China, and Japan forms one influence-subsystem in the Far East, with Australia being taken into account in oceanic Southeast Asia and China dominating the mainland; a quadrangle of Russia versus China and India versus Pakistan dominates South Asia. A pentagon of American versus Russian and British versus French versus German influences competes in West Europe; a subordinate quadrangular competition of Germany, Poland, Czechosla-

[19] The following European powers are omitted on grounds of being overshadowed by two or more substantially richer neighbors: Spain, Netherlands, Belgium, Rumania, Switzerland.

[20] Omitted: Denmark, Hungary, Austria.

[21] Omitted: Yugoslavia, Norway, Bulgaria, Finland, Iran, Greece, New Zealand.

[22] Omitted: Portugal, South Korea, Peru.

[23] Omitted: Singapore, China-Taiwan, Malaysia, Ireland, North Korea, South Vietnam, North Vietnam, and (notably) Cuba.

vakia, and East Germany is found within the Russian sphere in East Europe, like the secondary competition of German, British, and Swedish influences in North Europe. Italy has secondary influence to her north and east, and somewhat more in the Middle East, where Turkey, Israel, and three Arab states are the chief local competitors. France versus Italy, and in their shadows Algeria versus Morocco, are leading influences in North Africa; Nigeria overshadows West Africa, Ethiopia and the Sudan compete in East Africa, and South Africa dominates the lower tip of the continent.

This abstract deduction of influence from wealth and location bears some conviction; but evidently military capabilities, extant servitudes and alignments, statesmen's will to influence the external environment, and other power factors have enlarged the actual influence of the United States, France, China, and Cuba while diminishing the role which this paradigm suggests for Mexico, Colombia, Venezuela, Britain, Germany, Japan, East Europe, Turkey, Australia, Sweden, Italy, Nigeria, Ethiopia, and Sudan. Let us next consider, then, how the ranking of the oligopoly of economic production is actually transformed into a pattern of political influence.

We have inferred from the inequality of capabilities an operating inequality of influence. Such an oligarchy of world political influence is in actuality to be found; but it is not in complete and one-to-one correspondence to the oligopoly of economic capability.

An analysis of the actual scale, activity, and success of these states' recent foreign policies would surely put the United States and Russia at the top. Britain and France have a second rank, diminished by the nearness of American and Soviet power, diminished for Britain and somewhat augmented for France by factors of leadership and capacity for collective action. Germany and Japan would rank low, because of the historical consequences of World War II (defeat, occupation, and disarmament); they have no nuclear weapons, and Germany at least is closely watched by its neighbors. China's recent activism followed by passivity can be attributed on the one hand to an idealistic and willful ideology and leadership, on the other hand to the internal problems and preoccupations of that leadership and to internal disorders that have cut its collective capacity (and possibly its GNP as well). China's failures are partly due to close containment by one world power and conflict abroad with the other. Italy bears the repressions less of World War II defeat than of being located in West Europe, with three greater powers in the region and the United States evidently present; Canada similarly lives in the shadow of the United States; India and Pakistan live in one another's, and in those of Russia, China, and United States containment.[24]

Poland, East Germany, and Czechoslovakia are deactivated less by their mutual neighborhood than by their fear of Germany

[24] Still, of the three (India, Canada, and Italy), India has probably sustained the largest world role, precisely because of the conflicts among its three major "shadows."

and, primarily, their subordination to Russia. Brazil and Mexico play smaller roles than one might expect, less because of the United States' sphere than because of their own internal economic preoccupations (and successes). Nonetheless, both have external influences, the one mainly on its Argentine periphery (which also provides a countervailing influence), the other in Central America (where the United States weighs even more heavily). Sweden is strong enough to pursue a classic neutrality and a Scandinavian policy, but the ties of its neighbors to the two giants restrict the sphere of the latter, and Sweden's lack of the most modern weapons constrains and limits the former. Australia lacks influence because of its geographic isolation and small population; Indonesia is confined by its internal collective-action weaknesses and preoccupations, the United States' presence, and the neighborhood of China and Australia. South Africa has developed a sphere of influence of its own, rigidly contained beyond a certain line by the hostility of most African governments to its forms of polity and policy. Turkey, Venezuela, Colombia, the Philippines, Chile, Morocco, and Algeria are contained by great-power influences in their region, and by internal preoccupations.

The United Arab Republic (Egypt) has a leadership that has been extremely active and ambitious in foreign affairs, partly because of capability, even more because of the personal "consciousness" of Nasser. More often than not its ventures have been unsuccessful, due to the frustrating presences of the United States and Britain, to the rather selfish and unhelpful presence of Russia, to the UAR's low collective-action capacity and the contrary high capability of Israel, and to the general want of the wherewithal to achieve goals of a very high scale. Nigeria has grave inner problems, lacks traditional foreign goals and willful leaders, and is short in collective-action capacity. Thailand's traditional goals of independence and local expansion have been compromised on the one hand by the presence and menace of China and communism and on the other by a desire to maintain an international legitimacy and a certain pride in being the only noncolonial state in Southeast Asia. Israel's active policy has been directed at mere survival, and has been successful outside its region, but only militarily successful within it. No settlement with the Arabs is in sight, and population and territorial shortages make the question of the future survival of Israel, despite its high developmental level and collective capacity, still moot.

Thus, there is an international oligarchy of influence, but it is even more tightly stratified and even smaller than the international oligopoly of economic and military capability. This is due to three facts: (1) The United States and, to a lesser degree, Russia are world powers, whose presence is felt in most regional subsystems, of which they are often the chief members. Their interests and presence thus reduce the natural (expected) scope or sphere of influence of other states, all the more if only one of them is present in any region without the countervailing influence of its opponent. (2) The influence of any state is reduced through the existence or location in its region of several powers of the same rank, even more if those powers are hostile and if attention must be concentrated on their long-lasting hostility.[25] (3) Most states are heavily preoccupied with internal problems of economic development and political decay, a preoccupation and problems that weaken their world presence.

So it is only under extraordinary circumstances that the narrow oligarchy of world influence has been temporarily and partially upset. A third or lower ranked state wishing to pursue policies of a broad scale has had to have the forbearance of both superpowers from forcibly recruiting it to their blocs. It has required internal and regional conditions benevolent enough to enable it to give less than full time to domestic politics and immediate problems of resisting foreign enemies. It has required either a long, ingrained, and traditional independent policy or an ambitious intellectualistic or emotional, charismatic or slightly insane leadership. And even when all these conditions have been met, such policies have been marked by very uneven success and rather high risks.

Means or capability factors, 3: rankings and oppositions; impact of general capability rank on state policy

Rankings

We have seen that, of the factors of state power, it is the means that are most intriguing and examinable. It is very desirable to be able to evaluate all these capabilities at once, and, to a limited degree, it is possible to do so. The preceding section employed GNP statistics in discussing the world capability structure. And a recent study[26] has suggested the presence in fact of a high relationship (from country to country) among certain key statistics: population, population times energy production, national income, Gross National Product, energy production, defense expenditure, and total energy resources potentially available. This high relationship on the one hand suggests that power potential (long and short run) tends to be actualized; on the other hand, it justifies the use of the more readily available figures for Gross National Product (GNP) as rough initial indicators of a single power "status" or ranking. This ranking must, of course, be speedily modified by reference to military systems actually possessed and under development, and (so far as practical) by reference to the organs of foreign political action.

But the fact that the oligopoly of economic capabilities also

25 Which long enmity the long presence and countervailing balance of the two giants often tends to keep alive by preventing its final resolution through military force.

26 R. J. Rummel's Dimensionality of Nations (DON) Project: See R. J. Rummel, "Oblique Rotated Factor Tables for 236 Variables," March 1, 1965.

describes the balance of military power and that there is a large, partial correspondence between economic and military rank seems to point to the possibility of a tentative ranking of states by a single qualitative capability variable. Using gross and intuitive indices of relative capabilities, military and economic capabilities being taken as a lump (as they can be for very limited purposes), we can say that in the world of 1969 the United States is definitely the first-ranking power and the Soviet Union the second, but that the privileges of being first are very restricted indeed. Furthermore, there is a substantial gap between the capabilities of these two world powers and those of a group of third-ranking states (China, Germany, Japan, Britain, and France),[27] and another fair-sized gap between this whole oligarchy and a rather larger set of regional great powers in East Europe, Latin America, Southern Africa, the Middle East, and South Asia.

Oppositions

The international power structure is complicated by the deep and bitter three-way hostility among the United States, Russia, and China and by the independent antagonism of France for the United States and Britain. It is somewhat simplified by the current and long-lasting passivity and inwardness of Germany and Japan, the increasing withdrawal from world to European politics by Britain, by the recent (but perhaps periodic) internal disorder and preoccupation of China, and by the regional, local, and primarily internal concerns of many regional great powers. The capabilities of withdrawn states are less relevant for *immediate* comparisons and policymaking and are less available for use by allied states or blocs.

The first- and second-ranking powers are hostile to one another. The United States has no friend or ally of equal or greater strength, and possesses a mass of relatively weaker or much weaker allies, dependents, clients, and willy-nilly members of the "free world." The Soviet Union has no friend or ally of equal or greater strength (consequently it conducts a policy as independent as America's); it has a smaller mass of dependent, allied and semiallied states and Communist parties. The United States is stronger economically than the Soviet Union (in that it produces more goods and services), and stronger despite the fact that it appropriates a smaller proportion of national product for central-government use; but this economic strength, though it is an object of state policy and though in the long

---

[27] The following table may emphasize this point. Estimated 1967 GNPs and rough estimates of planned defense expenditures (Defex) for 1968 or 1968–69 from *The Military Balance 1968–1969*. All estimates converted to billions of United States dollars.

	United States	Soviet Union	Germany	Japan	Britain	France	China
GNP	807	358	125	116	110	104	75?
Defex	79.5	39.7	5.1	1.1	5.4	6.1	7.0?

run its changing balance can be made decisive for outcomes in international politics, is poorly and indirectly connected to United States policy objectives, tactics, and (especially) outcomes. American economic capabilities are highly "flexible," in the sense that production can in time be shifted from one good to another, but they are far from thoroughly mobilized for foreign policy use: they present long-term possibilities.

Militarily, the United States has the capabilities to destroy the Soviet Union, but not to survive that act; nor can the United States conquer or occupy its adversary. The Soviet Union is in the same case vis-à-vis the United States: it can destroy, but neither survive nor conquer. The military superiorities of the United States are more apparent in the worldwide mobility of its conventional forces, as a result of a network of treaties, bases, seapower, and airpower. The Soviet Union is able to mobilize and to deploy, certainly through Europe and probably on its other frontiers, armed forces for nonnuclear (and possibly limited nuclear) war superior enough in quantity and/or quality to those available to its potential adversaries that it might in such a war conquer and occupy Germany, Manchuria, and Sinkiang (possibly France, not Britain, probably not Central and South China or Japan). But because of the bipolar nuclear stalemate of mutual deterrence, Russia's great military capabilities are more useful for maintaining the status quo than for changing it.

To the degree that the two giants are mutually opposed, their joint superiority in capabilities over the rest of the international oligarchy is largely irrelevant to policy, and their individual superiority over any other actor is partly negated by the tendency of each to deter serious or unlimited measures by the other against any third party.

Rank and policy

The Soviet Union. The military and general status of the Soviet Union—which, despite vast changes in military technology, holds fundamentally the same *rank* as it did 20 years ago—has permitted it, and at points tempted it, to strive for the first position with varying but persistent energy. Russia has resisted with some success the designs of the United States for general and specific settlements of disputes round the Soviet periphery; it has held off the plans of American statesmen for Soviet-American cooperation in which the Russian junior partners would implicitly abandon their worldwide goals; it has achieved dominance in East Europe, and then moved back from dominance to primacy without yet having to retreat further; it has slowly expanded Russian influence in the Middle East and elsewhere, and it has maintained material support and fraternal relations with many "Communist" ideological-power movements abroad. The secondary status of Russia has been reflected in practice by the failure of most of the dramatic and ambitious thrusts that it has made or supported abroad, in Iran, Greece and Turkey, Berlin in 1948, Korea, and Cuba in 1962; but Russia's second rank has also been reflected in its ability to shake off failure and renew pressure, and in its ability to make significant but limited gains in influence by supporting one or another party to disputes (Middle Eastern, South and Southeast Asian, Latin American) that it did not necessarily provoke.

The United States. The economic, military, and general status of the United States has enabled it (and the absence of friendly European world powers or truly neutral great powers elsewhere provoked it, and of independent and hostile world powers permitted it) to contemplate a world policy of containment of Russia (and then of China and of polyform communism), and to undertake it, and largely to carry it out. The want of absolute preponderance over *all* its opponents at once has given that policy severe jolts: China, 1948–49; Korea, 1950–51; Indochina, 1954; Cuba, 1961; and Vietnam, 1965–? The loss of Communist and "free world" cohesion has led to some cutting back of the pressure for containment of Russian influence, especially on Russia's southern borders. American military resources have been large enough to support most decisions to weather or win through specific crises; the world fabric of commitments, almost imperial in scope, has stretched thin and sagged without tearing. But the proliferation of independent and semi-indigenous, yet hostile, communisms in the 1960s, along with the unwillingness of either Russia or China to reach a general settlement, has steadily raised the cost of containment. And United States economic capabilities in the 1960s have been increasingly hard pressed, despite steady growth, to meet domestic and foreign demands simultaneously, while the demands of containment for capabilities (and attention) have sapped and deadened United States ability to carry out more "idealistic" developmental-aid policies abroad (and at home).

The United States–Soviet arms race is a contest in the efficient employment of economic capabilities to create military capabilities sufficient at least to sustain the nuclear stalemate and the spheres of conventional military dominance. The danger of hostile nuclear predominance is the first threat guiding policy. The danger of hostile conventional predominance that will tempt the opponent to take advantage of the balance of terror or to test nuclear deterrence of conventional war is perhaps the second guiding threat.

After these imperatives are met, there is the chance of stealing a march that will remove the opponent's key nuclear "unit veto" (for example, by means of an antiballistic missile system) or degrade his conventional sphere (for example, the long Soviet buildup of seapower), both offering opportunities where the more demanding problems offered threats. There is the infrequent chance to rule out of bounds some area of arms competition (for example, an unlikely locale like Antarctica or a futuristic one like outer space). There is currently the need for both sides to pursue a secondary arms race with China, the chance for the Soviet Union to exploit breaches in the containment barrier by extensive arms aid to favorites abroad, and the demand for the United States to devise counterinsurgency systems of combat for "free world" states menaced by polycentrically controlled or independent "Communist" rebellions. All these capability policies are responses to perceived threats and opportunities, but also to general ideas of the obligations of a first-class power and of the total expenditures on foreign military and other commitments that one's economic capabilities will permit.

The United States capability position displays certain marked weaknesses, five greatest and most persistent.

(1) America is unable to construct, indeed even to conceive of, the credible first-strike counterforce capability and the civil defense or antimissile defense facilities that would nullify the Soviet ability to destroy United States population and industrial centers by a thermonuclear second or first strike. Unable to overcome this limitation, United States policy has adjusted to it rather thoroughly from 1950 onwards by (a) rejecting all lines of "rollback" or "liberation" that have involved military support for revolutions against regimes that the Soviet Union has taken within its proclaimed sphere; (b) developing contrasting strategies of "massive retaliation" and "graduated deterrence," both designed to avoid or terminate war crises with the Soviet Union over forcible attempts to alter the world status quo, by dissuading the Russians from beginning, entering, or fully committing in such crises.

(2) The United States conceives of, but does not possess and may not be able to construct, an antimissile-plus-civil-defense system that would nullify the growing Chinese nuclear capability. Policy has been adjusted to this threat by the decision to develop a "thin" antiballistic missile (ABM) shield that may not be sufficient; other adjustments, more radical, may be enforced if it is later judged insufficient.

(3) United States capability for general thermonuclear war, and limited nuclear-and-conventional war in Europe, is much superior to its capabilities for nonmodern, nonnuclear, mobile conventional war (Vietnam), for counterinsurgency support, for "pacification" and "revolutionary development," and for ideologically-politically-morally based forms of "people's war" in general. This weakness is particularly significant against noncentric, polyform, revolutionary communism, and for United States promises and alliances in Southeast Asia and Latin America. The weakness has been met in Latin America and outside Vietnam by early and rapid counterinsurgency aid, which fosters temporary local successes, and by economic-social-political development aid, which is sporadically successful but costly, underfinanced, strategically backward, and of varying effect. The weakness provokes opponents, raises costs, and lowers chances of success in these subconventional encounters, and makes more probable the expensive and risky attempts to resolve the defeat or

stalemate of counterinsurgency by escalation to conventional-war levels, a solution that cannot be applied in too many places simultaneously.

(4) The adaptable United States economic capability is perennially overstrained and overcommitted; the technique for managing its growth, although reasonably well conceived, is subject to partisan interruptions and decisions. Growth itself, although well sustained through the early and middle 1960s, is still too slow to meet ever faster-growing domestic demands and the needs for long-range, intensive, flexible foreign commitments. Despite the success of containment, United States economic weaknesses prevent extensive positive policies and sustain the constant risk that United States military capabilities will be so overloaded as to cause a general recession of commitments, with incalculable consequences.

(5) Even more seriously, American peacetime power is far less advanced, organized, and financed than American wartime power. This is reflected in an aid policy of limited concept and success, in America's possession of an imperium without much American or foreign sense of its legitimacy, and in the failure of a recognizable world political movement to develop around any of the possible legitimizing bases of United States ideology—capitalism, democracy, progressive development, anticommunism, liberalism, conservatism, and so forth. The result of this lack of peacetime or political capability is reflected in relative American paralysis in the face of nonmilitary threats to its influence or objectives—the erosion of British power, the defection of de Gaulle, the passivity of Germany and Japan, drifts toward political crisis in Greece or towards neutrality in Turkey, and so forth. This lack is apparent also in the American tendency to operate politically in a subterranean manner and on elites (through the CIA) rather than openly and on masses; in appeals for legitimation to the corrosive ideology of nationalism or the contrary-to-fact principle of equality of states; in a tendency to seek military solutions late in crises because of the lack of theory, influence, legitimacy, and capability to achieve political solutions earlier.

The last three weaknesses reinforce one another and account in part for the policies of various "independent" opponents of American objectives, as for the widespread failures of American deterrence of war at the subconventional level, for the resort to military solutions, or larger military solutions, of various United States foreign policy problems in the 1960s, and for neoisolationist counterpolicies in various American opposition groups.

China. Chinese policy has been affected by the great discrepancies between Chinese desires and potential on the one hand and actual Chinese capabilities on the other. It has been affected by the partly illusory but partly real prospect of using the dissemination of moral-ideological-revolutionary-strategic notions as an instrument to frustrate American deterrence and technology—counterposing spiritual-collective against material capabilities. The Chinese sense of their legitimate claims to territory (primarily against Russia), to national influence (primarily in the American-defended arc from India to Japan), and to ideological influence (both in the world Communist movement and in revolutionism within the underdeveloped Third World) is rather grand. The Chinese population is immense and hard working; the Chinese territory is large and rich in resources. But the economy—despite, and perhaps because of, attempts to rush development—is still backward and mostly agricultural; the military, although large, is chiefly a conventional land force with a restricted technological base and radius of foreign operation and a still rather limited and primitive nuclear capability. Actual Chinese capabilities are far from sufficient to reunify China, impose local suzerainty, regain lost territory, control the Communist movement, or revolutionize the world. But Chinese potentials permit and feed the ambitious objectives that current capabilities frustrate, and redirect a certain amount of that ambition into a drive to reach the power status that might satisfy it. Hence the impetus toward hyperrapid industrialization, and the more patient and successful movement toward nuclear weaponry. The export of Maoistic insurgency doctrines, if limited by a certain rigidity of those doctrines, has had a stimulating impact upon what is now a largely multifaceted, independently developing, and mutually supporting world "revolutionary" movement, well salted with centers and quarrels and heresies. That movement, if not a limb or docile tool of Peking, shows a rewarding anti-Americanism and provides a source of harassment and strain on the capabilities of China's larger enemy. Thus political and technical innovations, stimulated by weak material capabilities and great expectations, have in part redressed Chinese weakness and permit the entertainment of somewhat grander short-term hopes than the more immediate material factors would sustain.

Germany and Japan. German and Japanese foreign policies are virtually beyond explanation in capability terms since the middle 1950s. They bear instead the marks of defeat, occupation, disarmament, artificial revolution, implanted but rooted "democratic" political systems, and in general the extreme national weakness of the late 1940s. Polycentrism and increasing independence have not stimulated them to active policies but rather to withdrawal, dependence, passivity, modest aspirations of regional interdependence, and concentration on economic growth. Their policies are those of weak states, much out of line with the capabilities of economically great and progressive powers. Their future policies are more likely to be interesting than their past in the sense that their activation, in whatever direction, would have profound regional repercussions. The instability of the discrepancies between their great economic capabilities and their almost nonexistent independent military capabilities, and between their economic capability (and military potential) and their objectives, successes, and influence, suggests a profound future instability of relations and configurations in their areas. At the same time, their very limited recent policy objectives support the notion that immediate external objectives are likely to alter in some close relation to their levels of military capability.

France. France, on the other hand (despite its significant increases in nuclear capabilities and the diminution of its untenable and draining overseas military engagements since the middle 1950s), provides an illustration of the principle that a regional power can have world objectives and can achieve certain limited successes attributable scarcely at all to its material base and almost entirely to the will and animus of a leader. If France had the resources of Belgium, de Gaulle would attract less notice; and if the Fifth Republic were as paralytic as the Fourth, he would be more restricted in his external discretion. But, given that certain material and political strengths and weaknesses both permit some ambition and deny its easy achievement, it is still remarkable how far recent French policy has depended on his leadership and how his departure seems certain to lead first to severe limits on the further achievements of current policy and then to calculable diminutions or modifications of objectives. France's relative economic inferiority has constrained its leader to seek a form of military parity, not yet achieved, in the nuclear-deterrent area only. If even this should prove too expensive, some modification of objectives and tactics seems likely, but whether this will involve more Europeanism, more isolation, or a change of alliances no one observing the gyrations of Gallic alignment proposals can say. But it appears clear that in one sense French policy has responded to a capability imperative, that is, to the perception of an actual or potential United States preponderance since 1962, and to the classic balance-of-power advice to oppose whichever state appears to move toward primacy. French success in shaking off and in harrying the Americans is in turn proportional in part to long-term economic improvements and military retreats that have made independence from United States aid and influence more feasible, in part to the recession of Soviet pressures (and of the consequent need of a United States alliance), and in part to the weakness of American capabilities and the strength of American inhibitions in the area of peacetime diplomatic, political, and economic manipulation.

Britain. British policy since the war presents a picture of more or less steady withdrawal of commitments, scaling down and regionalization of increasingly economic objectives, increasing dependence, and decreasing independent success. All are partly the results of relative or absolute secular declines in economic output and military capabilities[28] and probably also in absolute capacity for collective action. In short, changes in British policy appear to have been very much dependent on changes in British power.

---

[28] And a reorienting of the latter toward nuclear weapons, useful mostly to persuade the United States to take British advice seriously, and useful for that to a very limited degree.

So there is a sometimes simple but usually rather complex relation of foreign policy to capabilities, in these cases at least: but a clear and dominant relation nonetheless.

Means or capability factors, 4: rank and imbalance; some formal and informal hypotheses

Rank

The preceding discussion of the specific effects of contemporary capability rank on foreign policy leads logically to a more abstract and theoretical discussion about the kinds of propositions that may generally be true of capability and policy. First one asks: What is the significance of world capability rank? Even with all the qualifications that must be introduced into specific rankings, any measurement or estimate of material capabilities will eventually confer upon an actor certain relative international capability ranks or power statuses—one in the world system at large, another in the smaller regional and local subsystems of which the state is a member, and another in its relations with each other state with whom its ties are strong and close.

Assuming, then, that an analyst has prepared a rank or status list, what are its consequences? Can we make generalizations? One might begin by proposing that a relatively high capability status will in general mean a higher latitude of discretion, that is, a broader range of policies that a state can pursue with a high chance of success. Let us say that one normally expects states that rank very high in their level of material capabilities to be better able to enact their policies than states that rank lower than they. This normal expectation is strong enough so that events that defy it require special explanation.[29] Thus, the failures of the United States since the war are rather more surprising and more in need of explanation than its successes.

The notion of a normal expectation that events will move in a certain way can be expressed as a hypothesis about the relationship between capability and policy. But various conflicting hypotheses can be entertained, because it is not clear in many cases what we ought normally to expect to happen in world politics. Therefore, I shall set down for examination some conflicting hypotheses that represent conflicting normal expectations.

[29] And that is all they require, because this generalization is a generalization about explanations. It says that the successes of a high-ranking state will require less extensive and detailed explanations than will those of a low-ranking state, because the successes of the strong state will usually be attributable to its capabilities. Thus, it is here alleged that the success of the weak (and the failures of the strong) are peculiar events in need of special explanation when they happen. This is not the same as saying that "stronger states always overwhelm weaker states"; therefore, the American failure in Vietnam 1961–65 and 1965– is not a counterexample that refutes the generalization.

Hypothesis 3.0 (null hypothesis)

On the whole, the fact that some states are strong and others weak has no striking and systematic impact on the objectives, the content, the quality, or the outcomes of their foreign policy.

This proposal defies common sense, which need not mean that it is untenable. But what are the alternatives? Two have already been suggested.

Hypothesis 3.11

The higher the capability rank of a state, the larger is its chance of success in the pursuit of any given policy.

Hypothesis 3.111

The higher the capability rank of a state, the larger is the scale of the objectives it can pursue with a given chance of success.

And we will want to give a hearing to some paradoxical counterhypotheses.

Hypothesis 3.12

The higher the rank, the lower the chance of success for any given policy.

Hypothesis 3.121

The higher the rank, the smaller the scale of objectives with any given chance of success.

A three-way theoretical argument can take place. The supporters of 3.11 can argue simply that if a state has great resources in general, one should usually expect that they will be applied in specific cases. Hence, more economic resources should mean more success in diplomatic bargaining, more military resources should mean more success in combat, and so forth. Furthermore, the expectation that they will be applied successfully if necessary should lead to greater foreign adjustment to, or even deference to, the views and demands of the powerful state. The supporters of 3.0 (the null hypothesis) will argue that so many other factors will have to be taken into account, and will intervene between capabilities and out-comes, that the influence of capabilities will turn out to be quite inconsistent, muddled, unclear, remote, and secondary to other fac-tors. And the proponents or 3.12 may contend that the higher the rank of the state, the more menacing it will appear to its neighbors and the more they will tend to combine or pool their capabilities against it, thus increasingly denying it a chance of success.

Similar problems arise when we talk of other relationships between capability and policy.

Hypothesis 3.21

The higher the rank, the more active the policy.[80]

3.31

The higher the rank, the larger the scale of objectives of the policy.

3.41

The higher the rank, the more policy tends to seek dominance over the international system.

3.51

The higher the rank, the more policy tends to seek the homo-geneity of the international system (the establishment of similar regimes abroad).

3.61

The higher the rank, the more policy tends to seek the mainte-nance and stabilization of the world political, territorial, and eco-nomic status quo.

3.71

The higher the rank, the greater the adaptability, coherence, sta-bility, and flexibility of policy.

All these hypotheses are contradicted by 3.0 (general null hypothesis); each can be directly reversed (for example, 3.22, the higher the rank, the less active the policy); some are not mutually

---

[80] That is, the larger the number of situations in which decisions to take action are made by the state.

consistent (for example, 3.51 and 3.61). Some arguments, convincing or otherwise, could be brought forward for each, some cases raised as exceptions to each, and some cases claimed in support of two or more inconsistent hypotheses. But where, then, does this argument lead us? One must arrive at one's own opinion. Each one must pass judgment; each analyst is free to believe or to disbelieve each of these hypotheses on the basis of abstract argument. The more cautious readers will select, accept, and believe some of them only after adding reservations, and will accept some others only as interacting parts of a multiple-factor explanation.

The best use of such hypotheses, once they are accepted in theory, would probably be as normal expectations. The analyst decides to "believe" them, to give them a try, because they sound sensible and convincing. He then tries them on cases.[31] When a normal expectation is contravened in some case, it becomes necessary to explain why it failed, and then to reevaluate the expectation in the light both of its failure and of the explanation of that failure.

Imbalance

Next, it is worth our while to note some further hypotheses, phrased informally, that will reveal some slightly more sophisticated notions of the impacts of capability on policy. It is here alleged that there is a destabilizing influence or pull exerted on foreign policy objectives by imbalances between (1) objectives and capabilities, (2) military and economic capabilities, and (3) capability rank and what might be called "influence rank" (a status measured by the chance for success in policies of grand scale).[32]

The imbalance between objectives and capabilities. This imbalance is displayed on the one hand by China (or perhaps America), on the other by Japan (or perhaps Germany). Objectives that a state is not capable of attaining tend over a long time to produce failures and, consequently, either a retrenchment of world objectives or a new capability policy designed to correct the imbalance by achieving adequate power. On the other hand, available reserve capabilities very much larger than are actually employed in seeking state goals tend to provoke foreigners to voice awe and great expectations or to make attempts to "awaken," align with, and utilize the sleeping giant: all these perceptions and responses in turn are likely to awake proportionate ambitions. Yet cases have been known (especially following wars) where the achievement or abandonment of objectives leaves states without goals and with a large unused surplus of military force. Instead of adjusting objectives upward, the capabilities may be adjusted downward as a consequence of the

---

[31] See the section on research papers at the end of this chapter.

[32] It has already been contended (in "War, cold war, and peace," p. 44) that imbalance between peacetime and wartime capabilities has a similar "pull."

perceived imbalance. So, in short, objectives may be disproportionately larger or smaller than capabilities, and the imbalance may be adjusted by a striking change in either; many changes in foreign policy are to be attributed in part to a decision to resolve such a tension.

The imbalance between military and economic capabilities. This imbalance leaves a state overarmed or underarmed.[33] Such an imbalance is not easy to measure. One appropriate statistic is defense expenditure as a percentage of GNP.[34] Another approach matches GNP rank with defense-expenditure rank: by this, China, France, Poland, Czechoslovakia, and East Germany appear overarmed, with Japan especially, and also Germany, Canada, and India, underarmed. And there are probably several overarmed regions (for example, the Middle East and the confrontation arc of China's northern, eastern, and southern frontier). Overarmament is of course a drain on the economy, but is a stable drain in that it seems usually to be the result of a perceived long-term, intense threat.[35] Thus, China (aside from its immense ambitions) perceives the two greatest states of the world as its particular enemies; Poland, East Germany, and pre-Dubcek Czechoslovakia (aside from their dependent status and their leaders' diffidence of their populations) have felt threatened by the mere existence of West Germany, as France has by the spheres of influence of America and Russia. China, France, and East Germany also have notably dissatisfied leaders (see Chapter 4), of a type prone to see their environments as highly threatening. Until the threat abates, the economy collapses, or softer leaders decide to meet threat by a soft line, overarmament is unlikely to subside. Underarmament is, similarly, a benevolence to the taxpayers, who are likely to resist its redress (as are those who benefit from government nonmilitary spending), but it is probably less stable than overarmament even so. Germany, Japan, and India are all relatively better armed than they were 15 years ago, in part because of external pressure not to be power vacua but to look like "responsible" great powers, in part because of frustration of basic objectives by better armed states, in part because of perceived external threats. The last two pressures at

[33] In one sense, the whole world system is overarmed, along with most of its regions and member states: but see the next two footnotes.

[34] As a rule of thumb, states with more than 10 percent of GNP expended on defense are probably overarmed, and those with less than 4 percent underarmed, in today's world; but both these thresholds are right for powers with large GNPs, and should fall rapidly for powers with regionally large GNPs, locally large GNPs, and small GNPs.

[35] One might contend that any armament is overarmament, since it would be better if all production could be devoted to personal consumption and social uplift. But in a world of many states, statesmen habitually perceive the environment as threatening in principle, if not in fact at the moment; and this heterogeneous, nationalistic, and revolutionary world of states is a threatening environment for most of its members; hence, one can speak only of relative overarmament.

least, in an unjust and threatening world, make underarmament in general rather precarious.

The imbalance between capability and influence. This is often perceived in terms of the strength of a state's voice in international relations; it is also a delicate question. If one could measure actual world influence (for example, by international outcomes of crises and conflicts according to a state's expressed desires), that of the United States, although far from meeting American desires, would probably rank first; the USSR, France, and Britain, in that order, would probably cluster next, with China, Germany, Japan, and India following. But the gaps between those clusters are probably larger than those between capabilities, so that many great powers are actually also powers with small world influence. In this sense, there is always less influence than capability would seem to warrant, even on the first level of the world power structure, and far more so below the first level. This suggests a condition of perpetual perceived frustration that is likely to aggravate almost all members of the system, and to inflame foreign relations for those states that do not adapt their objectives to it. Adaptation to the frustrations of low influence includes turning to (1) goals shared jointly with members of a coalition concentrating a preponderance of world or regional capabilities, (2) goals that are noncompetitive with those of greater states, such (perhaps) as independence and isolation, and (3) goals that offer possibilities of wide cooperation and mutual advantage, for example, economic cooperation for development and growth. States that fail so to adapt objectives—and often even those that have adapted goals—will repeatedly be found to be fixated on or oscillating among objectives that are never achieved, with frustration consequently a sort of steady state.

All these points and hypotheses add some complexity and detail to the basic principles that (1) capabilities condition success, (2) capabilities therefore both affect and are affected by objectives, so that (3) a state's recent and present foreign relations can in large part be understood as functions of its capabilities. But they merely clarify, extend, and complicate these basic principles, without fundamentally altering them.

Research into problems of capability and policy

The student of foreign policy ought not automatically to rest content with the generalization of one or another analyst; too much is at stake and too little firmly known for such acceptance of the judgments of others to be justifiable. The question then arises of how one might, in an orderly and methodical manner, do research into the actual impact of capability on policy in given cases. The answer to the question *How?* in turn depends upon the answer to the question *Why?*

Obviously, there is an academic answer to the question of why one should study the relationship of capability and policy. We want to know because we want to know, and that is reason enough. We are sure that there is a relationship, we are sure that it is important; we do not know its precise nature, but we have strong suspicions about that nature. Therefore we ought to inquire on a case-by-case or a comparative basis, at any rate in an empirical manner, exactly what that relationship is.

But there is also an answer of some civic or public or policy relevance. In the public discussion of foreign policies, there are strong tendencies to ignore capability, to treat it as an issue irrelevant to or separate from policy, or to have vague expectations that high capability rank will more or less automatically translate into high success in the attainment of policy objectives. All of these tendencies are of doubtful merit. It would be very desirable to have informed publics take seriously the issue of the relations between objectives and capabilities. It would be equally desirable to have governments and policymakers sharply aware that nonmilitary capabilities can be, and perhaps should be, as deliberately controlled in the interest of policy as are the military means of influence. But in order to support such serious concern, there must be facts, the results of relevant inquiry into and informed judgment upon cases of the actual relations between power and policy. And in order to have such facts at last, it is necessary to map the beginnings of a road of inquiry that might lead to them—to ask the questions whose answers might be those facts. And the next step toward providing convincing answers is "trying it on": the setting out by organized and self-organized groups of students and analysts of policy, as well as by individuals, to see if such questions seem to fit the data publicly available, and vice versa.

Three kinds of inquiry seem to be appropriate: (1) comparisons of the capabilities of opposed pairs of states, (2) investigation of specific and neglected factors, and (3) examination of the capabilities of one state in their relationship to policy. All are desirable, but not all are equally feasible.

The most plausible manner of examining the relative capabilities of two states whose objectives are in conflict is by examining a specific past crisis or series of crises in their relations. If such a crisis has had a definite outcome, especially an outcome of clear success for one side and clear failure for the other, then it is appropriate to go to the journalistic, polemical, and scholarly works written about that crisis and to extract from that literature the explanations given there. The writers will usually have done more than narrate the sequence of events; they will also have put forward explanations to account for the outcome of the crisis. Every analyst will have to judge these explanations, to accept, wholly or in part, or reject them. From these explanations the analyst can select those that relate to the relative capabilities of the states involved and weigh them against those that employ other factors to account for the crisis outcome. By so weighing capability and noncapability explanations of one case and another, one comes to sense where and in what degree the conflicts of our day are conflicts in which power governs success.

At a much more theoretical level, the analyst should study the specific factors of "political" capabilities and the "capacity for collective action." Such study will not be easy, even to begin. It must be theoretical and very speculative too; little is told by governments about the organization and operations of their "political" branches and little is truly known about how a collectivity gains and loses its capacity for action. Collecting data about political capabilities must probably be left to political specialists, and examining the nature and fluctuations of collective capacity left to sociologists and social psychologists.

The scrutiny of an individual state's capabilities is easier to begin. That scrutiny can be of various types: (1) explaining a notable success or failure of that state's recent policy by reference to capabilities and other factors; (2) explaining specific state objectives, again by comparative reference to capability factors and others; (3) a general overview of the capability weaknesses of a state, the constraints these weaknesses place on its objectives and their successes, the degree to which these capability weaknesses can be controlled and overcome, and the objectives that the strengthened state would be liberated to pursue. The third type of inquiry is the most complex and advanced, requiring a familiarity with a broad range of the foreign aspirations of a state, its past failures, and the whole pattern of its power; it is a topic suitable for essays, summarizing the results of extensive research. The first two types of inquiry require a decision to accept event x as embodying a failure, or to consider goal y an actual objective of foreign policy. The study of the second topic, the influence of capability on specific goals, involves a reference to the public and the official debate about that goal, in order to determine whether actual or necessary capabilities were taken into account at all (and where, and to what degree) in the formulation of the goal, and to evaluate the realism and seriousness of the consideration of capability-objective relationships.

It is the first topic, explaining a state's recent success or failure in terms of capabilities, that lends itself most to consideration by those whose interest is centered on the recent policy of a single state. The analyst must take a very recent decision, set of crisis decisions, or line of policy, now over and fulfilled in the sense that it has either succeeded and become obsolete through success or failed and been abandoned. Thus, in United States policy, one might study the failure of intervention in Cuba in 1961 or its partial success in the Dominican Republic in 1965, the partial success of the 1962 Cuban quarantine, the limited success of the 1963 move toward détente with Russia, the failure of the limited Vietnamese escalation or the Vienna summit or the Berlin deterrence of 1961, or any of a number of more ambiguous outcomes.[36] The analyst must then ask these questions: What was the success or failure here? What was gained and lost? What caused it? How far were capabilities implicated?

The last question is central, and breaks up into several different lines.

1. What capabilities were used in this case? Which of them were used up and which merely diverted so that for the time they could not be used elsewhere? What, then, were the capability costs? Were the costs offset by any temporary or lasting capability gains or reinforcements?

2. How far did the general image of United States power or capability rank shape policy objectives by leading to the assumption that certain goals were risky, impossible to achieve, or easily within our grasp? How far did the possession, or want, of specific capabilities seem to permit, or to rule out, objectives? And how far did capabilities influence the alternative lines of policy that were considered and chosen, by making some appear practical and others too risky? Did a wide or a narrow range of possible objectives and decisions seem to lie open on the basis of capability alone?

3. How far did the outcome depend upon the actual material capabilities brought to bear by both sides, whether actually deployed and used or merely wielded in threat or promise? If the outcome was failure, what change in capabilities used or threatened appear in retrospect to have been necessary for success? Were these capabilities readily available? Supposedly but not actually available? Available too late or in irrelevant places? Theoretically possible but never generated? Or simply impossible to acquire and therefore out of the question?

Such a study can be carried out, although with considerably less data about the thoughts of leaders, for the recent successes and failures of states other than the United States. If properly and painstakingly handled, it will say something general as well as specific about the impact of power upon policy.

Procedures for ranking capabilities and explaining policy

Most readers of this volume will doubtless be less interested in undertaking extensive theoretical research into capability and policy than in proceeding to collect information about the capabilities of some state in order to judge thereby the specific impacts of its capabilities upon its policy. Sources of such information are suggested elsewhere in this book.[37] An outline of the steps through which

---

[36] It is easiest to approach the evaluation of crisis policy, since crisis and crisis policy tend to have the clearest points of termination.

[37] See Research Guide and Bibliography.

one may reasonably move and the tasks logically required at each step is perhaps in place at this point.

1. Start with the GNP of the state and its world and regional GNP rank, as a provisional index of general capability rank. (See p. 53, "Rankings," and p. 49, "Oligopoly.")
   a. What are its main opponents and supporters? Are these alignments in part explained by capabilities? Do they tend to neutralize or to reinforce the ego-state's capabilities? (See p. 54, "Oppositions.")
   b. What is the scale of its objectives? Is that scale in part explained by capability? (See p. 55, "Rank and policy," and p. 61, "Rank.")
   c. What is its general world influence rank? What is the degree of success of its overall policy and of its recent initiatives? Are relative influence and success explainable by capability? (See p. 50, "Oligarchy.")
   d. What is its rank in defense expenditure? In armed forces and army manpower? Is this ranking explainable by GNP rank? (See p. 53, "Rankings," and p. 39, "Conventional force capability.")

2. Take note of any oddities or apparent imbalances.
   a. Are objectives out of proportion with capabilities? Explain, and anticipate possible future effects of any imbalance. (See p. 64, "Imbalance.")
   b. Are military capabilities out of proportion with economic capabilities? Explain and anticipate. (See p. 65, "Imbalance.")
   c. Are influence and success out of proportion with capabilities? Explain and anticipate. (See p. 66, "Imbalance.")
   d. Is the base complex disproportionate to the means complex? Explain, note impact on policy, and anticipate. (See p. 33, "Base," and p. 35, "Base.")
   e. Does the capacity for collective action magnify or nullify the means complex? Explain, note impact on policy, and anticipate. (See p. 33, "Capacity," p. 35, "Capacity," and p. 47, "Flexibility.")
   f. Can other discrepancies be accounted for by reference to flexibility of means, or to political means? (See p. 47, "Flexibility," and pp. 33–34, "Means.")

3. Explore military capabilities.
   a. Is this a first- or second-class actual or potential nuclear power? Is it deterred by another nuclear power? Does nuclear status explain objectives, influence, success, or other capability weaknesses? (See p. 37, "Nuclear force capability.")
   b. What is the world and regional rank of its army and armed forces in manpower and cost? What proportion is tied down

by local enmities or foreign commitments? How mobile are the remainder? What is the quality of available and potentially available fractions of conventional forces vis-à-vis the most likely opponents? What objectives are actually and potentially sustained by the presence of conventional force? (See p. 39, "Conventional force capability.")

c. How substantial and flexible are its insurgency and counterinsurgency capabilities? How do they match with allies and opponents? What objectives are permitted or barred to pursuit (with reasonable chance of success) by strengths and weaknesses of subconventional forces? (See p. 40, "Subconventional force capability.")

d. How balanced are the peacetime, wartime, and cold war capabilities of this state? Explain, note impact on policy, and anticipate. (See pp. 42–47.)

4. Note any remaining oddities or unexplained events.
   a. Explainable by reference to very specific kinds of capability strengths and weaknesses? (See pp. 57–58.)
   b. Explainable by reference to noncapability factors? (See Chapters 4–7).

When the researcher into one country at one moment has fairly completed this schedule of inquiry, he can justly say that his work is done. When a multiplicity of such researchers have done such work, the comparativist's work will but have begun. He will seek an impressionistic yet extensive "test" of extant hypotheses (for example, those presented in this chapter) to substantiate, refute, modify, qualify, extend, or detail them. And from extensive and comparable research into cases, he may also derive or generate new hypotheses about capability and its relation to policy.

References

Aron, Raymond, *Peace and War,* trans. Richard Howard and Annette Baker Fox. New York: Doubleday, 1966.
The Military Balance 1968–1969. London: Institute for Strategic Studies.
Kahn, Herman and Anthony J. Wiener, *The Year 2000.* New York: Macmillan, 1967.
Russett, Bruce M., Hayward R. Alker, Jr., Karl W. Deutsch, and Harold D. Lasswell, *World Handbook of Political and Social Indicators.* New Haven, Conn.: Yale University Press, 1964.

4

Will and prescription

The substantial and significant differences between the foreign policies characteristic of strong and weak states are almost matched in gravity and consequence by the disparity between policies that do and do not bear the impress of strong conation—of active will.[1] Policies that result primarily from conscious and deliberate choice and those primarily attributable to confirmed habit, inconsideration, inveterate practice, or "prescription," may and should be contrasted in principle. The contrast is between policy created by pure "will" and

---

[1] Because of historical peculiarities in the evolution of the discussion of the subject of "will," it is perhaps advisable to approach it roundabout. There is a song:

> I know an old lady / Who swallowed a fly
> And I don't know why / She swallowed the fly;
> Perhaps she'll die.

But, refusing to die, this old lady instead swallows a spider (to catch the fly); and this is only the beginning. Bent on clearing her innards of their tormentors, she swallows a rat (to catch the spider), a cat (to catch the rat), and so forth, and this vigorous, persistent, and remarkable series of swallowings ends only with:

> I know an old lady / Who swallowed a horse.
> She died, of course!

Now, that old lady had a certain remarkable determination, and it was the end of her. A literalist will declare that she died of an excess of horse; but we would be just as correct in declaring that she died of an excess of *will*.

This chapter deals with the operation of will in foreign relations, a zone wherein it is always important when present, and wherein its workings are sometimes as disastrous as they were for the old lady—and for the same reason of imbalance between will and capability.

characterized by conscious, original, and decisive action and policy established by pure "prescription" and characterized by the continuity and momentum of inertia, the legitimation of tradition and history, and the durability of routine. This is an ideal-typical contrast: it is so extreme that we need not expect ever to find anything in real life to match it. All policies will contain a certain proportion of conscious, deliberate decision and another proportion of matter-of-fact continuity. But the proportions will vary strikingly from state to state and from time to time. When they change, policy will also change strikingly, and so will the *kinds* of explanations of why policy is what it is.

Three central concepts are introduced in this chapter, the concepts of *will, prescription,* and the V (for *volition*) *phenomenon.* *Will* is presented as the label for an *objective* political phenomenon, where we find in combination *independence, demand, action,* and *resolve. Will* is always associated with certain particular individuals in a political leadership. *Prescription* is the label for the common element in a set of widely varied and otherwise ill-assorted political processes: it is the living presence of the past in current policymaking; it is that sanctification of tradition, that bureaucratic inertia, that permits us to explain a decision of today by referring to the policy of yesterday and saying "Nothing has changed"; it is the persistence of memory. The V *phenomenon* is a special manifestation of will in the political life of a state, in which there appear not only "independence, demand, action, and resolve" but also special kinds of *leadership, ideas, rhetoric, centralization, drama,* and *conflict.*

Will occurs in politics when independent leaders appear on the stage, making clear demands and taking resolute action to obtain them in the face of great obstacles. The V phenomenon occurs in politics when a strong leadership characterized by a special type of personality engenders unity of action in the ruling circles of a state, creates an atmosphere of high drama through the manipulation of heroic or revolutionary rhetoric, centralizes the control of national potentials in the hands of the state, and embarks on a course of rhetorically and actually intense international conflict as the result of the leader's conscious and logical elaboration into action of a dramatic vision of the world. Volitional decisions have a vivid and garish hue, reflected both by contemporary journalism and by antiquarian history, that sets them off from the background of gray and motiveless routine determinations; thus will and V both *contrast* with prescription. But the three stand in a more complex relation than that of polar opposition, for will and V also both *override*[2] old prescription and *create* new prescription.

These assertions are complex, and must be presented with care and with qualifications. This chapter therefore begins with a set of propositions that summarize its argument. It goes on to detail the

[2] Whether by harnessing or by extirpating it.

ideas and the objective indicators of will and the V complex. The V complex is examined in particular in its relations to foreign policies and policy changes. Procedures and hypotheses for researching V are suggested, with specific references to states that should measure high on any scales that might be set up to measure V. A brief note on two possible patterns of origin of high V is included, and the chapter ends with a consideration of how the overall explanation of a state's foreign policy should be affected by the apparent current or former presence of the V complex.

Propositions about will, V, and prescription

The burden of this chapter is contained in the following propositions.

1. *Will* is a term that has a complex but real meaning: it corresponds to a certain part of human experience.

2. Will is a phenomenon not only of individual psychology, but also of the social process of group decisionmaking.

3. Will has certain objective indicators by which it can in effect be measured.

4. Because will is subject to measurement, we may speak of it not only existentially (as being present or absent) but also in gross quantitative terms (as being present in larger or smaller amounts).

5. Will is encountered frequently and significantly (in extra large doses) in foreign relations, as a quality of policy decisionmakers that they demonstrate in their decisions.

6. In foreign policy decisionmaking, will appears most strikingly as a portion of an even larger and recurrent complex of significant phenomena, which we may label V (for *volition*).

7. This V complex is measurable in its parts and in the correlation of those parts, if not as a whole.

8. The presence or absence of the V complex, and of will within it, is the most important factor, after capability, in accounting for foreign policy.

9. The presence or absence of V is, consequently, to be searched for (systematically, when that becomes possible; impressionistically, as things stand now) by those who seek to explain the foreign policy of any state.

10. When and to the degree that V exists currently, in the *present* of the policy to be explained, its causal impetus should be expected to override the various influences that share the common characteristic of prescription.

11. *Prescriptive* influences on foreign policy include, as main examples, (a) the psychocultural dispositions and habit patterns of mass publics and of long-established conventionally selected elites, (b) restrictive and conservative institutional structures, and (c) legitimate and customary decisionmaking routines.

12. To the degree that V is present, it deflects all these prescriptive influences and, conjointly with capability, virtually suffices to account for the content, quality, objectives, and success of policy.

13. Where and to the degree that V is not to be found in the present of policy, two conclusions follow: (a) Current policy *must* largely be explained in terms of prescriptive factors; (b) it *may* be accounted for in substantial part by reference to periods in the *past* where V was high.

14. Past V is to be searched for in periods of great decisions and great changes of policy, when old precedents were broken by men whose decisions made new precedents that still endure.[3]

15. When V existed in the past, it may have occurred in *bursts* or in *tides*.

16. *Bursts* of V are major precedent-breaking decisions clustered in brief periods and separated by long periods of stable policy.

17. *Tides* of V are represented in the history books by major decisions and changes at one time that were modified and extended by a series of decisions succeeding the earlier at a distance not of months or weeks but of years or decades.

18. Where V is tidal, present policy will have historical layers: the general line will trace back to a policy of several decades before; intermediate goals and regional general lines will be traced to more specific decisions of a few years past, which apply the logic of the initial policy to new circumstances.

19. To trace a present policy back to past episodes of high V is only to say that all *mystique* turns into *politique,* that the radical and rationalistic ideas of yesterday become the bureaucratic shibboleths of today, that will becomes routine, and that the power structures, procedures, and common notions that in combination sustain a stable set of national objectives and reactions are the result of the reception, embodiment, institutionalization, bureaucratization, and ritualization of long-past will.

[3] Even if only as recollections within the political culture, which may at some point permit the reinstatement of a precedent now disused in the political arena.

The will phenomenon

The word "will" covers in common usage a multitude of things. Webster's Third New International Dictionary can serve as a guide through that multitude to its operative essence. As synonyms, Webster's presents us with *desire, wish, inclination* (especially the desire to act in a particular way, as contrasted with the means or ability), *choice, determination, intention, insistence, persistence.* But "will" often also suggests the power of choosing and acting in accordance with a choice, the power of controlling one's own actions—self-control, self-direction. "Will" may be used to indicate the act of willing, choosing, or determining, settling indecision and mental uncertainty, or the total conscious process involved in choosing and effecting a decision. And, finally, according to Webster's, "will" may refer to the directing of action toward a goal clearly known in advance and requiring an effort to overcome obstacles or contrary desire.

By calling "will" a complex phenomenon, I mean to suggest that it is worthwhile looking for all these features in combination as well as separately. By suggesting that it is roughly quantifiable in practice, I am suggesting that we can find indications that several features are present in a given foreign policy decisionmaking apparatus (or any other decisional body) at a given time.

Will

High	*independence*
High	*demand*
High	*decision*
High	*persistence of action*

The first such feature in *self-direction* (*autonomy, self-determination*). Some decisional actors are not independently able to choose and act, but are subject to external forces, while others lack practical independence because their mutually vetoing institutions, stalemated processes, and fragmented political culture make it meaningless to speak of their having a single decisionmaking unit. There can be more and less unity, more and less independence of decision; some actors are very united in action and very independent. Criteria can surely be developed to provide evidence of this easy and widespread impression, and thus to measure the first feature of will, self-direction.[4]

The second feature of will is *desire, wish, inclination.* Some

---

[4] For further queries intended to be used to organize the investigation of self-direction, see Chapter 7 for external penetration; Chapter 5 for cultural homogeneity; Chapter 6 for the loci of decisionmaking and the separation of powers; Chapter 7 for decisional style and social homogeneity.

actors may have no strong and lucid desires, but a conflicting multitude of small wishes, a muddle of oceanic longings, a mélange of repressed strivings, or a repertoire of reflex reactions. To find actors high on this second feature of will, we look for clear, conscious, express, strong, salient *demands*.

The third feature of will is *choosing* or *determining to act* in a particular way. Some actors never transform their desires into behavior designed to fulfill them. The measures of this third aspect of will would then be the occurrence, frequency, saliency, continuity, and costliness of decisions to take action for obtaining goals.

The fourth feature of will is the *persistence* and *insistence* of effort in the face of obstacles and opposition, despite threats, risks, increasing costs, and a significant chance of failure. Some actors make decisions and abandon them lightly, while others take losses and are resolute. Therefore, to estimate this fourth aspect of an actor's will, one must look at the size of the obstacles and the degree of resistance to the decision, and at the time and resources spent in implementing that decision despite those obstacles and resistances.

Will in politics, then, is the complex phenomenon of independent and persistent demand, decision, and action against resistance. Its objective indicators are: lack of external penetration and internal paralysis of the decisional structure; clear and strong demands in the political talk of the governors; evidence of deliberate decisions in behavior designed to procure these demands; and evidence of substantial resistance to these demands and of behavior persistently directed at overcoming resistance and obtaining goals. Now the subject of will in politics, as will is thus defined, is a study all in itself. Even in foreign policy we could readily spend volumes finding, recounting, explaining, and judging the incidence, occasions, causes, and results of extreme will. But there is a more striking species of will in foreign policy, which demands our special attention.

The V complex: nature and symptoms

The phenomenon of will in foreign policy has certain recurrent and characteristic companions. Taken together with will, these form a multiplex and intriguing phenomenon. Since will itself is described here as a complex, this larger multiplex phenomenon, of which will is the essential center, can conveniently be labeled the V (for volition) phenomenon. This section will present an ideal-typical, extreme image of the V complex, combining several features of elite psychology with various characteristics of state behavior in words and deeds. This ideal-typical V complex will be an imaginary prototype to which actual states and policies may be matched, against which they may be rated, and by which they may perhaps be understood.

The V Complex

> Centralization of decisionmaking; internal unity in action
> The Leader; his special personality
> Verbal behavior: hostility and demand
> Observer-descriptions: dangerous ambition
> Observer-explanations: intention, not habit
> Mobilization of national resources
> External conflicts and violence
> Real and militant, often Revolutionist or Challenger, roles

Unity of action

The high-V state will commonly display a high centralization of decisionmaking in the hands of a Leader who stands as a monarch or a tyrant to his associates. These associates will not appear as independent and jealous feudal barons, nor as representatives of coordinate institutional or personal checks and balances. They will stand for compliance, not for resistance or bureaucratic sabotage; will perform as subordinates, as instruments.

Personality type

The Leader (perhaps, but uncommonly, the collective leadership) will reveal, if ever he is tested, a complex psychology mixing intelligence, ego strength, dominance (as opposed to submissiveness), superego strength (as opposed to dependency), venturesomeness, tough-mindedness, nonconformity, experimentalism, self-sufficiency, self-integration, and tension; he will be notably lacking in fear of threat and proneness to guilt or resignation.[5] Under anxiety, he will be unlikely to withdraw, waver, or conciliate.

Verbal behavior

If the statements of the representatives of a high-V state are studied and measured by content analysis, they will have specific characteristics. Strong *motivation* (repeated reference to goals, desires, and ideals) will be found, in close combination with strong *perception of frustration* by outsiders and *perception of hostility* on the part of these outsiders. Deep *dissatisfaction* with the frustration will appear, along with strong *hostility* toward the frustrating outsiders, and numerous *denunciations, threats,* and *accusations* against them. There will be a high expression of *intention to act,* and the leaders will frequently perceive and describe themselves, their roles, and their regime as *innovative* and *active*. There will be unusually fre-

[5] These categories are derived from the personality studies of Raymond B. Cattell, e.g. *The Scientific Analysis of Personality* (Baltimore, Md.: Penguin, 1965); see p. 365 for a listing and explanation of these traits.

quent *prophecies* or forecasts of victory for the ego-state and of frustration, defeat, or destruction for its enemies.[6]

Observers' descriptions

A state displaying extreme V complex in foreign policy will be described, or its leaders will collectively and individually be represented, in a certain language. Observers—journalists, academicians, official and unofficial commentators—will speak of its independence, its drive, its animus. Leaders will be called vigorous, zealous, spirited; or obsessed, fanatical, driven, overreaching. Its policies, whatever their contents, will be called novel, radical, extreme, daring, reckless. Such policies will involve great hopes, large costs, larger risks, debatable chances of success, and a high price of failure.

Intentionalistic explanations

Where V is high, observers and historians will tend much more often than is usually the case to attribute the verbal and physical behavior of the state in question to the inferred intentions of its leaders, to the presumed contents of their consciousnesses; and to attribute these in turn to the inferred structure of their psyches, to hypothetical mental events, and to their biographies. There should be especially frequent explanations of action by intention rather than by reference to routine, to habitual dispositions to react in given ways, or to the interplay of controlling interest groups.

Physical behavior

Physical behavior of a state with a high V complex will be characterized (unless verbal behavior is effective in securing desired outcomes) by a higher than average degree of external violence and a high degree of conflict behavior initiated and carried out against opposition. There should also be either a high and steady or a rising degree of exploitation of national resources for political purposes, as reflected in the government budget, the defense budget, the size of the armed forces, and so forth.[7]

The V complex: consequences for policy

The physical behavior of a state affected by the V complex and the verbal behavior of its leaders suggest the impact of V upon foreign

[6] These categories reflect the construction of quantitative measurements of content by Robert C. North and his colleagues in *Content Analysis* (Evanston, Ill.: Northwestern University Press, 1963).

[7] These categories reflect the statistical collections of R. J. Rummel, (The DON project), and of Bruce M. Russett, Hayward R. Alker, Jr., Karl W. Deutsch, and Harold D. Lasswell, *World Handbook of Political and Social Indicators* (New Haven, Conn.: Yale University Press, 1964), and others.

policy. But that impact should be made more explicit. Where objectives are set and decisions dominated by one deliberative volition, the V hypothesis implies, foreign policy will be, and will be perceived as, "revisionist" or anti-status quo. World politics will be, and will be perceived as, a source of discontent, injustice, and frustration. Objectives will seem difficult to fulfill, but will be intensely desired and demanded. Certain foreign states will be seen as hostile, standing in the way of the demanded satisfaction of desire, and their hostility will be returned with interest. The ego-state, probably self-perceived as having broken with and discarded a previous humiliating acquiescence in or subordination to things as they are, will feel as if it is on the move. And indeed, watchers on the outside will believe that it is on the move: the objectives of the leadership will seem novel, clear, and large (despite intense argument over the actual substance and relative novelty of these objectives); the leaders will seem to be coordinating all the necessary and available forces in pursuit of their hearts' desire. When its goals are not swiftly attained, the V-complex leadership will precipitate frequent and intense verbal battles, and perhaps more violent crises, by its demands, its *démarches*, its persistent attempts to gain a favorable issue in spite of resistance.

The V complex: hypotheses and their testing

It is a thesis of this chapter that the complex phenomenon labeled *will* and the even more complex phenomenon labeled V will in fact be found in the history and practice of foreign relations. But the main point of the thesis is the allegation that the presence or absence of an extremely strong V complex will be, when we come to explain the contents and quality of that policy, next only in explanatory power to the *capability* of that state. This thesis risks being tautological, since the ideal and composite representation of the V-complex phenomenon includes characteristics that *are* contents or qualities of policy, and that cannot, in consequence, be used to *explain* policy. To avoid a tautology, this thesis must be restated as *the unity of V*.

The unity of V

All the separate parts of the V phenomenon will frequently be found to exist together as a whole—the high centralization and unity of action, the type of leader, the hostile verbal behavior, the awed descriptions by observers, the high resource exploitation, the high foreign-conflict behavior, and the revisionist policy. And the psychology—the intentions and logic of the leaders—will explain the policy. Observers will use intentional, not dispositional, explanations. Thus V will frequently occur, and its parts will be united *in space and time* and *by causality*.

Other hypotheses about will and V

Several conflicting hypotheses may reveal some further controversies about will and the V phenomenon beyond the dispute over their mere occurrence and frequency or intensity of incidence.

Hypothesis 4.11

States displaying high will tend to have disruptive, anti-status-quo, revolutionary-or-imperialist foreign policies.[8]

Hypothesis 4.12

States displaying high will tend to display policies active in defense of the status quo.

Hypothesis 4.13

States displaying low will tend to have status-quo policies.

Hypothesis 4.01 (null hypothesis)

There is no relation between the will of a state and its attitude toward the status quo.

Hypothesis 4.21

States displaying high will tend to have a high degree of effectiveness in foreign policy.

Hypothesis 4.22

States showing high will tend to receive more and larger defeats in their foreign enterprises.

Hypothesis 4.02 (null hypothesis)

There is no relationship between will and the effectiveness or success of foreign policy.

[8] This and each of the following hypotheses may be amplified by substituting "V phenomenon" for "will," and thus proposing a relationship between the larger whole and its parts rather than between its central part and the consequences of that central part.

Research on V

In order to examine the connections, if any, between the V phenomenon and the contents and quality of policy, research should examine, in detail and one by one, cases where superficially the latter might seem to proceed from the former. More than the speculative hypotheses above should be tried, as they may be too gross. One might discover that the indicators of V go most often together with large results, great gains and great losses; one might find V associated with the most active policies, both defensive and aggressive.

To examine these relations, studies of V should focus on periods of novelties and of adventurous policy, periods that culminate in disastrous setbacks or major successes. The researchers may then scrutinize the politics of such times for the following: (1) the preeminent influence of new men of a special character; (2) an increased centralization of state resources and of the decisionmaking process (with perhaps increased speed, volume, scope, and coordination of decision); (3) a rise in the political saliency of personalities (as opposed to institutions, routines, or received and general opinion); (4) alterations in the content of official statements and inspired reports—toward a novel world view, toward dissatisfaction, hostility, and activism, and toward definitions of enemies, objectives, and means that are clearer, more concrete, and different in scope from previous definitions.

But of more immediate interest to the researcher will doubtless be the testing of the main thesis. He must ask whether, at any time, for any country, by comparison with previous and later posterior phases of the history of policy, the phenomenon V has been present, and if so, whether its consequences have been as significant as is here maintained. Where the presence of V is discovered, the order of its parts and precedents might well be described so as to see, for instance, whether a rise in foreign-conflict behavior preceded a change in the contents of official statements, or whether deep internal disturbances, the waxing of a foreign power, external threats and ambitions, or some other antecedent and stimulant appeared to evoke V. But first of all the researcher must see if, where, how intensely, and for how long the phenomenon did exist, according to the marks herein set down and by comparison with other states at the same time and with other times in the life of the same state.

Cases of high V and their scrutiny

To seek specimens of foreign policies justly attributable to the V-complex phenomenon is, since the prototype is an ideal pattern, to seek comparatively striking but nonetheless incomplete instances. Once one has decided that in a given state's policy certain broad objectives and lines of action are established and dominant, these must be traced back so far as is possible to specific political decisions made in specific circumstances. The more easily the pedigree of policy can be discovered, the more current policy is the issue of a few recent decisions or the brain child of a few men, and the more radical the departure of current from traditional policy, the more likely it is that a concentration of volitional indicators will be discovered at the birth-point of current policy—the more likely, in other words, that V will be found in the past of current policy. The more recent the establishment of the current general line of policy, the more likely that those indicators of V will still be present. And the more novelty and concentrated decision in a policy at a given moment, the more appropriately does explanation focus on the specific desires, principles, political doctrines, plans, analyses, and psychic aberrations of a charismatic leader or an organized and conscious ruling elite.

When these clues are followed in recent history, the lineage of American foreign policy reveals a crucial germination in the years of 1947–50, the palmy days of the Truman Administration, with later major overlays in the détente policies of 1955 and 1963 and the Vietnam decisions of 1961 and 1965. Soviet policy shows a double nature and a double trace, to cold war decisions of the 1940s and to coexistence decisions of the middle 1950s. French policy has undergone a calculated evolution since 1958, British policy an uncalculated devolution since 1945, German and Japanese a most gradual emergence since the collapses of 1945; the developing and very will-full Chinese policy of the early 1960s has undergone external and internal retrogression since 1965.

Today one would expect to find among the great powers most evidence of the V phenomenon in the work of de Gaulle; similar symptoms should be found in Chinese policy 1960–65, and in Russian and American policy at the outset of the cold war. If international "crises" truly reflect in practice all the connotations that term calls up, then there should be brief but severe increases in the several manifestations of the V complex on all sides in all of the many such crises that have characterized this postwar era. And the policies of such states as Cuba, North Vietnam, and North Korea ought to show high levels of willfulness on all indicators at many periods, if not continuously since the establishment of their still-persistent regimes.

A case of moderately high V:
the containment policy

It is impossible at this point even to begin the long, energetic inquiries that will be required in order to give a full account of the V complex in recent history. But they might be prepared for by reviewing one of the cases that ought to provide the clearest evidence of the V phenomenon to see whether it seems in fact to be likely to yield acceptable results.

The American policy of containment is currently applied to the Soviet Union, to China, to lesser Communist states (independent or satellite), and to Communist parties, armies, and movements in non-Communist states throughout the world. The policy evolved from one consciously adopted by a few men in the highest places of the executive branch in late 1946 and early 1947, which was ratified (as foreign policies are habitually "ratified") by congressional appropriations and in national elections. These men had for some time expressed resentment and dislike of the extensive dominion and the colonial policies of the Soviet Union in Eastern Europe, hostility toward the Communist parties that were its agents abroad, apprehension at the scale of its land armaments, skepticism about its leaders' intentions, and suspicion of its ruling movement's future drives.

Except for President Truman, the chief among them, who had come to office suddenly 2 years earlier on the death of his predecessor, the arrival to predominant influence of these men was rather gradual. Still, in less than 2 years' time from April 1945, there were new men in the key seats of power, and the policies of Harry S Truman, Dean Acheson, George Kennan, and others were very little like those of Franklin D. Roosevelt and Harry Hopkins. These men worked out by degrees the objective of containing, in Europe and the Middle East first, then in Asia, the expansion of direct and indirect Soviet influence, and the techniques of containing it through economic, military, and covert and overt political aid to its local opponents and through the threat and use of collective or national military force where aid would not suffice.

The American Administration lacked a charismatic semidivine Leader of the stature of the Stalin of the time (or the Mao, Castro, or de Gaulle of later years), and did not discard the limits of the Constitution, the power of Congress, or the regularity of elections. But its Soviet opponent supplied enough dramas, challenges, and confrontations to evoke an occasional, serviceable, and basically unnatural unanimity between the Administration and its Congresses, a unity expressed in aid bills, in treaties ratified, and in large increases in military force and expenditure. The policy of opposition to Soviet designs led soon enough to budgetary and military commitments, exchanges of warnings, threats, and denunciations, war crises, and war (Korea 1950–53).

Except for the low salience of a Leader, America in 1947–50 did seem to display much conformity to the V pattern. Furthermore, its policy of the present shows symptoms of past V. To this day, current acts of state are explained in official and scholarly circles as workings-out of the deliberate intentions of the men of those years. In their time, their ideas were original and somewhat shocking; now these ideas have become received doctrine, stock in trade, and ongoing bureaucratic reflex. The old ideas are incremented, deflected, softened, or elaborated by their successors; containment evolves into containment à la mode, with a topping of "competitive coexistence" or "peaceful engagement," but the basic doctrine is never abandoned. These former innovations have gone to routine. What were once the deliberate and reasoned analyses and choices of elites have become consecrated, vested, and lodged. They are consecrated in the political culture, in the shape of public attitudes and dispositions toward Russia and toward communist states and movements. They are vested in institutions, in the shape of the Central Intelligence Agency, the North Atlantic Treaty Organization, the world apparatus of American military bases and advisers and presence, the National Security Council, the U.S. Information Agency, the Agency for International Development, and the selected personnel and ingrained presuppositions of the Department of State, successive White House staffs, the continuing political establishment in high congressional posts, and both of the major party mechanisms that present and provide candidates for high public office. They are lodged in processes, under the titles of *maintenance of continuity, adaptation to circumstance,* and the *selection-out* or compromising of deviance by these institutions, through the traumas of succession and of altering challenges or capability balances.

At this date in America, the V complex of the days of containment's genesis seems highly institutionalized. Indeed, centralization is still great, and foreign-conflict behavior still high. But there is probably less strength of intention, frustration, dissatisfaction, motivation, and activism; there is certainly less perceived and self-perceived innovation. It may be that there is a natural process of diminution in institutionalized V, with innovation falling off first, activism next, will expressed verbally next, actual conflict behavior next, and centralization last of all, but that is yet to be seen and stands for future research to prove. But whatever the order by which V declines, it has clearly declined in the United States since 1947, and as the policy of that time has become precedent, the will of that time has become the prescription of the present.

Genesis of the V complex: two patterns

If V explains policy, we may well ask: What explains V? In part, surely, it is the chance or circumstance that puts certain ideas in the heads of certain men in high places at certain times. But there may also be certain typical situations that tend to evoke V. The issuing forth of American will in 1947–50 seems to have centered on an analysis of a new enemy and a new threat, and on the articulation of a new and greater objective. These acts of consciousness were in turn evoked by a striking change, over a few years, in the world distribution of power, a change that raised this state and its foe-to-be to unequaled preeminence, and by the adoption by Russia of a policy that might justly have been taken from external signs alone for one both imperialist and revolution-exporting. Perhaps such events will

appear as typical precursors of a waxing will; one might by comparison examine the antecedents and the character of American war
policy in 1941, British in 1940 (or against Napoleon), Russian policy
itself in the late 1940s, and for that matter the manner in which
William of Orange dealt with Louis XIV.

If these comparisons hold true, then we might propose that
one pattern of the genesis of will and the V complex is as follows:

Because of prior corrupt or short-sighted policy or because of
a shortage of equally high-ranking great powers, a foreign state
with high ambitions has come so near to predominance in the
international system as to demand a strong check, and a long,
deliberate, and steady check, if it is to be reined in at all. The ego-
state, a power of high rank, has a general line supporting the
status quo. By chance, it acquires as its chief executive a William,
a Churchill, a Roosevelt, or a man or set of men capable of such
analysis and consequential decisions as these men displayed. The
ego-state thereby becomes the extraordinary member that oper-
ates a semiautomatic balance-of-power system to check and to
contain the challenger.

There is another possible model of the origin of the V complex, which may be drawn as follows:

A period of internal convulsion is stopped by a rigid dictatorship
of one man, or of a few. In this case it is chaos and conspiracy,
if not internal war, that admit and impose centralization. On the
pretext of the universal validity of its ideology, the dictatorship
creates a system for that idea's external propagation, hardly distinguished from the institutions and processes set up for its internal maintenance; and/or, frightened or humiliated by foreign
intervention in the period of turmoil or by foreign domination before it, the dictatorship resolves and takes steps to expel, spite,
harry and weaken, or (for better security and greater satisfaction)
overthrow utterly the outsiders. This course is held tight, first
through the force of the overpowering personality and common
animus of the leadership, then through arranged and picked succession to the original leaders, and at last through inveteracy and
reception into the public consciousness and the state structure.
In this model, men out of power are first seized by grand ideas
and enmities, then seize power and enforce the centralization of
authority, and—perhaps at once—give official vent to their bitter
ideas, prepare the needed resources, charge foreign policy
sharply, and begin the struggle. Such an exacerbation of will
should end, if not in new convulsions, with a sequence: the departure of the Leader, slow decentralization of command, slower
moderation of physical behavior, lagging deescalation of words,
and eventual diminution of centralized resources.

Under the rubric of this model it would be worth the effort to compare de Gaulle, Mao Tse-tung, Castro, Ho Chi Minh, perhaps Kim Il Sung; also the early Comintern, Hitler, the French revolutionaries, and others of varied career and character but singular determination.

Will and the explanatory residuals of prescription

The V phenomenon has no single polar opposite. The term *routine* suggests a primary contrast, but not the only one, unless the meaning of routine is enlarged to encompass not only habitual and persistent bureaucratic behavior but also actions stemming from political traditions, the characteristic prejudices of the people and their rulers, and the whole general character of the political institutions and processes of the country. *Prescription* is the common element in all these opposites.

All these determinants are best understood as residuals: most often resisting by their inertia, they are sometimes overridden by a Promethean will. When they are so overmastered, they at first change their content to embody and to reflect the new influence. When the active innovation of will has ceased, these residuals perpetuate its determinations by reducing them to routines, traditions, and prejudices. They attain in turn a persistence and inertia of their own, and resist the new will of the living by building a lasting monument to the dead.

Policies emergent from a state where prescription dominates and will is at a discount must bear the double stamp of custom and caprice. They will seem familiar yet arbitrary; ingrained and conventional, they are also purposeless. When they are explained, the interpreter will make reference to a chain of causes or to chance, and not to a chain of reasons relating objectives to acts and means to ends.

How, then, should explanations that take will and the V phenomenon seriously be ordered so that they may also encompass these residual factors? The relationship may be demonstrated by reference to a specific case. No matter how widespread the attitudes from which President Charles de Gaulle made his policies were in France under the Fourth Republic, and no matter how long his policies may outlive him or how thoroughly they may become routinized dispositions and prejudices of post-Gaullist bureaucrats, parties, and publics, the essential aspect of any explanation of French foreign policy after 1958 will be "de Gaulle made *this* and *this* decision, and for *these* reasons." The explanation of the contents of the "Gaullic" consciousness may then evolve into (1) an examination of elite and bureaucratic resistance, sabotage, and routinization of de Gaulle's policies, (2) an investigation of Gaullist tendencies in French political culture or of prestige-seeking in historic French dealings with allies, or (3) a study of "monarchic" institutions and processes in the Fifth Republic and before. But all these factors are routed to or through that of will in decision. They lead to the questions of why de Gaulle reasoned as he did, or why and how he was able to impose his designs and to make them legitimate.

Thus, to take the phenomenon labeled V seriously in foreign policy is first of all to explain *some* current policies by reference to *some* personalities, *some* individuals—to their biographies, their reasoning, their ideologies, and their psychopathology. The world is populated only by individuals, but the concepts of political science permit us to dismiss virtually every individual as an explanatory entity in foreign policy. Almost all persons can be better (more truthfully as well as more briefly) dealt with by statistics on their numbers, productivity, and militarization (as capabilities), their opinions (tradition and political culture), and their political organization and functioning (institutions and processes). A few forceful contemporaries cannot be so dismissed. To them and to their decisions much of policy, and sometimes much of capability, institutions, and political culture, must be attributed. All ruling circles must be treated, at least formally, in this personal way when one writes a detailed *history* of *past* policy. Only some present and former ruling circles merit such personal treatment when the enterprise in hand is that of giving a general account of current policy.

To take will seriously is to expect to find some significant cases in history where the impact of institutions, established processes, and prejudices on policy was sharply overridden by the design and decision of a few men. At such junctures one expects to find the construction of grand objectives, a substantial mobilization and centralization of capabilities, an intensification of tensions, and a sharp breach with the policies of the immediate past. Such conditions have surely occurred and concurred in the past; when they have arisen, they have been of great moment. As far as they overbear in practice the weight of more persistent and more slowly evolving factors, so they must outweigh them in the accounts that explain practice. And even where there is a persistence of policy, perpetuated by tradition and by stability of political forms, that policy—even those traditions and forms—will commonly bear tracing to a *will* and a *decision,* long gone, made lasting (and an impediment to future will) by routines, institutions, and prejudices—in short, by *prescription.*

It is in this sense that the categories of prescription are residual to V in explanatory weight. They become important in proportion as personality and intentionality lose their momentousness. They are to be employed fully in explanation when a very recent and powerful will is not to be found, and partially when such a will, rather than overbearing all continuity and resistance arbitrarily and directly, acts—as it must—in part through persuasions, intermediaries, consensus-building, and established (or newly established but self-sustaining) notions, persons, roles, and channels.

References

Cattell, Raymond B., *The Scientific Analysis of Personality*. Baltimore: Penguin, 1965.

North, Robert C., Ole R. Holsti, M. George Zaninovitch, and Dina A. Zinnes, *Content Analysis*. Northwestern University Press, 1963.

Russett, Bruce M., H. Alker Jr., K. Deutsch, and H. D. Lasswell, *World Handbook of Political and Social Indicators*. New Haven, Conn.: Yale University Press, 1964.

5

Political culture

Contents: cognitions
          valuations
          affections
Relevant political culture: narrow or broad?
                               homogeneous, fragmented or compound?

Political culture and foreign policy

A polity's political culture is the pattern of its members' individual orientations toward politics. It is a pattern of cognitions, affections, and valuations. *Cognitions* are empirical beliefs, beliefs about what the actual state of political life is. *Valuations* are judgments of what ought to be, judgments about the goals that ought to be pursued in political life, the moral quality of political objects and events. *Affections* are feelings, often represented verbally by expressive symbols of attachment, involvement, alienation, rejection, identification, amity, enmity, and so forth, about political objects. The basic values, political ideals, emotional commitments, operating norms, and empirical beliefs about patterns of political action and interaction that compose a political culture are the subjective realm of politics, and function to give meaning to and guidelines for individual and collective behavior.[1]

We are interested, of course, in only those aspects of the political culture of a state that bear on its foreign policy and world role and that also influence or help to explain state behavior. The particular contents of political culture that are of interest in the

---

[1] See Lucian W. Pye and Sidney Verba, eds., *Political Culture and Political Development* (Princeton, N.J.: Princeton University Press, 1965), and Gabriel Almond and G. Bingham Powell, Jr., *Comparative Politics: A Developmental Approach* (Boston: Little, Brown, 1966), pp. 50–72.

study of foreign policy will characteristically include fundamental attitudes and orientations (cognitive, evaluative, affective) to the specific political objects of international politics. These objects include the world political system as a whole, one's own state and others, the individual and group incumbents of key national and foreign roles (and those particular roles and structures of roles), and specific current policies, issues, and problems. But the relevant cognitions will also include basic assumptions about the nature of man, politics, states, international politics, and the world system. The relevant valuations will include guiding principles and overriding demands that may set and explain general foreign policy and world political goals. The relevant affections will include emotive expressions about all these subjects.

Political culture versus relevant political culture

Let us assume for a moment that we are dealing with a political community that is completely homogeneous—one in which there are no social classes, no rulers or leading elites, no interest, opinion, or pressure groups. The problem of discovering the contents of the political culture of such a polity would be radically simplified by its lack of sociopolitical differentiation, and it would be easy to understand what was meant by political culture in a social context where all individuals had very much the same set of notions about politics.

If a political culture is a set of subjective orientations to politics, then we are justified in speaking of the political consciousness of an individual as his own private and personal political culture. If we grant that a man's ideas can be studied at all (by inference from his behavior, including, most particularly, his talk), then a researcher might reasonably seek to reconstruct an individual's subjective orientation to politics from his words and actions in various circumstances. If we next grant that ideas, inferred from verbal behavior, can often explain action, then a political researcher might reasonably use the inferred contents of a political actor's consciousness as partial explanations of his political behavior. Given these assumptions, a person's private political culture is both worth studying and susceptible to study. And if every member of a given political community were of a single mind, if the polity's political culture were perfectly homogeneous, it would be a simple task for the researcher to determine the specifics of that single mind's political culture—for a close study of the political talk of any man on the street would also demonstrate the ways of thought of the men in positions of trust and power, readily displaying the role of such ways of thought in the making of foreign policy. An easy job indeed!

But if we were to take all the inhabitants of all the states on the globe, and to extract from them all their judgments about foreign states and foreign policy, we would surely find no state with a single "mind." Great differences would exist among states in their degree of national consensus on such matters. In any state, some elements would be so general and widespread as to appear as a national "style"; others, more narrowly confined, would appear as the ideologies or "character" of particular groups; yet others would be so much more restricted as to be best described as the special features of certain frequently discovered psychological types; and a last set would be so specialized as to represent the beliefs peculiar to one or another individual person.

As soon as it is admitted that the political culture of any polity is likely to be multiplex and varied, the separate portions of that variety must be differentially treated as relevant to policy. The key question in the present is: Who is in power? More exactly, it is: Who has what influence over policy? For the relevant political culture of the present is the subjective orientation of those who actually influence policymaking.[2]

Relevant political cultures, narrow and broad

The first thing that the would-be researcher into the effect of a state's political culture upon its foreign policy needs to know, then, is the answer to the question: Whose political culture is relevant? In practice, the initial questions of our researcher will be: How concentrated is influence upon foreign policy? What persons, what roles make and affect decisions? Who controls, who decides, who governs? This inquiry, itself to be classified as an investigation into the political institutions of foreign-policymaking,[3] is supplemented by the question of how far the V phenomenon is present.[4]

To the degree that the V phenomenon stands out in a state's present foreign policy, *relevant* political culture should largely be studied by any explanation of that policy that examines the will and ideas of the dominating few; the notions in other minds than those of its ruling few must be referred to as impediments, as resistances that cause the leaders to go slow, to trim, to mediate their policies beyond their own desire and best judgment. But the less the V

---

[2] Just so, in anticipating future politics the relevant political cultures are those of the most likely successor personalities and groups. The future of relevant political cultures is, of course, a matter of speculation—speculation on who (what person or collectivity) will replace a domineering personality, on what young elite is in training to replace a persistently disposed ruling elite, on what recurrent ideologies or personality types have irregularly risen to power in the past and may therefore be expected to do so again.

[3] See Chapter 6.

[4] Or anticipated. Political culture is in part a matrix of dissatisfactions, complaints, and wants, some of which may not be articulated to the political system as demands. Widespread unarticulated or ineffectively articulated wants may presage a future seizure of will and forecast its policy content.

phenomenon is operative, the more it will be appropriate to refer in explaining policy to a political culture that is diffused and differentiated, widespread but segmented, and to characteristics of both the content and the organization of such political cultures as influence policy.

Thus one polar model of the political culture that is relevant to foreign policy represents extreme *centralization*. The more that decisional influence is in fact concentrated, the more attention must be paid to the particular political cultures of elite persons, roles, and institutions. When the V phenomenon is extreme, the intensive examination of the personality type, psychic disturbances, ideological expostulations, and special prejudices of one man may make up the main burden of a study of political culture in foreign policy decisions. But even then, just insofar as demands, suggestions, interpretations, and analysis filter up to the central decisionmaker through the agencies for political communication, those agencies will deserve to be examined in order to reveal the distortion of the flow of communication by the individual subjectivities or collective prejudices of agency members.[5] And, to the degree that policy requires popular support in the form of soldiers or taxes, the political culture of those social segments constituting the political base of the dominating few must be examined for the elements that explain why such support is rendered—and whether it is because of habitual obedience or charismatic hypnosis of that political base in all things, or because policy is attuned to ageless prejudices or legitimized by incessant current indoctrinations. But centralized institutions and processes, and in particular the intense presence of the V phenomenon, require that the main explanatory work concentrate upon the consciousness and character of certain individuals—an elite.

The more widespread the participation in foreign policy decisionmaking, the larger the relevant political culture. It will be a matter of course in any state for large numbers of the population to be legally or practically deprived of influence for reasons of age, sex, health, education, location, race, or subordinate condition. Some persons will be "parochials," with little or no awareness of the national political system. Many more will be "subjects," aware of the impact that the outputs of the national political system will have on their lives. There may be many "subject-participants," who have little opportunity to share in decisionmaking but who nonetheless have unarticulated political demands and see themselves as potentially engaged in the political process. And some persons will be "participants," who do in fact articulate demands and make decisions.[6] Characteristically, there will be far fewer participants, and more subjects and parochials, with regard to foreign than with regard to

[5] This study of the political culture of the institutions of communication could go hand in hand with a study of the structure of the process of information production and distribution; see Chapter 7, under "Political communication."

[6] See Almond and Powell, *Comparative Politics,* pp. 53, 59.

domestic policy. The participant "mass" whose political culture is relevant may be a relatively tiny political class, composed of members of a certain party, church, economic level, or other well-defined social stratum.

A very narrow relevant culture could be studied biographically and psychographically, man by man and mind by mind. Depth interviewing, psychological testing, and the analysis of individual writings and public statements would be appropriate. A mass political culture is most appropriately researched by public-opinion polling and attitude surveys on general principles and immediate issues of foreign policy, by extensive content analysis of consistencies and uniformities in public communications (editorials, reportage; public letters and petitions; official statements and documents; political speeches and writings of public figures; rumors, legends, myths, and folklore), and by political anthropology, studying the political socialization of children. In fact, in any given case, both narrow and broad groups' orientations will be relevant, the former being more relevant.

The only evident hypotheses about the substantive impact of the scope of relevant political culture on foreign policy are derivatives of hypotheses about the policy impact of concentration versus diffusion of influence on decisionmaking.[7]

Homogeneous, fragmented, and compound political cultures

All polities with operating governments must have a certain degree of uniformity in the relevant political cultures of their members. All relevant masses whose political socialization is not successfully designed to eradicate identity will show a certain degree of fragmentation. Thus all political cultures will be compound—partly uniform and partly fragmented—and should be studied as such. Nonetheless, we shall approach the study of compound political cultures by positing (again, ideal-typically) a polar dichotomy between homogeneous and fragmented political cultures. This is heuristically useful because, although both the unified and the diverse in political culture will be revealed by the intensive biography and extensive surveys here recommended as research techniques, it is not immediately practical to start such intensive and extensive work. More venturesome and impressionistic modes are in order to begin with, and in these modes the approaches to uniformities and to differences are not the same.

Furthermore, there are empirical differences among polities in the degree of homogeneity in their relevant political cultures. These are reflected, cursorily, in a typological variable extracted from

---

7 See Chapter 6, under "Loci of decisionmaking."

Banks and Textor,[8] where it is Raw Characteristic Number 31, "Political Enculturation." For any polity, we can ask the typological question: Is it "integrated . . . with little or no extreme opposition, communalism, fractionalism, disenfranchisement, or political nonassimilation"? Or has it a significant minority in such an alienated status? Or is it so nonintegrated or restrictive that a majority or near-majority is in extreme opposition, communalized, fractionalized, disenfranchised, or politically nonassimilated? The typology suggests hypotheses:

Hypothesis 5.11

The less politically enculturated a polity, the more its leaders will tend to seek external allies against internal opponents.

Hypothesis 5.21

The more complete a polity's political enculturation, the more stable and effective its foreign policy.

Hypothesis 5.01 (null hypothesis)

Variations in political enculturation are not connected to variations in the content and quality of foreign policy.

Homogeneous political culture

Assuming that the relevant political culture is a single system of empirical beliefs, values, and affections, some specific questions of substance may be asked. One of them relates to the degree of secularization in that culture. *Secularism* entails an attitude toward politics as pragmatic bargaining in a marketplace of give-and-take trading, where each participant accepts rough reciprocity as a norm to govern

[8] Arthur S. Banks and Robert B. Textor, *A Cross-Polity Survey* (Cambridge, Mass.: M.I.T. Press, 1963). Despite its sometimes controversial and sometimes vague definitions, this volume offers a set of explicit classifications that mostly seem empirical or, at least, evocative of a consensus of impressions. It permits significant contrasts of types and sets of states. Because of the great suggestiveness of such contrasts, I propose to employ them in constructing hypotheses wherever possible; because Banks and Textor have this field nearly to themselves, it is mostly their contrasts that will figure herein. In order to research these hypotheses in depth, it would be necessary to update the actual classifying done by Banks and Textor from 1963 to the present, and also to apply their typologies to categorize year by year (or month by month) the whole group of contemporary polities. This would permit correlation of, for example, kinds of political culture with kinds of foreign policy, and changes in political culture with changes in foreign policy.

outcomes of dealing, and in which empirical, specific, and limited objectives are sought—all within some more implicit and diffuse sense of the limits upon the bargainable and of excluded goals, actions, and deals. Secularism is contrasted with *traditionalism*, whose orientations are diffuse rather than specific, closed rather than open, and governed by rigid norms of interaction; it is contrasted with *ideologism* (for example, Communist and clericalist), where an explicit, specific set of political orientations and rules of conduct is spelled out to form a rigid and closed image of political life; and it is contrasted with *supersecularism*, which sets no visible limits to dealing and bargaining. One might reasonably hypothesize the greater adaptability of foreign policy directed by secular than by ideological, and by ideological than by traditional, orientations; and it is equally reasonable to propose the greater stability of foreign policy directed by ideological than by secular, and by secular than by supersecular, political culture.

This typology[9] is closely related to one proposed by Banks and Textor, "Ideological Orientation."[10] For any polity, we may ask the typological question: Has the regime committed the state and the whole polity to a single formal doctrine? To an overriding national goal (especially, for example, "development")? Or are the polity and regime committed merely to conventional procedures for the legitimation of new or changed power relationships and policies? Or are polity and regime so "situational" in orientation as to reject all ideological elements, making no commitments on doctrines, goals, or procedures? Once more, of course, one then inquires for any state whether its type of ideological orientation has any discernible effect on foreign policy; and if so what that may be. One might consider offhand as hypotheses the following:

Hypothesis 5.31

"Doctrinal" and "goal-oriented" (for example, "developmental") polities will tend to follow an elite model of relevant political culture.

Hypothesis 5.41

States with a choice of external allies prefer to choose partners of similar ideological type.

Hypothesis 5.411

Hypothesis (5.41) holds most strongly for states with doctrinal and least strongly for states with situational ideological orientations.

[9] Derived from Almond and Powell, *Comparative Politics*, pp. 58–63.

[10] *A Cross-Polity Survey*, Raw Characteristic Number 24.

Hypothesis 5.51

The more comprehensive a polity's ideological orientation, the more stable its foreign policy.

Hypothesis 5.61

Goal-oriented polities will show more dominance of the V phenomenon, doctrinal polities of institutions, conventional polities of the legitimate political process, and situational polities of an informal political process, in foreign policy decisionmaking.

Hypothesis 5.02 (null hypothesis)

Variations in ideological orientation are not connected with variations in the content or quality of policy.

These typologies are regrettably primitive. The study of the political culture of foreign policy, like the study of political culture itself, is not yet far enough advanced to permit the presentation of complex, convincing, and intriguing typologies. Consequently, both comparison and generalizations are lacking. New typologies will have to grow out of impressionistic classifications applied to extensive descriptive studies undertaken with comparative intent. Even these do not yet exist, for the most part; rather, we find more global judgments.

To the degree that the political community whose cultures we intend to study is indeed a homogeneous one, having only *one* culture, and that one of sufficient internal consistency and elaboration that specific decisions can frequently be derived by applying general principles to immediate situations, the researcher can expect that the significant elements of political culture, as they are judged by observers to have affected foreign policy, will be found filed in the literature of foreign policy studies under several traditional headings. Some accounts will declare that they have discovered stable national (or group) "myths," or fluctuating "national morale" or "national opinion"; others will seek to reveal special cultural-psychological traits, or "national character"; yet others will allege the expression of continuing "national styles" or "operational codes" in foreign policy.[11]

[11] See Gabriel Almond, *The American People and Foreign Policy* (New York: Harcourt, 1950); Walt W. Rostow, *The United States in the World Arena* (New York: Harper, 1960), Chap. 3ff.; Nathan Leites, *The Operational Code of the Politburo* (New York: McGraw-Hill, 1951); Ruth Benedict, *The Chrysanthemum and the Sword* (Boston: Houghton Mifflin, 1946); J. William Fulbright, *Old Myths and New Realities* (New York: Random, 1964); Hans Morgenthau, *Politics Among Nations*, 4th ed. (New York: Knopf, 1967), Chap. 9; Geoffrey Gorer and John Rickman, *The People of Great Russia* (New York: Norton, 1962); Robert E. Osgood, *Ideals and Self-Interest in America's Foreign Relations* (Chicago: University of Chicago Press, 1953).

The student of the homogeneous elements of a relevant political culture of foreign policy will doubtless begin by turning to these accounts.

The researcher's target, on the assumption or in the area of homogeneity, is the discovery of a well-defined national identity, a single national loyalty in foreign affairs, a single expected or demanded "legitimate" institutional structure and political process of foreign policy decisionmaking institutions, and a nationally valid collection of judgments, beliefs, emotions, and ideas about the actual world order, the proper world order, the subject state's (and other states') actual and proper world role and foreign policy. Until detailed empirical analyses of political opinion satisfy him, he must give his own impressions, and draw upon the impressions of others, as to the actual contents of the diffused and homogeneous relevant "national" political culture: his initial aids are the academic and objective historical studies of a state's "nationalism" or of official ideology.

When the researcher at last makes his way to primary sources, he will secure his most accurate data by widespread polling of attitudes. But if he is searching for uniformities, he will be most economical in his work if he begins, not with polls, but with the officially approved school textbooks on the history of the state's foreign relations. For just so far as the literate class is the political class, and so far as uniform political socialization takes place in the school rather than the home, an elemental and only partly deliberate and artificial condensation of the opinion and the assumptions of participants will be discovered in these volumes.

Fragmented political culture

Political socialization is the lifelong process by which orientations to politics are transmitted to and received by individuals. It begins in the family unit, continues in the school structure and peer group, and is maintained by employment experience, the mass media, and direct contacts with the political process. Heterogeneity and inconsistency in political socialization create a fragmented political culture, with shared common orientations being either nonexistent or shallowly rooted and unstable.[12]

The assumption of homogeneity in diffused political culture is proved out by an extensive survey of ideas, trends, and viewpoints. When true, it will be true only to a certain degree; and it may not be true at all. There will regularly appear to be contradictions in the relevant political culture, mutually incompatible outlooks and propositions and "isms" located in different groups, parties, movements, elites, and persons—or even in the same such group, party, and so on. Attempts to research a political culture of foreign policy on the assumption of homogeneity will normally, as they become more

[12] Almond and Powell, *Comparative Politics*, pp. 66–72.

extensive and precise, correct that assumption by discovering the contradictions of political culture: simultaneous, contradictory, and competing strands of thought about foreign affairs.

In a diffuse and homogeneous relevant political culture, the student of nationalism and national character is at home. In a sharply constricted and uniform relevant political culture, the student of elites, the biographer and psychobiographer, and the scrutinizer of monolithic and consciously elaborated ideological systems should come to the fore. It is in the study of fragmented political cultures relevant to foreign policy that the student of plural ideologies, the examiners of "isms" who poll and survey or interview and probe in depth, and the historians of foreign policy who extract and expound upon conflicting and countervailing national traditions come to the fore. These are the authors of the secondary sources that will provide the researcher with the suggestive hypotheses that will organize his work.

But where no prior judgment of the substantive contrasts within a fragmented political culture exists, or after prior judgments are exhausted, the student of foreign policy has again a secondary and a primary source to be examined before extensive polling and intensive personality study must begin. The secondary source is the bare detailed narrative history of the nation's foreign relations; one searches for contradictions in its foreign policy, in order to detect incoherencies in its political culture. Contradictions in the relevant political culture may express themselves as conflicting factions and their programs; these programs, even if not made fully explicit, should nonetheless appear as temporary *compromises* and internal *inconsistencies* in policy at one time, and as specific *alterations* or regular *alternations* of policy over time. Thus to locate in policy such compromises, inconsistencies, and so forth, will very often be a first indication of the presence of such contradictions (among many other things).

The primary material, consequently, is the official and immediate verbal behavior of the state. These official public documents constitute the most accessible verbal output of a state (the secret internal record is too belatedly released for our purposes). The exhaustive study of a fragmented relevant political culture then requires the scrutiny of the official verbiage of the state over time. Recurrent and contrasting themes will be sought by a content analysis, to display the cognitions, valuations, and affections; the basic desires, principles, assumptions, and symbols; the beliefs about states and the world that constitute relevant political culture. Where there is a public debate over policy (and that debate is sometimes carried on in the foreign press), its materials form the next object of scrutiny, in the same fashion. Such a study, which will reveal the degree of homogeneity as well as the directions of fragmentation, should crystallize a contrasting set of models of the desires, assumptions, and reasoning of which this public talk is the expression, just as the fluctuations of policy are the indicators of their impact.

Comparative foreign relations

Compound political culture

One expects, in fact, however extreme the variations in the degree of homogeneity or fragmentation from polity to polity, that there will be in most countries a rather homogeneous but diffuse basal political culture of foreign policy, with increasing specificity of subject matter bringing increasing variety of orientations (and these probably carried by fewer persons). In most cases, therefore, the techniques relevant to the study of both homogeneity and difference will need to be applied. For example, secondary accounts of the distinctive contents of Irish nationalism and primary studies of the world image provided in Irish textbooks should combine with secondary and primary studies of ambiguities in Irish foreign policy and contradictions in the official verbalizations and public debate of Ireland. These would at length lead to intensive studies of the thought of Irish leaders and extensive surveys of public opinion and content analyses of public communications, and at last to the study of political socialization in Ireland. Such is the long road to the comparative study of political culture and foreign policy.

References

Almond, Gabriel and G. Bingham Powell, Jr., *Comparative Politics: A Developmental Approach.* Boston: Little, Brown, 1966.

Banks, Arthur S. and Robert B. Textor, *A Cross-Polity Survey.* Cambridge, Mass.: M.I.T. Press, 1963.

Pye, Lucian W. and Sidney Verba, eds., *Political Culture and Political Development.* Princeton, N.J.: Princeton University Press, 1965.

6

Political institutions

Political institutions and foreign policy

Under the label "the influence of political institutions on foreign policy" we may properly place statements discussing the external effects of the character of the organization that makes foreign policy. The *political institutions* of a state are the significant and persistent organizations, ordinarily self-maintaining and self-stabilizing, that occupy a cardinal and commanding position in the society in that they contain those fundamental roles that make authoritative decisions for the state and its society. It is therefore of prime interest to students of political institutions to know (1) where, in the complex maze of roles that ordinarily makes up the ruling bodies of any society, the broadest and most authoritative decisions are made; (2) what autonomy those crucial centers have, with what others they share decisional authority, and by what others they are held responsible; (3) what regular and persistent characteristics are displayed by those personnel who are the occupants of key roles in those centers of decisionmaking. These considerations are interesting because they reveal the institutional context of the policymaking process. Consequently, in this chapter we shall examine the questions of the loci of decisionmaking, the constitutional and representative status of the regime, and the recruitment, tenure, and character of political leaders. In the next (and closely related) chapter, we shall consider the influences of noninstitutional aspects of social and political structure and of the structure of the policymaking process itself upon the substance of foreign policy.

Because the field of political institutions and processes has long been a preserve for political scientists, we possess a traditional viewpoint, an established manner of investigating institutions. Because the students of comparative government have concentrated so deliberately upon the study of internal politics, this viewpoint must be shaped and tailored to the study of comparative foreign policy. We lack sound and substantiated theories of the regular effects of different institutional factors on foreign policy; we may hope to develop them. But theories are only hypotheses that are well verified by comparative study of many cases, and hypotheses are only the speculative answers to significant and general questions. If we can present no theory, we can at least ask the significant general questions about the relations between institutions and policy, ask those questions that must be answered by speculation and by comparative study before valid generalizations can be made, and perhaps also present some speculative answers to these queries. But because studies that intend to be general and comparative often begin with one set of questions applied by many researchers, each to a single case, we will present here the questions believed to be generally significant in the form of a research schema intended to be applicable to any single case taken by itself.

There follows, therefore, presented in detail, a set of inquiries into those aspects of political institutions that ought to have the greatest regular impact on foreign policy, and that the researcher into the policy of a state therefore should (and normally will) describe in their connections with external relations, in order to permit a comparison that will eventually create general statements about the recurrent influence of political institutions on foreign policy. Three groups of questions are central, inquiries about (1) the loci of decisionmaking, (2) the status of the regime, and (3) the character of the leadership.

The loci of decisionmaking

Three basic questions must be asked in studying any country at any time: (1) Where are decisions made?[1] (2) Have the key points of decision changed over time? (3) What difference—if any—does it make that decisions are taken at point A rather than at point B? The first question is contemporary, merely descriptive, and difficult enough to answer. The last question, which asks what the significance of the *place* of decisions is to the *content* of decisions, is baffling and yet profoundly important.

---

[1] We must also and concurrently ask where decisions and decisionmakers are validated, that is, by what institutional locus the decisionmakers are held responsible for good performance in office. Are decisionmakers removed from office for reasons relating to their foreign policies? And does such removal, and the special political character of the removing organ, thereby affect external policy?

In order to organize a descriptive probe of the institutional loci of decisionmaking, we will need a further specification of the questions the surveyor of each country should ask. The following sets of questions, composing two descriptive survey schedules, provide a methodical scheme for ordering impressions and judgments of the status of institutions, first in governmental decisionmaking generally, then in foreign policy decisionmaking. After the descriptive questionnaires, there appears in logical order the question of the policy significance of such descriptions, followed by suggestions of evidence and hypotheses useful in answering that question of significance.

First descriptive survey. The first survey schedule employs the terminology and concepts of Banks and Textor.[2] The four following questions are asked about the state in question, and are to be asked twice, first as regards all decisionmaking in that state, then with specific reference to foreign policy decisionmaking. Each question has a limited and particular set of permitted answers. By adhering to these, the surveyor can insure the comparability of his answers, as well as that of his questions.

1. What is the general status of the legislature?
   a. Fully effective and "co-equal"
   b. Partially effective (limited by executive or military or a party)
   c. Largely ineffective (dominated by other institutions)
   d. Wholly ineffective (consultative or rubber-stamp functions only)
2. What is the general status of the executive?
   a. Dominant (throughout the government establishment)
   b. Strong (effectively dominant in a conventional "executive realm" only)
   c. Weak
3. What is the territorial power distribution?
   a. Effectively unitary government
   b. Limited sharing of power by regional authorities
   c. Effective sharing of power by regional authorities
   d. Effectively territorial government
4. What is the functional power distribution?
   a. Absent (general dominance of government by one institution)
   b. Limited
   c. Significant (effective separation or sharing of powers by functionally autonomous institutions)

[2] Arthur S. Banks and Robert B. Textor, *A Cross-Polity Survey* (Cambridge, Mass.: M.I.T. Press, 1963), Raw Characteristics Number 47, 48, 50, and 52. Where doubts arise about the assignment of a polity to one category or another, the 1963 codings by Banks and Textor may be helpful in suggesting where the lines of classification have in the past been drawn.

These questions are asked once of decisionmaking in general to provide background; they are asked again of foreign policy decisionmaking in the anticipation that different answers will emerge. For instance, we would not be surprised to find that legislatures will often be less and executives more effective in foreign than in domestic policymaking; nor should we be startled to find that both territorial and functional distribution of power are frequently significantly smaller in foreign than in domestic policy. And answering these questions will also indirectly help in clarifying the scholarly debate over the utility of distinguishing "foreign" from "domestic" policy.

If the answers to this series of questions seem revealing, they should then be asked again of the years of the recent and more distant past, so as to reveal trends and cycles. If these questions tell little that seems of interest, the surveyor may pass on to the next series.

Second descriptive survey. The second survey schedule is intended to encourage a longer and more detailed probing of the institutional structure of decisionmaking, and is derived from the work of Robert C. Fried.[3] It asks a series of questions about each of the following institutions: (1) executives, (2) legislatures, (3) courts, (4) foreign offices, (5) embassies, (6) the military, (7) the police, (8) the domestic civil bureaucracy, (9) regional authorities, (10) political parties, and (11) electorates.

The institution having been identified, it is ranked into a set of classes of institutional power, first in general and then with respect to power over foreign policy, as follows.

Power type	Control over government	Autonomy	Social control
1. Totalitarian	Total	Total	Total
2. Dictatorial	Total	Total	Large
3. Oligarchic	Shared with 1 or 2 others	Collectively total	Large
4. Strong	Shared with others including autonomous electorate	Large	Large
5. Independent	Shared with many others including autonomous electorate	Partial	Partial
6. Weak	Little	Variable	Variable
7. Captive	Variable	None	Variable
8. Ceremonial	None	Variable	Variable
9. Nil	Variable	Variable	None

These institutional power types are differentiated according to their share of resources and handicaps, classified under the rubrics of: (1) information; (2) expertise; (3) social power (class status);

3 *Comparative Political Institutions* (New York: Macmillan, 1966).

(4) popularity; (5) legitimacy; (6) leadership (skill and motivation in leading); (7) organization; (8) violence; (9) rules (power to make laws and constitutions, and power conferred by them); (10) economic power; (11) manpower, and (12) office (patronage control).[4]

It should be noted that control over government and control over foreign affairs will be the same for totalitarian, dictatorial, captive, ceremonial, and nil institutions, but that institutions whose general power type is oligarchic, strong, independent, or weak may have much more or much less control over foreign policy than that type might suggest.

A further extension of the same survey applies to those institutions of any state whose power type for foreign policy is oligarchic, strong, independent, or weak. Is the role of the institution that of a:

neutral agent and technical adviser on foreign policy?

divided defender of multiple interests?

coherent representative of a vested policy interest?

predominant controller of foreign policy decisions?

We may add the hypothesis that, where this extension is relevant, three patterns of institutional power over foreign policy are the ones most likely to emerge:

1. All relevant institutions are coherent or divided, none is dominant.

2. Parties are coherent, legislature divided, executive dominant, military and foreign office neutral.

3. Parties, legislature, military and foreign office are divided or neutral, executive dominant.

Consequently, the condition of each state may be recorded as one of these types, or as a minor deviation from one or another, or as a special case demanding a new category.

In any event, when all the institutions of a given state have been power-typed for foreign affairs, a pattern of institutional power for the whole state will emerge. The questioning may then be carried back over time, to unearth both trends in institutional power over foreign affairs and their significance in terms of changing patterns of content and quality of foreign policy, if any.

[4] For further elaboration of this scheme for survey purposes, see Fried, *ibid.*

The role of bureaucracies. Some further and special attention should normally be given at this point to certain bureaucracies, namely the foreign office, the military establishment, specialized agencies (for intelligence, clandestine operations, foreign aid, information dissemination, and so forth), embassies abroad, executive households and control organs, legislative staffs and reference services, and so on. These elaborate hierarchies, with their differentiated and specialized roles and functions, are the structures charged with the enactment of policy and the implementation—or enforcement—of decisions. But the function of decision implementation is so important and so demanding that bureaucracies will usually have especially large resources of manpower, organization, information, and expertise. Some will also possess large resources of violence, and all may have substantial resources of legitimacy, rules, office, and economic power (although normally they are handicapped in social status, popularity, and leadership). The persistent access of bureaucracies to their own characteristic resources may combine with frequent weaknesses of legislative and executive leadership, organization, information, manpower, and expertise to produce substantial entries by bureaucratic segments into the charmed circle of decision.[5] But these entries are so frequent that it will be important in any study to describe and classify the relations between the "administrative" foreign-policy bureaucracies and the "political" agencies. For this purpose, typologies of relationships are here supplied.

Any executive or legislature may stand in any or several of the following relations to its foreign policy bureaucracies, or segments thereof, on all matters or on specific issues, permanently or recurrently or on occasion:[6]

Initiator, monopolizing decisionmaking and enforcing bureaucratic implementation

Regulator, laying down general policy guidelines and delegating the decisions that specify these general lines

Energizer, pointing out areas for priority attention and seeing to it that a bureaucratic decision (whatever its substance) is made

Validator-modifier, awaiting initial decisions by bureaucratic agents and then approving or revising them

Monitor, acting, upon reports of a failure or malperformance, to reprimand, demand correction, transfer responsibilities, or relieve of office

Ceremonial legitimator, performing ritual and regular acceptance of bureaucratic decisions

[5] Cf. Gabriel Almond and G. Bingham Powell, Jr., *Comparative Politics: A Developmental Approach* (Boston: Little, Brown, 1966), p. 144.

[6] Cf. *Ibid.,* p. 158.

We may usefully distinguish, more broadly, among ruling bureaucracies, executive-dominated bureaucracies, legislative-dominated bureaucracies, and supercontrolled bureaucracies. The last type, the only one needing definition, is dominated by a separate bureaucracy specialized to precisely that role—a small, "political," diffusely competent organ ruling a large, differentiated, technical-instrumental service.[7] In a very complex modern polity, the presence or absence of such a superbureaucracy may mean the difference between controlled function and feudal disintegration of the entire administrative apparatus.

Assessing the results. When one of the descriptive surveys has been satisfactorily completed, its significance must be assessed. In other words, we must ask: Has the fact that some decisions or all decisions are made at one locus rather than another markedly accounted for the content or the quality of foreign policy being as it is? If so, how? What is the evidence? Two kinds of evidence seem central to such a judgment: It may be that there are known differences in attitudes—in foreign-policy political culture—at different loci in government; or past shifts in the institutional loci of decision-making may regularly have been correlated with actual changes in the content of policy:

This aspect of the inquiry may be structured as an examination of several alternative hypotheses.

Hypothesis 6.11

The higher the status of the foreign office, the more stable and less adaptable is the state's foreign policy.

Hypothesis 6.12

The higher the status of the foreign office, the more coherent is policy.

Hypothesis 6.13

The higher the status of the foreign office, the less will policy involve the use of force.

Hypothesis 6.14

The higher the status of the foreign office, the more policy tends to be reactive rather than active.

[7] Cf. *Ibid.*, pp. 149ff., 157, after M. Fainsod.

Hypothesis 6.21

The higher the status of the executive, the more stable and coherent is policy.

Hypothesis 6.22

The higher the status of the executive, the more forcible the policy.

Hypothesis 6.23

The higher the status of the executive, the less adaptable is policy.

Hypothesis 6.24

The higher the status of the executive, the more policy tends to be active rather than reactive.

Hypothesis 6.31

The higher the status of the military, the less will policy involve the use of force.

Hypothesis 6.32

The higher the status of the military, the more forcible the policy.

Hypothesis 6.41

The higher the status of the legislature, the less stable and less adaptable is foreign policy.

Hypothesis 6.42

The higher the status of the legislature, the more stable and adaptable is foreign policy.

Hypothesis 6.43

The higher the status of the legislature, the more policy tends to be reactive rather than active.

Hypothesis 6.01 (null hypothesis)

Varying status of institutions has no systematic effect on the content and quality of foreign policy.

Hypothesis 6.51

The greater the functional power distribution, the less stable, coherent, and effective the state's foreign policy.

Hypothesis 6.52

The greater the functional power distribution, the more adaptable is policy.

Hypothesis 6.53

The greater the functional power distribution, the less adaptable is policy.

Hypothesis 6.54

The greater the functional power distribution, the more policy tends to be reactive rather than active, isolationist rather than status quo, and defensive rather than expansionist or revolutionary.

Hypothesis 6.02 (null hypothesis)

Variations in functional power distribution do not affect content or quality of foreign policy.

These hypotheses may be used in comparing states at one time or in examining the changes in one state's policy over time. They reflect both common prejudices and intriguing possible denials of such prejudices (for example, 6.31 versus 6.32). They are to be treated as heuristic devices, which can focus inquiry somewhat more tightly than can the mere sets of questions (presented above) that inquire into the general significance of differing institutional arrangements. If a hypothesis seems correct or flagrantly mistaken, it may stimulate an attempt to test it; if it seems only plausible, it may stimulate a comparative investigation. Whatever its seeming, it is intended to work only as an instigator and a provocation to inquiry and research.

Status of the regime

Following the pattern of providing both a set of questions and a set of possible or hypothetical answers to those questions in order to organize inquiry, we may turn as matter of inquiry to the subjects of the effect of the constitutional and representative status of the regime upon its foreign policy.

Constitutional status of the regime

Under this head,[8] one asks first for a description of the limits, if any, on the domestic social control exercised by the regime. This will by indirection tell how free the state is to make its foreign policy without reference to norms and limiting standards legislated by preceding regimes or inherent in a conventional or written charter; also how much at liberty it is to treat the goods and persons of the members of its society as instrumental to policy and hence, at discretion, susceptible to mobilization, employment, and expenditure in foreign adventures.[9]

Three answers are permitted to the descriptive question. The regime may be called *constitutional* if its government is restricted in ordinary conduct by reference to norms that stipulate individual rights and majoritarianism. It is *authoritarian* if there is little or no such effective constitutional limitation on the arbitrary exercise of rule, but if the customs of the country and the practice of the regime differentiate between some conventionally bounded "political" and "social" spheres, with arbitrary government being largely confined to the former and large areas of daily life (family, religion, intellection and discourse, economy, cultural matters, and so forth) being reliably immune to interference. It is *totalitarian* if neither constitutional nor social bounds restrain it, and it broadly exercises power in all spheres of human life without regard for individual or majority rights.[10]

Such classification of the regime is only a beginning. One must specify any limits that are alleged; more important, one must note all recent changes in the constitutional status of the regime. And at last one begins to ask how, if at all, the status and its changes are judged to have affected the content and quality of foreign policy. Here again one asks if changes in constitutional status have been

[8] Banks and Textor, *A Cross-Polity Survey*, Raw Characteristic Number 26.

[9] This topic is distinguished from, but closely connected with, the degree of *actual* political mobilization engaged in by the regime (see Chapter 7).

[10] Evidently the classification of a regime is closely related to the power-typing of the institutions within it. Thus weak and independent institutions should characterize a constitutional regime, which might also contain one strong institution; strong, oligarchic or dictatorial institutions fit an authoritarian regime; oligarchic or totalitarian institutions must be present in a totalitarian regime.

correlated with changes in the character of policy, and seeks specific instances in which an otherwise satisfactory policy has been discarded because it ran athwart of vested ideas and interests oriented to limiting or resisting government. The general query of the influence of constitutional status on foreign policy may also be organized as an attempt to test a few alternative hypothetical connections.

Hypothesis 6.61

States with a choice of potential allies generally prefer constitutional to other kinds of regimes.

Hypothesis 6.62

States with a choice of potential allies generally prefer allies of regime status similar to their own.

Hypothesis 6.63

Expansionist and revolution-exporting states are more often than not ruled by other than constitutional regimes.

Hypothesis 6.64

Totalitarian regimes are more effective in mustering national power for external goals than constitutional regimes.

Hypothesis 6.65

Totalitarian regimes are less likely to follow policies of defense of the territorial and political status quo than are nontotalitarian regimes.

Hypothesis 6.03 (null hypothesis)

No relationship exists between the constitutional status of a regime and the content or quality of its policy.

Representative character of the regime

Under this head,[11] the question is asked of how representative the regime is in form and content, with particular regard to elections.

[11] Banks and Textor, *A Cross-Polity Survey*, Raw Characteristic Number 28.

Four answers to the question are permitted: "Broadly representative" (a broad-based franchise from which no large minorities are formally or practically excluded, selecting from more than one list elected representatives whose functions are more than limited or consultative); "limited representative" (a broad-based but nonetheless educationally or racially or regionally discriminatory franchise, permitting representation of the mass sector or at least of a very large minority); "pseudorepresentative" (single-list elections, and/or elected representatives ineffective with limited or consultative functions only); "nonrepresentative" (in form as well as in fact). After classifying the regime of a country into one or another of these slots over time, the question of the foreign-policy significance of a regime's representative character may be raised. The question may be examined with respect to specific limits or changes enforced on policy by elected representatives (especially as the result of new elections and of changes in elected officeholders), or changes in policy following a change in the representative character of the regime and emanating from the creation, invigoration, curbing, or expulsion of elected officials. Useful suggestive hypotheses about regular connections between representation and foreign policy include:

Hypothesis 4.71

States with a choice of allies prefer allies of the same representative character.

Hypothesis 4.72

The more effective is representation, the less stable and less adaptable is policy.

Hypothesis 4.73

The more effective is representation, the more adaptable is policy.

Hypothesis 4.74

The more effective is representation, the more the attention of policymakers tends to be concentrated on a few major issues while policy on other issues stagnates without adapting.

Hypothesis 4.04 (null hypothesis)

No connection exists between the representative character of a regime and its foreign policy.

Character of political leadership

In examining the effect upon foreign policy of the character of men holding leadership roles, we must scrutinize their stability of tenure, recruitment, *personalismo,* and charisma.

Stability of tenure[12]

This is a quantitative variable, applicable to each key post or leadership role, to all key posts collectively in every institution, or to all key roles collectively in a given government. Where we seek to find R (the rate of turnover) for a period of d years in e leadership roles that have been occupied in these years by f persons, $R = \dfrac{f}{de}$. Relevant hypotheses (aside from null hypotheses) will probably connect a high R with instability, incoherence, and ineffectiveness of policy, allege that either a high or low rate of turnover in key posts is connected with low adaptability of policy, and propose that states with low R will tend to be active (versus reactive), extraversive (versus introversive), and expansionist or revolutionary (versus defensive) in policy.

Recruitment[13]

The descriptive portion of this subject inquires whether recruitment to leadership posts is "elitist" (confined to particular racial, social, religious, or ideological strata), "moderate elitist" (largely but not wholly confined to such strata), or "meritocratic" (largely on the basis of achievement or performance criteria alone). More broadly, one must examine the social status of persons recruited to membership in the loci of decisionmaking: Do they represent a fair or a biased sample of the population, in terms of age, sex, race, wealth, social class, education, religion, nationality, language, section, and so forth? And what difference does it make to policy? Relevant non-null hypotheses might associate stratified leadership recruitment with stability of policy, or with reactivity and isolationism and defensiveness of policy, or with ineffectiveness of policy.

Personalismo

Personalismo is the tendency of the politically active sectors of a population to follow or oppose a leader for personal, individual, or family reasons rather than because of the influence of a political

[12] Cf. Bruce M. Russett, Hayward R. Alker, Jr., Karl W. Deutsch, and Harold D. Lasswell, *World Handbook of Political and Social Indicators* (New Haven, Conn.: Yale University Press, 1964), p. 101.

[13] Banks and Textor, *A Cross-Polity Survey,* Raw Characteristic Number 45.

idea, program, or party.[14] It may be pronounced, moderate, or negligible within a polity's party and institutional system. A relevant non-null hypothesis might associate pronounced *personalismo* with instability of policy.

Charisma

Leadership charisma[15] as an institutional feature is pronounced, moderate, or negligible insofar as specific political leaders are held in regard and obeyed because of the widespread belief of the governed in the extraordinary qualities of each specific person. Relevant hypotheses might declare that the more charismatic the leadership, the more power can be mobilized to support any given policy, and consequently the more effective is policy; or that the more charismatic the leadership, the more policy tends to be active, expansionist, or revolutionary.

Conclusion

Research that follows this framework for inquiry into the effects of political institutions on the substance of external policy merely involves the selective reading of journalistic country-reporting, and of political-scientific and historical country studies in foreign policy and in comparative government. Such studies will contain either statements or evidence about the effect of institutions on policy. They should contain substantially more evidence of changes in policy, as well as evidence of the kind needed in order to classify and reclassify regimes under the typological variables herein adapted from Fried and from Banks and Textor. But in most cases the researcher will have to make the judgments and find in primary materials the substantiating evidence needed to connect institutions and policies.

References

Almond, Gabriel and G. Bingham Powell, Jr., *Comparative Politics: A Developmental Approach.* Boston: Little, Brown, 1966.
Banks, Arthur S. and Robert B. Textor, *A Cross-Polity Survey.* Cambridge, Mass.: M.I.T. Press, 1963.
Fried, Robert C., *Comparative Political Institutions.* New York: Macmillan, 1966.

[14] *Ibid.,* Raw Characteristic Number 44.

[15] *Ibid.,* Raw Characteristic Number 46.

7

Political processes

Political process and foreign policy

Political processes are the recurrent operations that produce political information, demands, and decisions. Processes have two intriguing aspects: what they are like (their form, shape, or structure) and what they make (their yield, product, or *output*). Under the title of *political process and foreign policy*, we therefore ask not merely what the structure of the process of foreign policy decisionmaking in a country is, but what impact the character of that process has upon the outputs of that process. What effect does the *procedure* of making policy have upon the *substance* of the policy that is made? And, interpreting the subject more broadly, we also ask for a description of the structure of the *inputs* (of information and demand) to the decisional process, and for an explanation of what effect the structure of these inputs may have upon the decisions and the policy that are outputs of that process. Not stopping even there, we treat social structure and process as generating inputs to a system whose outputs then become the inputs to (and the demands made upon) the policy-making process. We ask what impact, mediated through the demand-making and decisionmaking processes, these social phenomena have upon foreign policy. This study may be illustrated by a diagram.

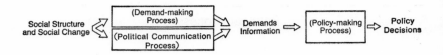

It is here suggested that the character of policy is in part a function of the character or style of the policymaking process; and if *A* is a partial function of *B*, then to understand *A* it is worthwhile to investigate *B*. The student of foreign policy ought therefore to examine *decisional style.*

It is further suggested that a nation's foreign policy is a product of the domestic demands and the information that are put into the policymaking process, as well as of the style of that process, (and its institutional skeleton, its lasting dispositions, the personalities of its controllers, and their perception of and the reality of the external challenge and the state's capability to respond). Furthermore, those demands and that information have form as well as specific content. Both must be scrutinized. Demands are structured by the *kind* of social groups that habitually express and coordinate them; information is structured by the scope and caliber of the media that transmit it. The student of foreign policy ought therefore also to be a student of *interest grouping* and *political communication.*

The specific content of internal pressures on the decisional process is highly variable in any state. Yet any state may be the locale of a few extremely significant social regularities, in particular of recurrent patterns of *social heterogeneity, social modernization, political mobilization,* and *external penetration.* Where a clear and distinct type of heterogeneity, modernization, mobilization, or penetration is present, the student of foreign relations must ask what, if any, impact that type of social condition has upon the content and quality of foreign policy—through the demands thereby inflicted on, the needs thereby made plain for, and the capabilities or weaknesses therewith conveyed to the decisional process.

The foreign policy decisionmaking process

To examine the decisional process in foreign policy, one must know the loci of decisionmaking: Who makes key decisions, and where are they made?[1] Knowing this, we can then ask *how* decisions are made —or postponed.

We are not interested in the mere description of policymaking processes. There is a descriptive tradition in foreign policy analysis

[1] See Chapter 6.

that seeks comprehensive narratives and analyses, for their own sake or as background information, of how policy is made; this tradition has little concern with the relation between process and output. But our keynote question is: Precisely what effect does the *nature* of the policymaking process in each state have upon the *substance* of the policy that is made in that process? Thus, in a study of the American decisionmaking process, we are in pursuit of a balanced description of those comparable features of the policy process that most strongly contribute to making United States foreign policy the type of policy it is rather than some other type. Is there a specific and recurrent style of policymaking that leads to especially stable, adaptable, coherent, or effective policy? Or to a policy well balanced with available capabilities? To an active, a status quo, or a revolutionary policy? This is what we wish to know.

Questions of style

Thus the relevant questions for us become questions of *style*. How does a problem come to be perceived as a problem, immediate or long run? How is the relevant information defined and collected? How are alternatives generated, elaborated, culled, chosen, and legitimatized? What is the chain of connection between a decision to take action and the action taken? How is a general decision translated into the employment of specialized techniques, the allocation of fiscal, material, and human resources into operation? How is information on implementation and on results fed back into the decisional system, and how are adjustments made? All these are questions that can be answered only when the locale of decisionmaking is known, but they are questions of style. And it is indeed the style of decisionmaking for which the investigator must search once he knows where decisionmaking goes on.

Now, "style" in decision is at present so little elaborated a topic of study that order and classification are hard to come by. Still and all, some distinct characteristics of decisional style are subject to relatively objective assessment.

Speed. The most obvious of these is speed, the rapidity with which decisions are made (and action taken) upon the presentation of a challenge. Speedy decision may, unfortunately, imply either of two opposed conditions—efficiency in the decisional process or pathological simplism in the ideologies of the decisionmaker. Indeed, it may indicate both. One might reasonably begin analysis, however, from the contention that speed in decisionmaking increases the adaptability and effectiveness of policy but decreases its coherence and stability.

Pattern of decision. It may also be possible to penetrate the pattern of arriving at agreement, as it appears to operate at the highest levels of government. Decisions may reveal a predominant pattern of *struggle, emergence, despotism, coalition,* or *consensus-building.* Decisions may be reached as victorious or compromise outcomes in a clash of "rival sovereignties," virtually independent, equal, and hostile participants in the decisional process (always actors representing factions, interests, institutions, or bureaucratic segments). Decisions may evolve as the unconsciously coordinated outcomes of the activities of independent sovereignties with separate spheres of influence. Decisions may be the final determinations of one heroic, authoritative, or tyrannical sovereign who has received supplications, petitions, and advice. Decisions may be reached as the result of a coalition of chieftains, a collection of virtually independent, equal, partly cooperative sovereignties, large enough to override rivals without serious clash. Or decisions may be reached as the result of an executive's construction of a consensus, an "executive-centered 'grand coalition of coalitions.' "[2] The latter patterns seem more likely to produce stable, adaptable, coherent policies than the former.

Still, the typology is far from sufficient. The systematic study of style and policy will have to generate further types of significant decisional procedure, different ways of making a decision that make a difference to the substance of the decision that is made. And, as if the elusiveness of the subject matter were not enough, the student must deal with further difficulties. He must cope with the difficulties posed by *differentiation of the policy process* and by *information shortages.* The former presents him with multiform style, a plurality where he wishes to discover simplicity and unity. The latter constricts his ability to observe the subject at all. If the first is a serious problem, the second is a nearly fatal flaw.

Multiform style

Foreign policy decisionmaking may be, rather than one overt process, a set of several overt processes. One must ask, therefore, if there are not different policymaking styles and processes for global, regional, and country policies.[3] These may be made at different levels or in different places, and consequently display a multitude of forms. Again, it is one thing for a state to administer and adjust the administration of stable and continuing programs; it is another for it to anticipate the developments and contingencies of the future and to prepare against them, yet another to perceive and respond to the sudden focusing of attention, the increases in activity, in anxiety,

[2] Gabriel Almond and G. Bingham Powell, Jr., *Comparative Politics: A Developmental Approach* (Boston: Little, Brown, 1966), p. 141, after R. Dahl. Cf. Robert A. Dahl, *Who Governs?* (New Haven, Conn.: Yale University Press, 1961), pp. 184ff.

[3] For instance, America's world policy, its Far Eastern policy, and its China policy.

and in the stakes of the game, and the speeding up of events that characterize action in crisis. Are there not contrasting decisional styles in each of these cases? Are there not "functionally" differentiated policy styles, so that "national security," "foreign aid," "political warfare," "information," and "diplomatic" policy are made in different ways? Where there are such differences in styles and their impact on policy, they must be explained. And the greater, the more ambitious, bureaucratized, and externally active a state is, the more surely will its policy styles be multiform.

Information shortages

But research into the decisional process of states, except for certain heavily studied periods of the recent United States past and even fewer episodes in other Western states, is a matter in which self-scrutinizing governmental commissions of inquiry, the foreign research sections of intelligence agencies, or even the best foreign correspondents have infinitely better access to needed information than do political scientists. Looking at American policy, it may be possible to find certain long-lived policy programs that will repay close study: unclassified aspects of national security policy; aid, trade and tariff, and information policy, to some degree. Or one might examine past crises that produced large quantities of documents, of "inside" journalism, and of memoirs intended to advertise or to apologize for the writer-participant's role. The case most awash in verbiage is surely the Cuban missile crisis of 1962, but the Berlin blockade of 1948–49, the containment decision of 1946–47, the Marshall Plan, the decision to intervene in Korea in 1950, and the Cuban crisis (Bay of Pigs) of 1961 are also affrays of some note, with considerable coverage. Yet these materials are far from complete, and are for one country alone.

The obstacles to systematic and comparative study of decisional processes are great. The multiplicity of policy styles in a complex state is a difficulty that can be handled; it requires only a greater effort. But both the special question we are asking (not simply "What is style?" but "What is style to policy—what difference does it make?") and the restriction on the data necessary to answer it in detail have a chilling effect on inquiry. They imply that global and impressionistic judgments are the ones most likely to be made in inquiries into the effect of the policymaking process itself on its own outcomes; and with global and impressionistic judgments, which are generally best made by participants or lifelong observers of a social process, we must rest content.

Given this restraint, it would probably be most efficient for the casual inquirer not to organize his questions in too tight, rigorous, and demanding a manner, since detailed and verifiable information is not likely to be forthcoming. Let him simply ask himself: In the American, British, or any other foreign-policymaking process and decisional style, is there any great and significant and persistent handicap or support to stability, adaptability, coherence, effectiveness, and/or balance in policy? Or any character predisposing to reactive or active, status quo or isolationist, expansionist or revolutionary policies? And, keeping the topics of speed and of decision-pattern in mind (along with any other topic on which he has constructed a significant typology), let him ponder what information he can find, and render tentative judgment.

If the casual inquirer is to rely on his own impressions, the systematic inquirer must also rely on impressions—but not his own. For his task will simply be to put these same quesitons to as many of the most intelligent and best situated observers of a decision process as he can persuade to speak—whether they be officials or ex-officials, native or foreign journalists, current or former political leaders or diplomats. So he may study indirectly what he cannot reach directly, and study to learn as well what regularities, occurrent in his data, bespeak regularity in the subject itself.

Political inputs to the policy process

In the last section we examined the very nature of decisional process and its effect on its own outputs; here we will study the inputs of information and demand to that process and their impact on its outputs. More narrowly, the group structure that articulates and aggregates demands, and the structure of political communication in a general sense, are brought under scrutiny here.

Interest articulation

The descriptive question here is, By what groups are interests articulated, that is, voiced and transmitted from the individual and private sector of the political culture into the public sector of political life? As usual, the question must be asked twice, once about the articulation of political demands in general and again about the articulation of foreign policy interests. If these results are interesting, the question must be asked for the past as well as the present.

Interests may be articulated primarily by individuals (acting for their own pecuniary, career, or ideological interests), by anomic, nonassociational, or institutional groups, by political parties, associational groups, or specialized mass-media structures. Thus one procedure for comparative study is to ask of each polity which *kinds* of actors articulate interests, and which kinds have primacy in interest articulation. Individual members of a small decisional elite and their cronies frequently articulate their own interests to that elite. *Anomic groups* are mobs, acting through nonorganized rioting and demonstrations, highly changeable in structure and working, and representing "spontaneous" breakthroughs of social groups into the political system. *Nonassociational* (ascriptive) *groups* are kinship and other (ethnic, regional, religious, status, class) groups that are normally entered by birth and that voice their interests informally and intermittently through traditional heads of family or sect or through individuals and cliques operating as spokesmen. *Institutional groups* include legislatures, executives, armies, bureaucracies, churches; these are groups that are nominally specialized to other political functions but that may (as wholes or through possibly competitive fractions) articulate their own interests or those of groups in the society. *Associational groups* are organizations explicitly set up to formulate and transmit the interests of a specific set of persons or groups; they are structures specialized precisely for the articulation of interests.[4] *Mass-media* structures are, ideally, autonomous organizations specialized to political communication, which may transmit demands as well as information.

Such a hypothesis as the following might emerge from examination of interest articulation in terms of these four categories:

> If domestic interests in foreign policy are articulated chiefly by anomic groups and parties, policy is least stable and effective; if by associational groups or individuals, it is more effective and stabler; if by institutional groups, most effective and stablest.

It is more to the point, however, to move rapidly from structure to substance, and to ask what the satisfying foreign policy would be for interests that are *inarticulate* and those that are *unsuccessfully articulated*. Only a small segment of the content of any political culture will be articulated as interests; who are the voiceless?[5] Only a small segment of the content of any compound or fragmented political culture can be successfully enacted into policy, however well articulated it is; who are the voices in the wilderness? This leads naturally to the question of what the *pattern of success* in getting demands made into foreign policy may be. What articulators of interest are regularly successful in getting their interests satisfied as policy? Frequently successful? Occasionally successful? Successful

[4] Arthur S. Banks and Robert B. Textor, *A Cross-Polity Survey* (Cambridge, Mass.: M.I.T. Press, 1963), Raw Characteristics Number 33–37. The authors ask whether interest articulation by associational and (separately) by parties and by nonassociational groups is significant, moderate, limited, or negligible; whether articulation by institutional groups is very significant, significant, moderate, or limited; and whether articulation by anomic groups is frequent, occasional, infrequent, or very infrequent. These raw characteristics are derived from Gabriel Almond and James S. Coleman, eds., *The Politics of the Developing Areas* (Princeton, N.J.: Princeton University Press, 1960), pp. 33–35.

[5] In this connection, one must know how far autonomous opposition groups are tolerated, that is, how far certain interests are denied legitimate articulation, and which interests these are. Banks and Textor (*ibid.*, Raw Characteristic Number 30) distinguish among polities where no genuinely autonomous opposition groups are tolerated, where they are informally tolerated outside politics, where they are free to organize but limited in ability to oppose, and where (though extreme opposition groups may be banned) they are free to organize and able to oppose.

under certain conditions, in certain places, at certain times, within certain limits, on certain issues? The pattern of regular success, if there is any, helps to account for the particular policy of the state in question. Furthermore, if the successful articulators or the pattern of success can be described as types, comparisons may be made and regularities may emerge.

In any case, the inquiry is not complete until one has asked and has said (impressionistically where necessary, objectively where possible) what impact the pattern of interest articulation has on the content and quality of foreign policy, in general and comparable terms.

Interest aggregation

Aggregation of demands[6] is the grouping, combining, and compromising of them—screening them down into relatively few alternatives or choices, major and general policy alternatives that then become the objects of choice for the final decisionmakers. The question is, once more, what groups do the aggregating and have done it, in domestic and foreign policy? Political parties? Institutional groups —legislature, executive, bureaucracies, military? Does this screening systematically select or "select out" certain kinds of alternatives well before the decision process? And is there any regular impact upon content and quality of policy from the fact that one rather than another group does the aggregating of foreign policy interests?

Party system

Now, to the degree that political parties either articulate or aggregate interests relating to foreign policy, they deserve a somewhat closer scrutiny as a system. Banks and Textor once more provide classifications, convenient to the purpose, of party systems examined for quantity, stability, and quality.[7]

1. How many parties are there?
    a. One, including fusions and national fronts (all others non-existent, banned, or nonparticipant or adjuncts in electoral activity)
    b. One dominant (opposition numerically ineffective at national level, although separately participant in electoral activity)
    c. One and one-half (significant opposition, unable to win a majority)
    d. Two (reasonable expectation of party rotation)

[6] Banks and Textor (*ibid.*, Raw Characteristics Number 38–40) ask separately whether, in the given polity, interest aggregation by parties, legislatures, and executives is significant, moderate, limited, or negligible.

[7] *Ibid.*, Raw Characteristics Number 41–43.

    e. More than two (if parliamentary system, coalition or minor-
ity government normally mandatory)

    f. None; or all parties illegal or ineffective

2. How stable is the party system?

    a. Stable (all significant parties stable and organizationally
nonsituational[8])

    b. Moderately stable (relatively infrequent or nonabrupt system
changes, or mixed situational-permanent party complex)

    c. Unstable (all parties unstable, situational, personalistic, or
ad hoc)

The nature of the party system is more closely examined by a
conglomerate and specified question about the quality of the party
system. We know of one-party or one-party-dominant systems, with
elitist membership and ideological tone (corporative—Spain, Portugal—and Communist states); one-party or one-party-dominant
mass-based parties with open membership and no specific ideological
content; two-party or multiparty systems where parties are regional
or regional-ethnic in basis, and those (Cyprus, Malaya) where they
are wholly ethnic or communal; two-party or multiparty systems
whose members range from mildly class-oriented to representative of
a spectrum of doctrinaire ideology; unstable party systems, where all
significant parties are called into existence temporarily to serve the
electoral or legislative interests of persons and cliques; one-and-one-
half-party systems where the minor partner is class-oriented, regional, ethnic, or doctrinaire and the majority party broadly aggregative; two-party systems where both parties are broadly aggregative,
competing to appeal to a largely overlapping constituency of articulated interests.

    The quality of the party system will probably serve best to
indicate which aspects of social heterogeneity and which set of articulated interests are generally most significant in policymaking in a
state and therefore most worthy of an examination that intends to
check out the significance of such interests in the making of foreign
policy. It is unlikely that the nature of the party system will have an
important and independent impact on foreign policy.

Political communication

At this point we inquire about the structure of the process for
communicating political information regarding foreign policy, and
the consequences of that structure for policy. The descriptive query
is, What are the foreign policy media, the information channels that
carry to the loci of decisionmaking current intelligence, indirect
reports of internally proposed long-term principles or goals or plans,
reports on relative capabilities, and possible or recommended alterna-

---

[8] *Situational:* organized around particular short-lived issues and, therefore, as
organizations, evanescent.

tive lines of action? What are the channels for locating and testing possible consensus for tentative policy and for mobilizing consensus behind actual decision? This query intends to supply the description of the links that connect the loci of information collection and those of interest articulation and aggregation—which may be examined as roles in groups rather than as integral groups—with the loci of decisionmaking, and these with the loci of decision validation. Is it possible that the number and connections of channels, and the volume, accuracy, completeness, speed, and noisiness of transmission of information through these channels affects the adaptability, stability, coherence, and effectiveness of policy? It would seem so; but it remains to be determined in fact.

Data that researchers can have fair to good prospects of gathering at this point in time relate first of all to the mere volume of mass communication and the size of its potential audiences: the number of newspapers in the country; radios and television sets *per capita;* percentages of population literate, with primary, secondary, college, and graduate education; volume of newsprint consumed; daily newspaper circulation *per capita.*[9] These relate rather more to "social modernization," discussed later, than to the subject at hand.

We may reasonably hope to render judgment, however, upon the degree of *liberty* of the communication structures from the control of the political leadership, and also their *autonomy* from control by particular political interest groups in the society. The structures so evaluated must include, moreover, not merely the specialized and differentiated *mass media* but also the political *input structures* (interest groups and parties as articulation structures), the *governmental structures* themselves (institutions—especially bureaucracies, but also legislatures), *traditional social structures* (interest articulators for nonassociational groups), and *informal face-to-face contacts* (individual articulators). The liberty and autonomy of these articulators are now considered, however, with respect not merely to their ability to state their own interests and demands without manipulation but also their ability simply to transmit information. With reference to all these sources on foreign relations (where the foreign office, the military bureaucracy, and any specialized intelligence institutions have a major role), one also asks (and is forced to guess) about the *homogeneity* and *volume* of the information received by the final decisionmakers.[10] How much information do they get? And how much variety, contrast, and clash of views does that information contain?

The presumptions here are three.

[9] See Bruce M. Russett, Hayward R. Alker, Jr., Karl W. Deutsch, and Harold D. Lasswell, *World Handbook of Political and Social Indicators* (New Haven, Conn.: Yale University Press, 1964), "Communications" and "Education" sections.

[10] Almond and Powell, *Comparative Politics,* pp. 167–86.

1. The freer and more autonomous the communication structures, the more accurate their product.

2. Some unspecified "moderate" heterogeneity of received information will provide both a fair prospect of accuracy and a minimum chance of confusion; too much homogeneity means that biased reports will go unchallenged; too much heterogeneity will leave the decisionmaker unable to make sense of things.

3. Some unspecified moderate volume of information received will provide both a fair chance of accuracy and a minimized chance of overload; too little information will encourage simplistic and unrealistic decisions; too much will swamp the decisionmakers and lead to decisional lag.

Liberty and autonomy in the structures of political communication and moderate volume and heterogeneity in the substance they transmit should all aid in making policy more coherent and more adaptable.

Inputs to the political process from social structure and process

Under this head and classification is found the search for whatever regular impact the general character of society has upon the foreign policy of the state. Such regular impacts are, where they exist, transmitted indirectly and through interest articulating and aggregating mechanisms. The most notable such impacts upon foreign policy are the destabilizing and activating effects of social modernization, the policy-stabilizing and effectuating qualities of political mobilization, and the policy-aligning and insulating results of external penetration.

Social heterogeneity

At least six social configurations are at issue here.

1. One must ask how far wealth, *property distribution*, is stratified and unequal; this can be approached through a quantitative index of inequality of income distribution, of landholding,[11] or of inheritance; it may also be attacked by an examination of the economic class structure and of the potential for and actualization of individual movement into other wealth-strata than those into which one is born. Occupations or income sources may be examined here, but primarily in order to distinguish rich from poor strata and secondarily to determine different types of interests derived from different relations to the means of production.

---

[11] See, for example, Russett *et al., World Handbook*, pp. 237–47.

2. In this polity, what is the degree of *sectionalism* (the phenomenon whereby the cohesion of the polity as a whole is appreciably challenged or impaired by the distinctive and self-conscious identification of a significant percentage of the population with a sizable geographic area in which it lives)? Negligible (no significant sectional feeling)? Moderate (one group with strong sectional feeling or several with moderate sectional feeling)? Extreme (one or more groups with extreme sectional feeling)?[12]

3–6. What is the degree of *religious, racial, linguistic,* and *ethnic homogeneity?* Very high—85 percent of the population of the same faith, race, language, and nationality (or tribe), no significant single minority? High—85 percent majority, a single significant minority of 15 percent or less? Or low—no majority or 85 percent or more?[13]

With the polity so classified and its wealth, sectional, and other configurations described, we may next ask what, if any, impact is made upon the content and quality of foreign policy by these cleavages. Such an impact may involve the existence of differing external interests and conflicting foreign policy orientations on the part of various interest groups and group coalitions. If these compete and are compromised in forming state policy, then they are the interests articulated by the demand-making process, and their substance and structure will largely explain the content of policy. If they alternate, they will explain both the substance and the instability of policy. If one strong group is regularly suppressed by another, it is likely that this suppression will explain why certain alignments are made and others are not, and why alignments are apparently stable but actually only as stable as the balance of coercive force between the competing social forces. And if heterogeneity is expressed as energy-absorbing violent or extensive social conflict, it is likely that this will prevent (and explain the absence of) any single, stable, coherent, and effective foreign policy adapting to changes in the external world.

Social modernization

Under this label is proposed the study of polities according to their historical type and their stage of *political modernization,* following C. E. Black;[14] according to their correspondence to two models of the international relations of a state in social transition (*economic revolution* and *social revolution*), as these are developed by A. F. K.

[12] Banks and Textor, *A Cross-Polity Survey,* Raw Characteristics Number 32.

[13] *Ibid.,* Raw Characteristics Number 16–18.

[14] As represented in Banks and Textor, *A Cross-Polity Survey,* Raw Characteristics Number 22 and 23.

Organski and by Charles McClelland; and according to their type of *political development and decay,* as proposed by Samuel P. Huntington.

Political modernization is progress toward a united, organized, national and industrial state.[15] Black's historical types of political modernization actually distinguish the degree and independence of the modernizing process. His historical types are five:

1. Early European or early European derived[16] (early modernizing European society or offshoot), modernizing without a model but with essential continuity of political and territorial structure.

2. Later modernizing European society or offshoot,[17] where political structure and territory were fundamentally reorganized and where national identity was a prime and overshadowing issue for several generations when modernizing leaders seized power.

3. Non-European "autochthonous,"[18] self-modernizing, never directly ruled by more modern societies, having a long tradition of effective government, with the force of external example driving the struggle between traditional and modernizing leaders inside the established framework of territory and institutions.

4. Developed tutelary,[19] with well-developed institutions, which commenced modernizing under the direct tutelage of a more advanced society.

5. Undeveloped tutelary,[20] with poorly developed institutions, which commenced modernizing under the direct tutelage of a more advanced society.

Black's stages are four: (1) pretransitional, (2) early transitional—entered transition since 1945,[21] (3) midtransitional—

---

[15] This definition is stipulative, and intended to be value-neutral. Others may be stipulated, and are, in large numbers.

[16] France, the United Kingdom, Benelux, Switzerland, the United States, Canada, Australia, New Zealand, and South Africa.

[17] Ireland, Scandinavia, Southern Europe, Eastern Europe, and Latin America.

[18] Afghanistan, China, Ethiopia, Japan, Nepal, Thailand, Turkey, and the USSR.

[19] North Africa, the Middle East, South and Southeast Asia, Korea, Mongolia.

[20] Black Africa.

[21] Black Africa and Southeast Asia.

entered transition prior to 1945,[22] (4) advanced transitional—transition completed.[23] The transitional phase is one of active struggle between modernizers and traditionalists, involving a fundamental social revolution that creates a politically organized society with an industrial way of life. This social revolution is begun by the infiltration into the elite of modern ideas, to the point that political leaders assert a determination to modernize and so to cause a profound and systematic social upheaval. It is not terminated until the institutions associated with an agrarian way of life are effectively and decisively broken with and the political struggle comes to involve rival programs of modernization.

It is by no means clear how these types and stages might affect the external policies of the states within them. Perhaps early modernizing and all nontutelary states should have more successful policies than later modernizing and/or tutelary states, tutelary states less independent policies, and advanced states more stable and successful ones. At any rate, certain hypotheses have been offered that relate the relative and absolute *social* transitionality and advancement of states to their relations with other states and their transactions with their whole international environment. To these we now turn, in hopes that their propositions may make useful the catalogues that will be all that emerge from applying Black's and Banks and Textor's classification schemes to state behavior.

McClelland suggests that modernization tends to lead to revolutionary transformations of national systems, followed by attempts of the revolutionized states to transform their international environment correspondingly, followed by attempts of the same states to stabilize their international environment. His hypothesis[24] distinguishes four stages in the foreign relations of a state that is undergoing extensive national transformation. Very briefly presented, these stages are:

1. Internal upheaval, provoking the intervention of outside powers

2. Internal reforms and power struggles, accompanied by isolationism in the revolutionized state and an attempt by other states to quarantine it

3. Stablization of the revolution at home and an attempt to spread it abroad through propaganda and force

4. Routinization of the revolution at home, deescalation of foreign involvements, and a policy of the status quo abroad.

[22] For example, Bolivia, Colombia, the Dominican Republic, Ecuador, El Salvador, Haiti, Honduras, Nicaragua, Panama, Paraguay, and Peru.

[23] Europe, the USSR, North America, Australia, New Zealand, East Asia, the Middle East, North Africa, and some of Latin America.

[24] Charles McClelland, "Systems and History," *General Systems* (Yearbook of the Society for General Systems Research), III, 1958.

This model has a certain simplicity and logic: our purposes do not require us to test its general applicability. Since its stages are not intended to provide a catalogue of slots into one of which every state must fit, the surveyor of comparative foreign relations need only ask whether in fact the state he examines is adequately and reasonably described as being in one such stage, and as having passed through its predecessors. If so, the stage itself becomes a description, McClelland's whole hypothesis an explanation, and the next anticipated stage a possible projection (all at the most general level) of the foreign relations of the state.

Organski proposes that a fast rate of modernization may create an imbalance between a state's material capabilities and its world influence (based on foreigners' lagging or outdated image—or its own premature image—of its capabilities), thus instigating the state to engage in active and hostile power struggles and in disruption of the status quo in order to end the lag and redress the imbalance. To elaborate slightly: Organski's hypothesis[25] applies to states that are close to the top of the world capability hierarchy, to great powers, although it could presumably be extended to regional subsystems and to the relations among the leading powers in these subsystems as well. For our purposes, it can be generalized and reduced to two parts.

1. There occasionally occur in economic history extreme imbalances of development, represented by economic-technological transformation localized in one state rather than uniformly present in all states.

2. When one state, previously a power of the second or lower rank, undergoes such a prolonged transformation, its new economic capabilities instigate it to challenge for influence and predominance the currently most influential power or powers, and a protracted conflict between them is to be expected.

Once more, this model has application to relatively few cases. The examiner will ask whether a state has undergone such a burst of economic development; if so, whether a drive for influence has been associated therewith, and whether such drive has led to prolonged diplomatic hostilities with a state formerly of preponderant capability and influence.[26]

Both these hypotheses are rather sweeping, in that they explain very large changes in state policy by reference to a single

25 A.F.K. Organski, *World Politics* (2d ed.; New York: Knopf, 1968), Chaps. 6–9, 14, and 19.

26 For further remarks on the general phenomenon of imbalances between capability and influence, see Chapter 3.

factor, albeit itself large and complex, of social modernization (socio-political revolution on the one hand, economic-technical revolution on the other). But their ideas are not strange or without merit and application, especially within an enlarged question-framework such as this where the other possibly central factors cannot pass unmentioned simply because of the saliency of the social upheaval isolated by these hypotheses as determinant.

Samuel P. Huntington uses two variables to classify polities with respect to four ideal types of political development and political decay.

Political institutionalization

		High	Low
Social mobilization	High	Civic	Corrupt
	Low	Contained	Primitive

The level of institutionalization of political organizations and procedures in a polity is the degree to which patterns of political behavior, organizations, and procedures are stable and valued. That level is defined by the scope of support, the adaptability, complexity, autonomy, and coherence of patterns of political behavior in the polity.[27] The variable "political institutionalization" in Huntington therefore examines the political organizations and procedures of a country as a whole, contrasting those that are strong, stable, valued, broadly encompassing the political activity of the population, adaptable, complex, autonomous, and coherent with those that are weak, unstable, confined in scope to a small minority of the populace, rigid, simple, subordinated to particular social groups, or disunited.

"Social mobilization"[28] is here indicative of political participation with the tendency to make demands on the political system. Participation is indirectly indexed by the degrees of literacy, urbanization, exposure to mass media, industrialization, and *per capita* income; it is more directly indexed by the proportion of the population that votes.

[27] For definitions, see Samuel P. Huntington, "Political Development and Political Decay," *World Politics*, XVII (1965), pp. 386–430.

[28] See the variable "political mobilization," *infra*. These are *not* the same. "Social mobilization" follows the concept of Karl W. Deutsch, "Social Mobilization and Political Development," *American Political Science Review*, 55 (September 1961) pp. 493–514. For relevant statistics, see Russett *et al.*, *World Handbook*, Tables 9, 10 (urbanization), 24 (voting), 31, 35, 37, 38 (mass media exposure), 44 (*per capita* GNP), 49, 53 (industrialization).

The four developmental types thus obtained particularly contrast modern, developed, civic polities (U.S., USSR) with corrupt polities (much of the Third World) having high and increasing participation rates but low and sometimes decreasing levels of institutionalization. One would expect the foreign policies of civic polities to be substantially more stable, adaptable, and coherent than those of corrupt polities.

Political mobilization

Banks and Textor[29] have tried to distinguish "mobilizational," "limited mobilizational," and "nonmobilizational" polities on a variable that they call "system style" and that intends to discriminate between (1) those states that have undertaken a political (not military) mobilization or partial mobilization of their human and nonhuman resources in order to meet what they have perceived as "compelling problems of national urgency," and (2) those polities that have not so mobilized.[30] Now, in a clear sense, this is a capability variable from the point of view of foreign policy. That is, one would expect mobilized social resources to serve to make the regime's policy more effective; and the effect of total or partial political mobilization should be to make the leadership conscious of a capability rank more exalted than economic or military statistics would appear to suggest, and willing to act in accordance with that consciousness. But political mobilization seems likely to have other effects, as well, upon foreign policy. It is likely to narrow the range of interest articulation (and therefore of articulation of opposition) as well as the range of organization of opposition; and the more extensive and intensive such mobilization, the less probable it is that social heterogeneities will affect policy, which is insulated therefrom by mobilization. Indeed, mobilization should (at least over the periods of its highest intensity) operate to diminish all extraregime initiatives and influence on foreign policy, and to sustain or to compel a centralization of the information-making, demand-making, and decisionmaking processes, and a reduction in the number of relevant loci of decision.

External penetration

Under this title we propose to ask of polities the degree to which concrete external actors (foreign powers, foreign nationals, formal international organizations, organized transnational movements, and so forth—as opposed to "foreign ideas") have achieved influence or

---

[29] *A Cross-Polity Survey*, Raw Characteristic Number 25.

[30] A quantitative index of the degree of mobilization may be provided by such statistics as "Expenditure of Central Government as a Percentage of Gross National Product," "Employed by Central Government and Public Enterprises as a Percentage of Working-Age Population," and "Military Personnel as a Percentage of Total Population." See Russett *et al.*, *World Handbook*, pp. 66–82.

dominance in their social life, and what impact (if any) that foreign influence has upon their external policies. Here the examiner must survey such relevant information as the date of national independence, length of tutelage, manner of achieving independence, cultural affinity and general relations with former suzerain power. The more recent, peaceful, and gradual the attainment of independence, the longer the tutelage, and the higher the cultural affinity—whether through extensive colonization or intensive assimilation—the more probable it is that extensive penetration remains. Similar queries must be asked about the last occasions of military occupation or derived artificial revolutionization. On the whole, the nearer in time, the longer, the more intense and thoroughgoing such occupation or revolutionization, the greater the likelihood of continuing penetration. (Incidentally, military occupation by victorious enemies and troop-stationing or "occupation" by allies during a war may be expected to have effects similar in kind if different in degree; the more war-shattered the military, political, and social structure of the state in question, the more influential an allied presence commonly is.)

It is "normal" for states to have their territory and government penetrated to a certain degree by other states. Thus it is expected that foreign interests will be articulated by foreign embassies on one's soil; but one extremely large foreign embassy, with constant and extraordinary access to the head of government or to other ministers than the foreign minister, signals special penetration. It is also expected that the foreign office will, through its network of embassies abroad, be turned in part into a device for articulating the interests of foreign states in the ego-state, reversing its intended function. Since this is normal, it is discounted. One looks instead for equivalent penetration in other institutions (especially the military and the police), and for signs that the foreign office entirely fails to secure the national interests that it articulates abroad, while foreign governments articulating their interests through the foreign office are successful. Furthermore, one looks for extraordinary modes of articulation of foreign interests—through foreign businessmen or generals stationed in the ego-state; through persistent expression of foreign views in a segment of the domestic press or other mass media; through ostensibly domestic political parties, churches, or other nongovernmental organizations and institutions.

Obvious signs to be sought in a survey of external penetration include the receipt of foreign aid, peacetime foreign forces and military bases and naval visits, touring foreign heads of state and missions, only a selected set of diplomatic recognitions and relations, foreign investment, foreign teachers, foreign trade, foreign university scholarships and admissions, foreign arms, and, of course and most evidently, foreign military alliances.

Not one of these is an infallible sign of external penetration of foreign-policymaking; they are merely clues, whose presence should stimulate further probing. One must ask to what degree such potential influences flow from one and only one foreign source, and to what degree such influences appear to be neutralized by the recipients' playing off one external power against another. One must ask how far each such input was voluntarily received, or even requested, and how far it is habituating (in that its continued presence seems to create a need—or a pressure group—that works in turn to sustain its continued presence). One must ask how directly each such external input bears on foreign policy in principle. More centrally, one inquires whether there is any specific evidence of current transactions in which policies or personnel or the very regime itself were sustained (or replaced) by foreign influence against extreme and nearly decisive internal (or foreign) pressures for their change (or maintenance).

And just where the physical and statistical evidence of penetration by one dominating outside power is greatest, or just where the penetrated state's reputation is that of a most servile puppet or satellite, one must conscientiously search for evidence of deliberate state resistance to, sabotage of, blackmail and bargaining about, or assertion of independence from that apparent preponderance—for the contrariness of the human animal is not to be underestimated. And since the degree of external influence upon a state's foreign policy (and its domestic policy, for that matter) is one of the hottest items in modern propaganda warfare, one does not want to attribute such influence sweepingly, blindly, or without material evidence.

But where external penetration is justly declared present, and if it could ever be complete, one would expect it to have three systematic effects:

1. **Alignment.** The penetrated state should consistently align itself with the penetrating state on international issues and disputes.

2. **Autonomy.** The pentrated state should leave the taking of foreign policy initiatives strictly to the penetrator, and should ignore its own traditional national interests (irredentist claims to annex certain territories, measures against customary foreign enemies) except so far as these suit the immediate needs of its penetrator.

3. **Insulation.** The penetrated regime should be quite unresponsive to the information and demands communicated to it by internal political process, and unaffected by the normally preoccupying and debilitating effects of social heterogeneities.

To the degree that there is penetration, then, there ought to be evidence of otherwise inexplicable deviations in these directions of the content and quality of foreign policy.

Conclusion

Effective comparative foreign policy research into the impact of political processes on foreign policy will require a survey of the decisional style, interest grouping, political communication, social heterogeneity, social modernization, political mobilization, and external penetration of a number of states. One student of the subject may hope at length to gain close familiarity with process and policy in three or four states, and then to do intensive comparisons across all the categories given above that seem relevant to any of the cases. But the appropriate preparation for such work, both for the student and for the study, would appear to be that of surveying first a single state, and then a fair number of states, on all these factors. Such a survey would use this chapter to give structure to judgments that are in the first instance expected to be, precisely, impressions of which sociopolitical process factors are most important and relevant, and which are least so. One asks first which factors seem relevant in one case, and then what their relevance and impact is; then the same questions are asked separately of a range of cases; and then, in the close comparison of answers and of cases, given general hypotheses may be sustained (or not), and hypotheses not given may emerge.

References

Almond, Gabriel and G. Bingham Powell, Jr., *Comparative Politics: A Developmental Approach.* Boston: Little, Brown, 1966.
Banks, Arthur S. and Robert B. Textor, *A Cross-Polity Survey.* Cambridge, Mass.: M.I.T. Press, 1963.
Huntington, Samuel P., "Political Development and Political Decay." *World Politics,* XVII (1965), pp. 386–430.
McClelland, Charles, "Systems and History," *General Systems* (Yearbook of the Society for General Systems Research), III, 1958.
Organski, A. F. K., *World Politics.* 2nd ed., New York: Knopf, 1968.
Russett, Bruce M., Hayward R. Alker, Jr., Karl W. Deutsch, and Harold D. Lasswell, *World Handbook of Political and Social Indicators.* New Haven, Conn.: Yale University Press, 1964.

part three

Analyzing and projecting problems
of foreign relations

8

The analysis of foreign policy problems

Every definite factual situation presents a number of *problems*.[1] A situation—normally an attitude, behavior, or action of a foreign state —is a problem when it presents a threat or an obstacle or an opportunity: in short, when it presents a challenge to the policy objectives and commitments of the ego-state. A new policy must then be formulated in response to the objectives and the problem.

Depth in the analysis of a state's major problems is usually a function of long familiarity with past intricacies of politics and policy. Perspective in such analysis is as important for the citizen, and more readily available. But perspective is acquired differently from depth: perspective is a function of familiarity with the simultaneous monologues of many conflicting analysts, whose mutual conflicts reveal individually unstated assumptions, biases, and shortages of evidence.

This chapter presents and discusses certain features of a method for researching and analyzing the foreign policy problems of a state. The elements of such a method require an organization, sources of information, questions to be asked of the data, and research goals toward which the questions are oriented. A certain form of procedure is therefore suggested here: (1) A research group, with members of sharply contrasting political views, to insure a broad

[1] See Feliks Gross, *Foreign Policy Analysis* (New York: Philosophical Library, 1954), pp. 134–41.

spectrum of sources, is to procure (2) sources deliberately selected from journalistic and partisan more than from academic accounts, to illustrate sharply contrasting perspectives, and to ask of them (3) a common set of analytical questions, as presented below, all in order to achieve (4) a uniform objective, that is, to outline for each broad problem a set of apparent possible alternative choices that the state in question might choose, and the costs and risks associated with each choice.

The description and explanation of existing policy requires us to look at the present and the past. But policy always has unfinished tasks, is always in process. At any moment, every state has to discover some method of responding to a set of new and old challenges, obstacles, and opportunities. These are the policy problems of the day. Students of foreign policy cannot be content with the fundamentally historical task of explaining the present from the past; they also require a method for looking forward from the present to the future. This chapter suggests an intellectual and organizational process—a collection of concepts and operations and standards—by means of which groups of persons studying a government's policy from outside (that is, without access to its internal documents and deliberations) may reasonably analyze the state's current foreign policy problems. Public discussion of current problems is often extremely backward, and academic discussion not much further advanced. Journalistic treatment in particular focuses on narrating background to the events of the day, collecting striking quotations, advertising or exposing the dramatic or scandalous. Partisan political discussion is full of vague rhetoric, self-justification, and denunciation. Academic and advanced journalistic accounts are often satisfied with identifying a problem as a problem by showing that it has a history; occasionally they will pose one or two possible solutions; seldom are these solutions subjected to any clear critical scrutiny.

The method suggested in this chapter (which I will call *problems analysis*, for brevity's sake[2]) makes use of all this journalistic, partisan, and academic debate as raw material. It attempts to carry relatively objective analysis as far as possible; it does not pretend to be able to provide immediate gratification in the shape of definitive simple solutions or galleries of heroes and scapegoats. Problems analysis requires a group to carry it out properly: provided that the natural tendency to take rhetorical postures and pass resolutions can be overcome, groups of great political diversity are as workable as those with high consensus.

The objective of a problems-analysis group is to take problematic situations as inputs and to deliver multiple policy *alternatives* as outputs. The more diverse the analytical group, the broader the spectrum of alternatives it can realistically consider; the more united

[2] And also to refer to the "problems approach" developed at the Brookings Institution, described in Appendix B of William Reitzel, Morton A. Kaplan and Constance G. Coblenz, *United States Foreign Policy 1945–1955* (Washington: The Brookings Institution, 1956).

the group, the more painstakingly it can dissect each alternative it covers. The disagreement within the group is most functional when it works to drive emotive rhetoric out of deliberations, and to compel the final statement of problem situations and the final formulation of alternatives in more concrete, precise, empirical, and objective language than their initial conception.

Although this method will most often be employed to study United States policy problems, it is generally applicable to the scrutiny of the problems of any state, with some obvious reservations: The state should not be so heavily penetrated by external influences that its foreign policy is nonautonomous or irrelevant; the state should not be so isolated or its current internal situation so chaotic that it can be said to have no foreign policy or no capacity to conduct a foreign policy.

The relationship of an examination of United States problems to their own interests will be more evident to Americans than the relation between those interests and a study of Soviet problems. But perhaps the greatest barrier to understanding (and anticipating) Soviet, French, or Chinese behavior in the United States is the inability to enter, or at least to mimic or simulate, the thought and the minds of the opposed decisionmakers. A problem analysis, based upon as many original foreign sources as are available, of the policy of a foreign state may have a special value in breaching the barriers that keep individuals trained within one political tradition from thinking (even experimentally) like their foreign counterparts socialized to another political culture and trained in another jargon. Thus, although the most natural introduction to problems analysis for Americans is through the study of American foreign policy problems, the full use of the technique will not be gained unless the analyst "tries it on" the problem of another foreign state with which he has some special concern.

The anatomy of a problem analysis

The language of problems analysis discloses the contents of the analytic process. The great and primary problem for any state at any moment is the problem of the *general line,* and it can be stated as a question: What ought to be the main goals we should seek, and the overridingly important commitments we should make, given the condition of the world system at this moment? But the state will also have the permanent problems of *regional* general lines (What form should our general policy toward Africa[3] take?), *country* general lines

---

[3] Or the Middle East, Latin America, Southeast Asia, the Far East, the Soviet Union, East Europe, South Asia, the Atlantic area. This particular division by areas is suitable only for United States policy: Communist China will define the regions of its policy rather differently, as will any other nation.

(What ought to be our Russian[4] policy?), *functional* general lines (What ought to be our defense[5] policy?), and of determining the proportion of leadership attention and of the governmental budget that will be allocated to foreign as opposed to domestic matters.[6]

Similarly, since policy is not made in a vacuum, any state will normally have to cope with new or recent specific problems (to generate *crisis* policy, that is, to create new policy lines), while also dealing with old and persistent problems (generating *program* policy, that is, altering and updating established and functioning policy lines); and no doubt preparing to handle problems that will be around for a long time to come (*planning* policy for the future, for the short range of 2–5 years, the medium range of 10–15 years, and the indefinite and indeterminate long range).

The input of a problem analysis is the problem *situation;* the output is a set of *alternatives,* a set of possible alternate *lines of policy.* A line of policy contains a statement of (1) *strategic objectives* or *long-term goals,* desired conditions that the policy is intended to bring about or foster,[7] (2) the current and/or probable *obstacles* or threats to the enactment of such goals;[8] (3) the *intermediate goals* relevant to overcoming these obstacles, with judgments of the moments in time in which they should be sought, the priority in terms of immediate attention demanded by each, their relationship to

---

[4] Or our policy toward China, Germany, France, Japan, England, India, Brazil, Argentina, Cuba, Mexico, Thailand, and so on: every state will have certain countries that are the chief foci of its foreign interest, and the chief targets of its policy.

[5] Or our foreign economic or social, informational, intelligence, or cultural policies; or policies towards arms control, international organizations, and so on. When one simply speaks of "foreign policy," there is an implication that the instruments in use are the diplomatic, political, and/or military.

[6] Some supposedly "domestic" problems are in fact also usually foreign policy problems of the highest rank. Thus a state's policy toward the national economy is a policy toward its own resources and capabilities for foreign affairs; and any state that has been "penetrated" (so that groups or sectors within it are the allies, agents, or sphere of a foreign power or powers) must consider its policy toward those sectors as a foreign, not just a domestic policy.

[7] Some general objectives that any state might have (for the world system, a regional subsystem, or a specific foreign country) are: withdrawal of commitments and isolation from foreign contact; sole, complete, and unquestioned dominance and control; general friendly relations without any specific content; nonalignment in all main conflicts; maintenance or abandonment, change or overthrow, of its own or a foreign or international status quo. The status quo is the condition that exists at the moment, and may usefully be subdivided—thus, states may wish to control the territorial status quo (the boundaries, coalitions, alignments, friendships, and hostilities or conflicts), the capability status quo (existing relative "power" and influence), the economic status quo (existing ties of trade, markets, supplies, and investment; existing distributions of production, productivity, and property), the political status quo (existing constitutions and regimes), and so on.

[8] Typical obstacles include powerful and hostile or intransigent blocs and states, regimes and leaders, political movements and parties and factions.

each other and to the long-term goals; (4) the appropriate kinds of *resources* to employ for overcoming these obstacles and reaching these goals, the *techniques* to be employed in mobilizing and utilizing resources, and the proposed amounts of *commitments* of resources in the service of these techniques.[9]

A line of policy will also (if well formulated) contain assessments of the certain and highly probable *costs*[10] that will be incurred in undertaking or sustaining this line of policy, of the probability or *chance of success* if the policy is undertaken, (and the index by which success or failure will be gauged), the *term* of the policy (how long are these commitments expected to last until "success" is reached or the policy is abandoned), the *fallback policies* in the event of failure, the *price of failure*, the *risks* or unintended possible bad side effects of putting the policy into effect, the *contingencies* or unforeseeable chance events that might in future occur to interfere with the policy, and the *insurance* available against disaster (that is, the actions and commitments that would raise the immediate costs of the policy while also raising its chance of success, lowering the price of failure, making risks less likely or less costly, and preparing to meet and weather contingencies).

Thus a policy problem is a situation requiring a state to choose from a limited range of ways of using power (or resources or capabilities): If the analysts agree on a prescribed objective, then a problem arises when the actual present (or potential future) circumstances are not very favorable to success in attaining that objective; if the analysts disagree on objectives, the problem may involve the same difficulties, but is complicated by the need to ask what actual feasible objectives exist, what the chances of achieving each alternative objective are, and what lines of policy are the most plausible routes toward each objective. But by the nature of the beast, a problem exists only where the circumstances of a situation make goals difficult to attain, or where different goals appear both desirable and feasible.

The things one expects to find in a problem analysis are, therefore, the statements of: a significant situation; a goal or set of possible goals, and the obstacles to the attainment thereof; a set of

[9] Typical resources and techniques may be classified as *diplomatic* (threats and promises, bargaining and trades with foreign rulers), *military* and *paramilitary* (organized force and violence), *political* (overt and covert activities of political support, political subversion, and political organization abroad), *economic* (gifts and loans of funds to foreign states and economic actors; channeling of foreign investments, trade preferences, and quotas and restrictions), *social* (technical aid personnel, Peace Corpsmen, community development volunteers, and so on), *informational* (propaganda directed at foreign elites and groups), *cultural* (exchanges of intellectuals, scientists, artists, students, and other members of national populations; displays of methods and objects of art, technology, and production), and so forth.

[10] The money, men, and material likely to be employed or lost, the time, energy, and attention to be expended, and the other things that might have been done or sought but will now be ruled out because they are in contradiction with this line of policy, or because the resources to seek them will have been preempted by this policy.

alternative possible policy decisions that would deploy (commit) certain resources in the attempt to achieve certain goals. So the job of the individual problems analyst begins when he selects a situation and declares that it is a problem, advances an objective as appropriate for the state in the situation, notes the main obstacles in the way of his proposed objective, and contends that some tools or means are immediately relevant for overcoming such obstacles.[11]

Organizing for problems analysis

As already suggested, a research group is probably better for preparing a problems analysis than is a single researcher. This is asserted with the assumption that this volume will be employed mainly by students of policy who are well outside government (that is, without much power, responsibility, or information beyond that available to others in the "political office" of citizen), and who study policy in order to reach opinions that they can understand, communicate, and argue. Such students must as individuals choose the alternatives that they will support on the basis of their own values. But it is very likely that their activity within a problem-research group will yield alternatives (for personal judgment and choice) that will be formulated more carefully, more precisely, more objectively than if one individual had created them. It is also likely that there will be fewer straw men; the points of disagreement, the values at issue, and the evidence relevant to the solving of empirical disagreements will be clearer, and the alternatives open will be more in number and analyzed in more detail. These are the points at which it seems that a well-organized problem-research group will probably outperform a single judicious researcher; and the need of a group to reach, not total agreement, but at least agreement on the grounds of disagreement, may contribute to the emergence of such single judicious researchers, in an area where even they are much needed.[12]

Sources for problems analysis

The researcher in pursuit of materials for a problems analysis is in need of the following: claims that a problem exists, and definitions

[11] This form of analysis tends to isolate problems one from another, and thereby to induce the analyst to forget that all of a state's problems at any moment are interlinked. In any government where a number of regional and functional specialists have a hand in a decision, they will make it their business to examine the implications that any alternative policy to deal with problem X is bound to have for the policy area that is their own speciality. Problems analysis has a formal place for this examination (in the section on costs and risks), and can generate it in practice to the degree that the analytical specialists talk to each other about one another's problems.

[12] See the Appendix at the end of this chapter for further remarks on organization.

of the problem situation; statements of objectives alleged to be actual, desirable, or possible; proposals, rejections, and weighings of policy lines, ranging from the broad "big picture" to the narrow-gauge and detailed.

Aside from the personal information and opinions of the analysts engaged in a given research, there are many sources that can be processed by analysts in search of such materials. The sources consist of the public debate, official, journalistic, scholarly, and partisan.[13]

Aside from the evident fact that those who have no access to the intelligence reports and internal proposals available to policy-makers must make do with what they have, the use of sources from the public debate may help problems analysts who are overwhelmed by the infinite number of possible problems, goals, resources, and policy lines to be found upon a simple exploration of the field of analysis. It is imperative for analysts to find ways to cut down the complex of alternatives they have to consider, and to confine their analysis to a few options. This narrowing of the range of choice may be accomplished by leaving most of the attempt to find creative and original choices (and definitions of problems) to individual participants in the public debate (who are better able to be creative than most groups in any case). The groups can then confine themselves to sifting the "outputs" of states, political factions, journals, academic writers; the researchers can comb this debate for alternatives, clarify and purify their statement, and then weld and fuse these discovered materials into a limited number of sharply defined selections. But this reliance on sources has certain costs, and need only be undertaken if the researchers are not ready and able to do the job in their own right. If they are prepared to imagine and to create, they need not merely evaluate.

[13] The American analysts focusing on the foreign policy problems of a foreign country will find certain standard sorts of sources: the foreign correspondence of the *New York Times*, the *Christian Science Monitor*, etc. (and the indexes thereto); the pronouncements of national representatives to the United Nations, especially at the General Assembly's general debate; official and opposition newspapers and statements in the national press; analyses by United States academicians and journalists, as indexed in the *Social Sciences and Humanities Index*, or the *Readers' Guide to Periodical Literature*. These will not usually provide all that he would like to know, but they will generally supply material enough for a reasonable and not incompetent investigation.

For American policy, there will be a wealth of sources, including all the above. Many books evaluating United States policy are published each year. Periodically, the views of the executive (for example, in the *Department of State Bulletin*) may be contrasted with opinions of various public figures (presented, for example, in *Vital Speeches*), opinions expressed in the legislature (for example, hearings of the Senate Foregn Relations Committee), the notions of columnists (for example, Alsop, Buckley, Evans and Novak, Frankel, Kraft, Lerner, Lippmann, Reston) and of the writers for a great variety of magazines (for example, *Atlantic, Harpers, New York Times Magazine, Economist* (London), *Time, Newsweek, U.S. News and World Report, Current History, Foreign Affairs, Orbis, New Leader, New Republic, Nation, National Review, Commentary, Ramparts, Dissent, Monthly Review*).

See Research Guide and Bibliography for a more detailed set of sources.

Frequent problems: studying the present through the past

Where an extensive public debate has not yet illuminated (or obscured) a contemporary problem, or where, as is quite normal, the whole of a current discussion has been skewed by transient prejudices and factions, previous problems of similar structure could provide some usable balancing materials. Similar types of problems occur to different states; it may then be useful to compare the choices seen and taken earlier by some state with those open to another or the same state later troubled by a similar problem. The special utility of a history of problems is to reveal alternatives and to suggest consequences of such alternatives that the current debate overlooks. A very broad typology of problems that have been taken up by one or more major powers in the contemporary period should make it easier for analysts to find past problems similar to those of their own period.

In other words, it appear that not only the problems of today but also the problems of yesterday are amenable to study according to the technique of problems analysis. Even to look for other ways of solving dead problems than were actually used has a contemporary value, if basic similarities in the character of problems exist, because the unused alternatives of the past will then constitute (broadly speaking) possible choices for the present confrontation of living problems. Thus, despite the dangers in reasoning from historical analysis,[14] the materials for the study of current problems include not only the specific contemporary background and public debate, but also the same background and debate plus the actual decisions and outcomes of significantly similar past problems. The group that analyzes a current choice in the making may find, in the history of foreign policy, useful, interesting, and plausible ways of defining the situation, notions of what resources are actually available and relevant, possible objectives in the situation, various lines of policy to secure objectives, and the possible consequences—gains and losses, expected and surprising. Not only are the outcomes of past choice (somewhat) better known than those of choices yet to be made; the internal documents of governments are also often rather more readily available when a decision has been made and disposed of. But in order to pick from the welter of history only the most relevant material, a fairly objective schema of classification is necessary.

The following schema is presented as another eclectic collection of variables of the variety already familiar from earlier chapters

---

[14] Which reasoning becomes nonsense when, for instance, the actual past consequences of one certain choice are presumed to be the *necessary* consequences of *all* such choices—for example, "After Hitler's demands at Munich were met, he increased his demands and his threats; therefore, to appease (nationalist) (socialist) (national socialist) (tyrannical) (imperialist) (revolutionary) (belligerent) (fascist) (totalitarian) (extreme) (revisionist) (German) [pick one or all] demands always provokes more of the same."

in this book. As usual, it is intended to be suggestive rather than exhaustive, and it combines the fairly obvious with the more remote. Some similarities will no doubt prove more useful than others for finding past parallels with present problems. It may seem at first glance for instance, that "crises" will be more significantly similar than "budgetary problems"; but this is not necessarily true. In any case, the following is a very broad typology of some problems that have been taken up by one or more major powers in the contemporary period.

"Domestic" capability problems

"New frontiers." An individual or group leadership, attempting to change national policy (perhaps rather radically), discovers that traditional objectives, policymaking institutions, and the constraints of the policymaking process do not automatically yield the economic, military, or organizational capabilities necessary to make good the new policy. Query: how to liberate policy from these restraints? *United States examples:* Truman and the European Recovery Program; Kennedy and a variety of novel policies. *Other:* De Gaulle and the reform of French military forces.

Popular support. A leadership finds it important to restore, sustain, or improve general popular support of foreign policy as a whole (to whip up mass enthusiasm, to regain idealistic vigor, to repair its public image, to build consensus, to recapture revolutionary dynamism), whether expressed in polls, votes, volunteer work, or public demonstrations. *United States example:* the public opinion crises of 1951–52, 1961, 1967–68.

New means. A leadership anticipates new types of international conflict and crisis, which will require that new organizational instruments, new systems of combat, or new politico-paramilitary capabilities be developed before the incidence of such crises if they are to be successfully met. *United States examples:* nuclear weapons; thermonuclear weapons; ballistic missiles; submarine-launched missiles; counterinsurgency forces; antiballistic missile defenses.

Power in general. A leadership determines that it is vital as a general means to a variety of vital ends that the state they govern should maintain or improve its position in the world power hierarchy, relative to its main rivals as they see them. *United States examples:* Rearmament under Truman, economic growth reform under Kennedy.

Bloc problems

Coalition and bloc formation. A challenge, or what is perceived by a state as a threat to itself and to others, leads the state to attempt to initiate collective action in response. *United States examples:* initiation of NATO, SEATO, CENTO, Alliance for Progress; collection and re-collection of allies for Korea, Vietnam, Cuban blockade. *Counterproblems:* preventing the formation of a hostile bloc, for example, the Warsaw Pact; fomenting breakup of a hostile bloc, for example, the Sino-Soviet rift.

Leadership and bloc maintenance. The leading state in an established bloc is challenged by a rival would-be leader or bloc-breaker, or by the tendency of alliances to fragment. *Example:* NATO versus German rearmament, Suez, the Common Market, De Gaulle. *Counterproblems:* seizing leadership in an extant bloc; shedding the burdens of a restrictive alliance.

Conflict problems

"Liberation." A leadership decides to promote radical alterations in the form and character of a hostile foreign government, by means of propaganda, covert aid, or military action. *United States examples:* Eastern Europe and the first Eisenhower administration; Iran 1951; Guatemala 1954; Cuba 1961. *Other:* a permanent problem of Soviet, Chinese, and Castroite foreign policy.

Containment of a state. A leadership decides that the growing influence or potential of another state constitutes a long-term direct or indirect menace, and sets about keeping that menace in check by confining its influence to extant spheres and territories, at most. *United States examples:* policy toward Russia since 1946–47, China since 1950–53, Cuba since 1961. *Other:* Russia versus China since the late 1950s; De Gaulle versus the United States since 1958 (or perhaps 1961). *Counterproblem:* to probe, penetrate, or burst the bonds of containment.

Containment of an ideology or political myth. A leadership sets about checking the spread of a hostile belief system. *United States examples:* policy toward "monolithic" Communism since 1946–47, the varieties of "polymorphous" Communism since the early 1960s. *Other:* Russia versus "broad democracy" in Hungary in 1956, "polymorphous" deviationism in Communist countries since the late 1950s, "socialist democracy" in Czechoslovakia in 1968.

Localization of a crisis. A leadership acts on a crisis abroad to prevent its exploitation by certain hostile forces that were not initially involved in the crisis, and/or to prevent the dangerously involving enlargement of the scope and intensity of the crisis. *United States examples:* Cuba in 1962; Middle Eastern crises since 1948; South Asian crises since 1947; African crises since 1960. *Other:* Russia and South Asian crises in middle 1960s. *Counterproblem:* how to exploit an external crisis, or to escalate it to one's own chance of gain; effective intervention in foreign revolutions, wars, civil wars, and mixed events.

147

These are problems of large scale, arising (as do so many) out of the alternatives chosen for action at the level of a world or regional general line. The cases that they bring to mind might be examined, when and as they seem parallel to a current problem, so as to secure from the sources that considered the old problem a variety of alternatives that may not yet have been raised to public notice in the current case.

Obviously, this scheme is not intended to exhaust the historical parallels that can be drawn between current and past policy problems. The scheme is allusive. The point here made is not that one should or should not argue by analogy that because line X was decided on and satisfactorily carried through by one state at one time, therefore line X is a decision for all situations. Rather it is that where an analyst perceives analogies in the structures of an old and a new problem, he can scrutinize the facts of the old to discover some possibilities for the new. The actual past decisions, the rejected past alternatives, the actual past outcomes, all have a value that is purely suggestive: they provoke and enlarge thought about the present.

Summary

This chapter argues for the employment of a technique of inquiry into current dilemmas of a state's foreign policy, *problems analysis,* as a means of gaining perspective on present and possible decisions of state. The body of the chapter is devoted to clarifying the way problems analysis is done, the concepts that it uses, and the kinds of recurrent problems that occur. The appendix to the chapter discusses more technical matters of the process, procedure, organization, and products of problem analysis.

Appendix to Chapter 8: mechanics of problems analysis

The best way to learn the mechanics of a problem analysis is to do one. When that is once accomplished, one can put together one's own handbook. But certain points of technical detail may be of assistance to those who intend to try problems analysis for the first time. This appendix therefore presents a summary of the process, a schematic table of procedures, some notes on group organization, and two kinds of papers that may form the final product of a group problem analysis.

Process

The first analytically trying step in the problem-analysis process is the definition of the significant situation that requires decision.

The situation may be a present condition, a real threat or opportunity, or a potential future reality (indeed, a whole branch of the policy studies of government planners is *contingency analysis*—the study of the policy problems that would face a government if some possible and important event were to take place). Whether actual or merely contingent, the situation is not a problem unless (1) it is *significant*, that is, it offers a threat or an opportunity to the values and world goals of the state in question, (2) it involves *choice*, so that the state is in a position to do different things about it, and (3) it involves a measure of *control*, so that the state in question has some chance of affecting the outcome of the situation by the action it takes or does not take.

For each situation and each goal a state has certain capabilities that are relevant. What these are the problems analyst must seek to determine. His question is, What facilities does the state have (or could it get) that could conceivably be employed to gain its actual or possible ends in this situation? To propose an answer, he must have some empirical notion of the "national power" of the state: its military and economic resources (as well as the resources that its friends and allies will or may commit for its benefit) and such less tangible goods as prestige and influence.

The objective of a problems-analysis group is to take problematic *situations* (as *inputs*) and to deliver multiple policy *alternatives* (as *outputs*). The more diverse the analytical group, the broader the spectrum of alternatives it can realistically consider; the more united the group, the more painstakingly it can dissect each alternative it covers. The disagreement within the group is most functional when it works to drive emotive rhetoric out of deliberations, and to compel the final statement of problem situations and the final formulation of alternatives in more concrete, precise, empirical, and objective language than that of their initial conception. And indeed, it is most important that the alternatives formulated by problems analysts be concrete, operational, as precise as policy directives can be, and phrased in language without partisan overtones. If each alternative the problem analysis yields could be conceived of as an instruction given by some specific government office to some other such office, such that some specific actions or statements would have to be done by some specific persons if the instructions were to be complied with, then the alternative is probably well formulated.

To each alternative the analyst must attach an estimate of the probable costs, the possible costs (risks), the possible gains, and the chances of success or failure of the associated line of policy. When these estimates are made (collectively if possible, more likely by each analyst separately), the job of problem analysis is complete. On the basis of his own scale of values and his own willingness to take chances, the individual worker may recommend, espouse, or reject each alternative line. But the weighing, and perhaps even the statement, of these alternatives ends the work of a group following this approach.

Procedure

The steps to be taken in a problem analysis can be schematized as follows:

1. Select the country whose problems are to be studied.
2. Locate its set of current problems.[15]
3. Select and define one for analysis. Decide whether to handle it as (a) goal-given or (b) goal-released.[16]

If (a) goal-given, subsequent steps are as follows:

4. Provide the background to show that the alleged goal is actually a goal of the state actor or its decisionmakers.
5. State the problem situation (giving evidence of a condition or writing the scenario of a contingency) that blocks or threatens the objective.
6. (a) Imagine as lines of action the tactical objectives, techniques, and commitments that might conceivably overcome the obstacle.
   (b) Verify the availability of the capabilities or resources relevant to and needed for each line of action.
7. Restrict the range of choice to the contrasting lines judged most feasible.
8. Attach statements of costs, chance of success, risks, sequences, and contingencies and branches, insurance costs, measures to be applied to determine "success," expected term of policy and times of review, and fallback policies.
9. Individually weigh costs and benefits of success against the risks and the chance and costs of failure; make recommendations.

If (b) goal-released, subsequent steps are as follows:

4. (a) Review prior and current goals, the current situation and trends, and actual possible capabilities.
   (b) Collect and catalogue proposed, theoretically plausible, and personally desired alternative objectives.
5. Review, reform, revise, and cull those goals for vagueness, ambiguity, impossibility or lack of capacity, irrelevance to the situation, and possible fusion, balancing, priorities, or alternations among them.

[15] Axiomatically, these include the problems of the world general line, regional general lines, country general lines, functional general lines, foreign/domestic attention, and program-crisis-planning policy. The specific current forms in which these problems arise will reveal themselves in the official and journalistic sources of the day. Priority in policy reevaluation is generally given to the crisis of the moment, to policies that have just led to failures in crisis, and to ongoing program policies that are not yielding the expected success at the expected time for the expected cost; occasionally (for example, after a change in government) all policy may come up for review.

[16] The decision is whether the research group is prepared to agree that a given objective is and should remain (for purposes of analysis) the target of the state as actor in the situation.

6. Select a very limited number of major, clear, plausible, relevant options.
7. Let separate groups or the whole seek maximum consensus on the *one* set of tactical objectives, techniques, and commitments of available resources most likely to lead to each of the contrasting strategic objectives, thus creating a restricted set of alternative lines of policy toward different objectives.
8. Attach statements (as in 8 above).

Organization

Given a problem and the formation around it of a research group, the organization of that group ought to be primarily in response to the tasks of a problem analysis and to the nature of the problem, and also to the size of the group, the time allotted to the analysis, the level of consensus among the members, their special interests and information, and so on. Some of these constraints will impose themselves without any special preparation; the most variable factors will be the division of labor and the specialization of tasks.

The character of the problem and the size of the group will determine whether the most appropriate specialization is by individuals or subcommittees, by region, function, subproblem, or time perspective (or a combination of these). But in all cases formations for four ends will be highly desirable: (1) "metatask regulation"; (2) a nonspecialized section or subcommittee; (3) duplication of responsibilities; (4) interspecialist communications. The first (performed by a coordinator or by the group) is the simple function, constantly in revision, of dividing the subject, assigning tasks and timetables, allocating effort and resources, and in general looking and working toward the conclusion of research. The second function involves the delegation, to a certain subset of the research committee membership, of responsibility for dealing with the whole subject problem and with the whole general line of policy toward that problem, responsibility for combining the alternatives provided by specialists into more complex alternative patterns of policy. Duplication of responsibilities (inefficient in an action organization) implies the assignment of reporting on a given, specialized or general, subject matter to two or more researchers (or subgroups) with strongly contrasting perspectives, to assure that varying alternatives constructed out of personal biases or viewpoints will be presented on each topic, to force debate and clarification. (Monopolistic responsibility would be likely to lead to peculiarly shaped alternatives that the whole group could neither endorse nor effectively alter.) Finally, the fact that even the nested breakdown of whole problem areas into their parts will not create a set of entirely self-contained segments makes it useful for specialists to keep up communication with others whose segments will probably overlap with their own when alternatives are finally set forth, so that the sets of alternatives presented by each specialist will be *as a set* compatible with sets advanced by the others.

The first task that the whole group must perform is the statement of the situation and objectives that constitute the problem. In attempting to perform this task collectively, they will discover whether they have or can assume a consensus or whether objectives themselves are in question. If they are, then the whole body should begin to examine alternative possible objectives, with partisans of each line speaking for it and clarifying it under criticism. With one or several objectives specified, the whole ought then to divide the subject into topical areas and assign the parts of the subject to the parts of the research group. These parts (which, if they are committees, may in turn subdivide, or sub-subdivide, their subject and themselves) will then discuss the alternative policies available within their scope, do research to find alternatives stated and clarified and argued, and on the basis of their researches and discussion report back sets of alternative lines of policy, which the whole will then fuse into one large and complex set of alternatives.

Every problem-analyzing group is likely to produce unique deliberations and therefore unique results. Sometimes there will not even be agreement on how to state the definition of the situation; very often, it will be impossible to agree on what the basic goals of a state, to be taken as given, actually are. Thus, the alternatives produced may be alternative problem definitions and alternative goals as well as alternative lines of policy. The most usual difficulty of this sort will arise when one analyst feels that a certain international conflict is the "responsibility" or fault of the state under scrutiny, and so inclines to define the problem as "the bad policy of state X, and the factors sustaining that policy," while another analyst chooses to put blame on a foreign actor, and so defines the problem as "state Y's resistance to the policy of X." But even this disagreement can be more correctly phrased as a set of alternative objectives; although the work of the first researcher will doubtless then be partly directed to the question of how the "bad" policy of X can be changed, he is not exempted from the usual criteria of goals, obstacles, means, and commitments, and the analysis of costs, chances, price, risks, and contingencies.

The character of the consensus among the members of the research group will and should determine the nature of its operations. The more they agree, the more they can devote themselves to analyzing intermediate goals, appropriate commitments, risks, contingencies, and insurance; the less they agree, the more they must elevate themselves to elaborating the case for alternate objectives and means, and to arguing the costs of policy, the chance of success, and the price of failure.

Despite the utility of group research, it has one unfortunate effect on some participants, in that they are driven to lose sight of the whole by their concentration on one specialized part. The disease of overspecialization is countered for the whole by the nonspecialist section; for the specialist, it can be met in part by his separate preparation (for that nonspecialist section) of a personal sketch of a problem analysis, which contains a short and unargued listing of the

152

general goals he thinks appropriate, the main obstacles and threats, the relevant resources, and one or two plausible ways around the difficulties, in broadest outline. This, if done once at the outset of work and once again while the whole group is debating the final report, can countervail the normal tendencies of specialization.

Outputs

The work proposed in Chapter 8 is a simulation of rational policy-formation. It can find its expression in two, sometimes three, research papers: the *problem paper*, the *alternatives paper*, and sometimes the *proposal paper*.

The *problem paper* presents a description of the situation. If objectives are given, it states them and poses the problem of what policy should be laid down and commitments made in order to alter the situation and achieve objectives. If objectives are not given, it poses the problem of what they could and should be, and what policy lines should be laid down and commitments made to support them. This paper may be a brief formal instruction (if only general lines of policy are to be reviewed, there is no need to identify specific problems; if the analysis is goal-released, there is no need to declare objectives); or it may be the complex product of an intensive investigation (into what are the specific objects of a set of decisionmakers and into what specific resistance confronts them). In either case, it is preliminary work.

The *alternatives paper* is written next. It contains the analyst's answers to the decisionmaker's questions—"What can I do?" and "What else can I do?"[17] The analyst may seek to find all the policy lines that are conceivable and feasible, or only a wide spectrum, a set of possibilities from which any one might be chosen. This paper is appropriately presented at a briefing (perhaps of simulated decisionmakers), where it is intensively scrutinized. The interrogators must ask how relevant the alternatives presented are to the objectives in question, whether the most feasible possibilities have emerged, and whether the alternatives represent an unbiased set. On the basis of this examination, the paper might be revised.

Or it might be followed by the *proposal paper*, individual or collective policy proposals. In this case the analyst chooses to recommend one policy from the set, presenting reasons and arguments in the light of all the influential variables: the international system, capabilities, leadership objectives and character, traditions, institutions, and political pressures. This paper may also be presented at a briefing, wherein the questioners will be most interested in to what degree the analyst's presentation of the nonpreferred alternatives is biased by his rejection of them, in how realistic are his evaluations of the costs, risks, price, chances, and contingencies of the preferred line, and in how well he has conceived that line's insurance, fallback, and review.

17 See Gross, *Foreign Policy Analysis*, pp. 134–41.

9

Methods of anticipating foreign relations

The planners of statecraft must seek to prepare for a future that they cannot fully predict but that they are not barred from contemplating. Social science is not a prophetic or precognitive discipline; it seeks to predict, but succeeds only very spottily. Predicting the future of international politics with detailed precision, theoretical justification, and consistent success is beyond us. But to *predict* what *will* happen and to *anticipate* what *may* happen are two different things. Anticipation deals with what is probable or merely possible. Anticipation fuses with statecraft in the bureaucratic activity of *contingency planning*. Contingency planning involves the decision to believe that a certain event is probable or possible and the decision to prepare a policy or even a program of resource allocation against that event. The peacetime army, prepared for the possible event of war, is the most immense result of contingency planning (as well as its largest user); but plans for government spending to prevent large-scale depression in the event of disarmament are also contingency plans.

This chapter discusses by what intellectual and organizational means groups of interested persons without access to classified material may reasonably work to anticipate the future course of a state's foreign relations. Like the previous chapter, it is directed at activating readers and conveying a sense of method rather than a set of conclusions; primarily, it aims to persuade students of foreign policy to do some systematic thinking, in groups even more than as individuals, about one or two possible futures of one or two actual states.

Some recent forecasts

Thinking about the future has only recently become a major activity on the part of a number of persons of some note, partly as an extension of the attempt to anticipate the possible challenges to United States defense policy in the near and longer future; that attempt to think ahead is in turn derived from the need to select weapons systems and systems of combat that are so long (and expensive) in the building that it would be impractical to wait until the challenge occurs and then construct them after the fact. This section summarizes some forecasts, the results of such recent thinking, that are already available, and evidently controversial; they include possible futures of United States foreign policy (offered by Herman Kahn) and of the international system (by Kahn, S. P. Huntington, I. de Sola Pool, and others). They are summarized and presented here not to foreclose but to stir up independent meditation on possible worlds and possible policies.

Kahn[1] lists fourteen alternative possible general lines of United States foreign policy, which are sometimes mutually exclusive, sometimes compatible with one another. These are sketchily summarized under his labels:

1. **Act of renunciation** (immediate, unconditional, total, unilateral, nuclear disarmament)

2. **Unilateral initiatives** (specific, unconditional, partial, reversible, unilateral concessions to the USSR and other opponents, to be continued if responded to and reversed if ignored)

3. **Minimum deterrence** (small second-strike nuclear forces to deter only nuclear attacks on the United States)

4. **Rule of law** (unilateral moves to improve international adjudicative machinery)

5. **Fortress America** (abandon foreign commitments and interests, and spend heavily for United States self-defense only)

6. **Accept the arms race reluctantly** (arm pragmatically, buying those weapons that seem useful, without trying either to win or to slow down the arms race)

7. **Follow technology or lead it** (push the arms race whenever technology seems to offer future advantage)

[1] *Thinking About the Unthinkable* (New York: Avon, 1962), Chap. 8.

8. **Not-incredible first strike** (seek some specific ability to destroy the enemy's nuclear system)

9. **Concert of powers** (cooperate with Russia to restrain China, to control nuclear dispersion, and to restrict the escalation of local wars)

10. **The aggressive democrat** (attempt to create or lead reformist or revolutionary worldwide "prodemocratic" movements)

11. **Credible first strike** (seek the ability to fight and survive a nuclear war)

12. **Protracted conflict** (prepare for and undertake a long and cold containment, counterpressure, and pressback versus communism)

13. **Win** (change or conquer the Soviet regime, by violence if necessary, by pressure if possible)

14. **Preventive war** (prepare to win through a thermonuclear preventive first strike)

Future-analysts might attempt to rank these in order of probable occurrence, updating them by addition and subtraction, blending them as seems appropriate, and to predict (on any of the four assumptions suggested beginning on p. 166) a set of most probable United States policies for some given year in the future. These alternative probable policies might then serve as first steps in various directions. If combined with various possible shapes of the international system, they would present a large set of general problems for United States policy: What sorts of capabilities, ideas, institutions, and processes would be necessary to carry out this line of policy in that international system? What specific decisions, what lines of area policy, what allocations of resources would follow? If the Kahnian strategies were crossed with a set of possible Russian or Chinese strategies and a projection of relative capabilities, we would have American-Russian or American-Chinese future problems viewed from either side: How should "we" (the United States or the Soviet Union or the People's Republic of China) act to implement *this* line in the face of *that* counterline with *these* available resources?

The other previews involve statements about the whole international system. Kahn, in "Alternative World Futures,"[2] speculatively constructs Alpha, Beta, and Gamma worlds. *Alpha worlds* are peaceful and stable, though various, and display the continuing year-to-year business of regional and middle-power problems of a world in which the great powers have reached arms-control agreements and assumed relaxed or defensive military postures. *Beta worlds* each

[2] Hudson Institute paper HI–342–B IV, April 1964.

contain special, defined, and lasting structural strains at a level of world significance: The Soviet Union loses control of the world Communist movement (recall that this is a 1964 paper), or Communist China develops a small nuclear delivery capability (ditto), or nuclear weapons spread to Japan and Germany, or the European Economic Community begins to exclude United States trade and investment, or new violent and unpredictable political movements disturb the underdeveloped areas. *Gamma worlds* are worlds in which a basic nuclear multipolarity, with major nuclear capabilities in France, Germany, Japan, China, and India and minor capabilities cheaply available to the next-ranking powers, is tested by crises.

Those seeking to capitalize on Kahn's work might judge Beta and Gamma worlds the ones most appropriate to create for the study of the future. They would then take an already apparent possible strain, make it "real," and then subject the world under such strain to a bombardment of various alternative or sequential crises. The anticipatory work having been done in the creation of worlds and crises, the analysts might then do a problem analysis from the viewpoint of any state. Or a large group of analysts might choose to run a simulation, playing the roles of the decisionmakers steering the states in the crisis, thus supplementing problem analyses from several viewpoints with running crisis analyses from the same viewpoints.

The essay by Herman Kahn and Anthony J. Wiener[3] contains a list of one hundred "almost certain" and "very significant" technical innovations likely before 2000 A.D., several of which suggest political speculation as a means to reducing historical surprise.

Numbers 23 (new or improved use of the oceans—mining, extraction of minerals, controlled "farming," source of energy) and 53 (permanent inhabited undersea installations and perhaps even colonies) suggest the possibility of a newly fruitful source of two-nation crises and "boundary" disputes.

Numbers 33 (new and more reliable "educational" and propaganda techniques for affecting human behavior—public and private) and 37 (new and relatively effective counterinsurgency techniques and possibly also insurgency techniques) suggest that states now apparently permeable by external subversion may become impermeable—or that some now clearly impermeable may be made permeable.

Number 36 (cheap and widely available or excessively destructive central war weapons and weapons systems) suggests Gamma worlds where any strain or crisis will be extremely dangerous.

3 "The Next Thirty-three Years: A Framework for Speculation," *Daedalus*, Summer 1967, 96, pp. 705–32.

Number 55 (extensive use of robots and machines "slaved" to humans), number 69 (individual flying platforms), numbers 78 (space defense systems), 79 (inexpensive and reasonably effective ground-based ballistic missile defense), and 98 (new and possibly very simple methods for lethal biological and chemical warfare) all suggest new forms of war that must be prevented or deterred, prepared against or planned for, and perhaps survived.

Kahn and Wiener, on the basis of a general trend projection (excluding major changes in the "old" nations, and making no allowance for surprise), project a world of 2000 A.D. containing some relative decline of United States and Soviet power, some further rise of Europe and China with a second rise of Japan, the emergence of new intermediate powers (Brazil, Mexico, Pakistan, Indonesia, East Germany, Egypt), much turmoil in the "new" and possibly in the industrializing nations, with some possibility for sustained nativist or messianic or other mass movements. This world presents us primarily with altered regional and power balances, plus a sustained or increased political effervescence in the third areas. Again, if specific contingencies or crises are then imagined within this general context, we have a set of problems for the states involved.

This "surprise-free Standard World" can be augmented by explorers of the future who consider plausible the major changes in the "old" nations that Kahn and Wiener rule out. These major changes include the phenomena (and the results) of invasion, war, civil strife, revolution, famine, pestilence, despotism and persecution, natural disaster, depression, economic stagnation, new mass movements, resurgent communism or fascism, political dynamism in the United States, the USSR, Europe, Japan, or a new middle power, economic dynamism and 10 percent growth rate in China, extremely cheap and privately available or continentally destructive nuclear technology, and so on. Some recurrences are listed here, some novelties; all are possible, and researchers can rate all for their subjective probability, then examine the highest rated and how it would alter the Standard World, what problems its occurrence would pose for statesmen in the Standard World, or how the altered world would perceive the problems that its likely succeeding crises and contingencies would create.

Kahn and Wiener have also set up *canonical variations*, specific major alternatives to their standard world.

I. More integrated worlds, peaceful and prosperous, with high political coordination:
   A. states oriented to problems of maintaining stability
   B. states oriented to problems of speeding economic development
II. More inward-looking worlds, fairly peaceful and prosperous, but uncoordinated politically:
   A. with an eroded Communist movement

B. with an eroded democratic morale and some Communist dynamism
C. with a dynamic Europe or Japan
III. Relatively troubled and violent worlds, in greater disarray:
A. with an eroded Communist movement
B. with a dynamic Communist movement and some erosion of democratic morale
C. with a dynamic Europe or Japan

Thus, students of the subject of anticipation who disagree systematically with the surprise-free trend projection can project in different directions to variant worlds, illustrate these variants with their own scenarios, and thus use Kahn and Wiener as base points for their own problems analyses.

Herman Kahn, in a separate report, also notes several specific scenarios, studies, and judgments that are individually suggestive.[4] One argues that "fascist" or "irrational manic movements" are reactions to modernization and acculturation, to increased rationality and technological control, and are therefore occurrences to be expected widely in the future. Another presents reasonable causes of tense United States–Soviet confrontation in the manner of the years 1947–62. Another suggests that Germany is now third largest nation in GNP and about twentieth in world influence, that this gap will close, that the key problems for Germany will be national reunification and world status, and that the world's problems with Germany will be those of absorbing her as a respectable full member of the international system. Each of these can be extrapolated and expanded on; each will yield a set of future problems, food for present thought.[5]

Eugene V. Rostow[6] presents three more intriguing worlds of the near future, based upon one general trend analysis and three distinct alternative United States policy responses.

1. A strong United States-led coalition protects and develops the Third World while containing and pressing cooperation from Russia and China.

2. A United States-Soviet team tries to maintain dual hegemony and nuclear bipolarity, seeking to contain and control China, but risking a division of the world along color lines, and the consequent defection of India and Japan to the Chinese camp.

[4] *Daedalus*, Summer 1967, pp. 938–40.

[5] The speculations that are summarized in *Daedalus* are presented full length in Herman Kahn and Anthony Wiener, *The Year 2000* (New York: Macmillan, 1967), Chaps. 3, 5, and 6.

[6] "Thinking About the Future of International Society," *Daedalus*, Summer 1967, pp. 922–26.

3. The United States withdraws from mainland Asia and is replaced by a Japan-driven China-Japan world power-complex of skills, resources, leadership, and manpower.

Each such world will have its special contingencies, dangers, threats, opportunities, and crises. If the student finds a probable world here, it can be illuminated and examined through an appropriate scenario or set of scenarios.

Samuel P. Huntington[7] hypothesizes that by 2000 A.D. American power and empire will wane, as China, Indonesia, Brazil, and some Middle Eastern and African regional great powers arise; this will be accompanied by numerous struggles between the rising powers and the United States, which will undermine and disrupt American politics while stimulating national alliances of peasants, armies, and intellectuals, and therefore national cohesion and institutional development, in the rising powers.

Ithiel de Sola Pool[8] predicts, seriatim:

1. A neutralist pro-European Economic Community France

2. Continued and wider but shifting violence in Southeast Asia

3. General decline of the drive and vigor of the world Communist movement

4. A major war in Africa with massive United Nations military intervention

5. Famine in China, followed by guerrilla war, Soviet seizure of Manchuria, and a deradicalized aid-seeking Chinese military dictatorship

6. A Soviet political crisis ending not in revolution but in fragmentation of the Communist Party of the Soviet Union

7. A German attempt to reunify, stopped by the United States and by the German border states

8. Regional federation in Africa, and confederation in Southeast Asia

9. A Western political confederation, including East Europe and Britain, but excluding Russia and the United States

10. "Token" nuclear proliferation

[7] "Political Development and the Decline of the American System of World Order," *Daedalus*, Summer 1967, pp. 927–29.

[8] "The International System in the Next Half Century," *Daedalus*, Summer 1967, pp. 930–35.

11. A new, very cheap, postnuclear weapon family

12. Several local wars in Asia, internationally contained

13. A shift in techniques of national-security maintenance from cruder and forcible methods toward subtler varieties of reconnaissance, intelligence, infiltration, and massive international corruption.

This series (which amounts to a "history" written from 2015 A.D.) can be followed by research groups as far as they find it probable, or branched from; it can be detailed, alternative branches or probable crises written up, and these possible situations subjected to problems analysis.

Pool's working groups[9] disagreed on various crucial forecasts, thereby identifying the points of disagreement as points of departure for future studies. Some saw the United States at the peak of its power today, and hence on the verge of a downward slide, with a growing number of middle powers likely to acquire a nuclear capability sufficient to destroy ten United States cities and thus able to frustrate the United States in the future. Others saw the United States moving toward a future peak of power, with a growing lead over second-level powers, because of the heavy American investment in research and development. Some saw the United States as increasingly accepting the routine obligations of a world policeman, others as increasingly unwilling to commit manpower and wealth abroad; there was disagreement about whether levels of United States arms expenditure and foreign aid would stay stable, increase sharply, or fall drastically as a result of shifts in domestic public opinion. Large-scale turmoil—war, revolution, and intervention—was generally expected at various points abroad throughout the future. And some major contingencies were identified: German reunification, a union of Europe, or a United States–Chinese rapproachement with heavy United States economic aid to China (all considered in terms of their profound effects on United States–Soviet relations); technological developments, as cheap power, weather control, cheap and easy equalizing weapons, cheap mass world communications and transportation, much improved food production and/or population control, and so on. These agreements, disagreements, and contingencies can all be employed by other previewers of the future, in exactly these forms, to lead into problems analyses of foreign policy.

As samples of guides to discussion of the future, we may take extracts from the papers for "Commission on the Year 2000" working parties.[10] These postulated the following tendencies: increasing ease of international transport and communications; increased moderni-

[9] *Daedalus,* Summer 1967, pp. 948–51.

[10] *Daedalus,* Summer 1967, pp. 980–81.

zation and social integration in developing states; many new intellectual or functional international organizations, and proliferation of weapons of mass destruction. The topics for discussion included the extent to which violent international conflict or domestic violence would be a major factor in world politics, the extent to which old Marxist and nationalistic ideologies and new ideologies based on poverty or race would wax and wane, the chances of transnational (regional, functional, intellectual) integrations, and the structure of the future international hierarchy of powers. And indeed these all belong in the studies of the students of the future of the world. In this instance, they are models of the kind of topics that other research groups might delimit, by a judgment on what current trends are of greatest significance, in order first to forecast the separate trends and then to meditate upon the worlds that the unions of these special trends reveal.

Finally, we can take note of the specific predictions for a 70- to 80-year future made by A.F.K. Organski.[11] Unlike all these others, they are made on the basis of a theory of international relations, from which Organski attempts to infer the future.

1. Nations will remain the prime units of action.

2. The world distribution of power will shift away from the West as a result of the end of empires and spread of industrialization; Britain and France will lose ground in the West to the United States. Russia, China, and India—in that sequence—will increase their power immensely.

3. Russia will level off at a point slightly below the United States level; China, sometime in the twenty-first century, will pass both Russia and the United States and become the world's most powerful nation; India, well into the twenty-first century, should pass the United States and Russia to become second in status.

4. Russia will not win world dominance, with or without a war; war with Russia is highly likely around 1990; China will gain world dominance with or without war, but a Sino-American war is highly likely before China's victory.

One cannot argue with Organski without first becoming steeped enough in his particular political theory[12] to understand it. Then, however, he might be believed in full or in part, argued with, rejected, or taken as limning a plausible and possible alternative future to be courted, evaded, or adapted to.

This has been a résumé of several major forecasts about

[11] *World Politics,* (2d ed.; New York: Knopf, 1968), pp. 483–90.

[12] See especially Chaps. 9 and 14 of Organski, *World Politics.*

international relations. Some are unilinear, some have several branches of equal probability, others have main lines and subordinate branches. There are some sequential artificial histories, some projections of trends to a definite point in time, and some contingent events of great significance. Analysts of the foreign policies of the future can use old forecasts in three ways: as models, as footstools, or as foils. Used as *models,* they show what some results of projections such as this chapter proposes might look like, and therefore how the projections herein proposed might be conjectured. Used as *footstools,* if they seem sound and probable, they will be incorporated whole into others' projections, which will build upon them by extending them, examining their implications, and illustrating them with scenarios of specific moments and crises; or, if they seem pleasant but not too likely, they will ingenerate a problem analysis of present policy designed to discover plausible lines of policy that may realize them. Used as *foils,* if they seem improbable, they may inspire rejection and an alternative forecast intended to overwhelm, outreason, and repudiate them; or, if they seem terrible, they may inspire a problem analysis of present policy, intended to suggest ways of averting such noxious futures as these.

The object of anticipation in comparative foreign relations

The particular business of students of foreign policy cannot be to write speculative narratives or trajectories of the international system merely in order to predict that system's future. They must focus upon specific states or types of states. Nor, in a field where the future is chancy, a bone of conflict, and an environment of policy, should anticipation be other than policy oriented. Previewing futures is of interest because we anticipate that the present may move into one such future or another; and since this book recommends a problem analysis of foreign policy in the present, those methods of anticipating the future that are treated herein will be tied to problems analysis in that we shall consider future situations as constituting future problems, and propose that contingent futures be constructed by anticipatory analyses only so that they may be examined for alternative courses of action through problems analyses.

Therefore, the anticipatory methods presented here all produce, as their final outputs, *problems.* It should be understood that these outputs are contingent future problems that *may* exist but need not, possible future perplexities that may yet become real, rather than real present problems; or they are real present problems, perhaps barely perceived today, that may grow strikingly and that, if they grow, will increasingly demand decision and action. But in both these cases the future as anticipated is also an item in the problems analysis of current policy; for the contingency of the future is, precisely, the threat or the opportunity against which sound long-range policy must prepare.

The methods of anticipation to be discussed could just as well secure, as their outputs, guesses at possible world roles of states, or future general lines of policy, or structures of the international system, or important future determinant factors of a state's policy. Indeed, they will do so, for a possible future expansion of China's world role or a radical change in the general line of United States policy would be as much problems for Russia as would be a possible radical de-de Gaullization of French policy or a dispersion of thermonuclear devices and delivery capabilities among middle powers for American policy. But to present all these conditions not as intriguing objects of speculation but as problems for the policy of a given state seems to get at their immediate practical and political significance. They become subjects of potential action, and of thought about action.

It is important to repeat that future problems do have an immediate significance: To long-sighted men they are *present* problems as well. Thus, attempting to anticipate possible problems of foreign policy maintains a certain practicality in a second sense, that of active relation to the present. The probable effects of a thermonuclear war in the near future, as they are anticipated today by government and other planners, form basic portions of the background material for discussing immediate problems (for example, escalation in Vietnam, antiballistic missiles, restrictions on nuclear proliferation, and so on). The grave implications of one possible event or trend (for example, the population explosion) may suggest that the problem should be mitigated in the future by being attacked in the present. The general benefit of another possible event may suggest that the opportunity for it to occur should be hastened. Any possible future situation that appears to be both portentous and fairly probable is legitimately seen and analyzed as a current problem as well as a future one.

Four viewpoints for anticipating the future: American and foreign; world and dyad

Most of those who read this book will no doubt be Americans. Americans who seek to anticipate the future of foreign policy might do so in any of four ways, depending upon the focus of their immediate interests. (1) They may view the United States from the inside, in the normal way, as the sole actor (ego-state) in a political environment that is composed of its problems. Viewing from within, they may (a) examine its future problems with the world in general, surveying the whole of American foreign policy; or they may (b) examine its specific *dyadic* future relations with a single partner from among such great states (and such great problems) as Russia, China, France, India, and so forth. (2) On the other hand, they may view the United States from without, from the point of view of some other state (again, such as China, the United Kingdom, and so on) for which the existence of the United States poses a problem; they may then choose (a) to concentrate on the specific future challenges that America will pose to, say, Russia; or they may (b) look from the Russian standpoint at the whole of a future international system, and choose to place the American challenge among the many that the world environment will put upon the Soviets.

The first two viewpoints (1a and 1b) will feel most natural to American students, the first to generalists, the second to area or country specialists.[13] Studying America, they will want to forecast its general line of policy (or possible different lines) and its world role in the changing structure of the international system; they will want to preview the lines, roles, and policy determinants of other states; from these they will wish to construct a list of likely United States problems in, say, 1975 or 1980. Next, working as problems analysts, they will try to educe alternatives for United States action in 1975 (or whenever); and, in the more momentous cases, they will also want to do a problem analysis for today, resulting in a set of immediately available alternative lines of policy to head off, speed up, or prepare against the future problems. This is all good and as it should be.

But there is much to be said for experiments that view the United States from outside, and the world as a whole through foreign eyes. There is a certain intellectual value, not to be overlooked, in the uprooting and revision of viewpoint required to achieve the sense of how a foreign state might perceive some future development. The most useful such "uprooting" might be achieved by a group of individuals who: (1) take a set of highly probable events of the near future; (2) try to assume the point of view of some foreign state that such events would deeply affect; (3) carry through problems analyses of each contingency; (4) wait until one or another occurs, and (5) then compare their own analysis with the actual foreign response. But this is an intensive exercise, to stretch the minds of future country-specialists. Country analysts with a more diffuse focus can still profit from a procedure that leads them to view the *futuribles*[14] of foreign policy—the same projected lines, roles, structures, and forces that United States-focused students view as United States problems—as the problems that they might be to the Russians or Chinese. Without the check provided by the attempt to predict actual Russian or Chinese analyses, and then to verify such prediction, it

[13] Evidently Britons will feel more at home "viewing" the United Kingdom, "from within," yet no doubt there will be some students who will be ready to view more than one state from within, with no feeling of peculiarity, alienation, or antipathy.

[14] Bertrand de Jouvenel's label for *possible futures*. See Bertrand de Jouvenel, ed., *Futuribles* (Geneva: Droz, Vol. I, 1963, Vol. II, 1965), which contains projections of the future domestic politics of Britain, Pakistan, Black Africa, and Burma.

would be impossible to say how successful the exercise was in providing the analyst with a Russian or Chinese point of view; but it would surely be possible to say how far it made him aware of the previously unconscious American-ness of his ordinary, and perhaps limited, day-to-day analytical standpoint.

Four assumptions about the future: stasis, trends, recurrence, and surprise

Intellectually, the construction of contingent futures requires us to make at least one unprovable assumption about what events or sorts of events will happen, and then to follow through both the logic and the probabilities of that assumption. Four great (and not fully consistent) assumptions can be employed to sum up the multitude of significant smaller assumptions that must be made and followed through for an exhaustive study of contingent futures on the basis of present knowledge and opinion. These four are: (1) the assumption of systemic stasis; (2) the assumption of trend continuity; (3) the assumption of probable recurrence; (4) the assumption of historical surprise.

The first, *systemic stasis*, is the most common among organizations and individuals who plan for the future on the basis of limited experience or very limited resources; it is presumed that all conditions in the environment (except those under the control of the planner) will remain unchanged while he plans, and while he acts (except as a result of his acts). The assumption of systemic stasis is obviously incorrect and certain to be disproved eventually; but, in the absence of reliable and precise prediction, it is the most economical of assumptions to make, and the shorter the time period for which it is made the more likely it is to be acceptable. The policy analyst who seeks to construct contingent futures on this assumption would specify it by assuming (for instance) that some basic tension (as between Russia and America, Russia and China, the United States and France, or America and China) will persist through some future date (say, 1980) unless there is deliberate action directed at changing it. In this case, the problems of the future merge with the problems of the present; hence the analyst may suggest the rationality of long-term planning in the present for the future. At the present date, one might, for instance, assume the continuation of the Vietnam war for 5 years without truce, victory, or withdrawal. The future problem then (for the United States or any other interested state) would be identical with the present problem, while the present problem would be amplified by the need to adjust current policy to the long-war prospect, whether by preparing to exploit that prospect, to endure it, or to prevent it.

The second great assumption, *trend continuity*, seems to be associated with liberal and reformist attitudes today (as the first is rather more associated with conservative and administrative viewpoints). These associations are quite independent of the intellectual validity or utility of either assumption. Consequently, political-philo-sophical biases should not preclude using these assumptions for the construction of futuribles; nor should political prejudice operate to exclude the third assumption simply because it attracts extreme pessimists and political quietists, or the fourth because it marks chiliasts, prophets, dreamers, and utopian visionaries.

The trend-continuity assumption implies the projection into the immediate, definite, or indefinite future of a trend that is visual-ized as a graphed straight sloping line or increasingly sloping curve, thus:

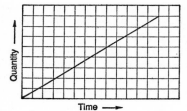 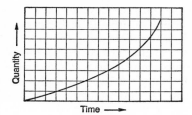

The most obvious such trend is shown on graphs of world and (some) national populations, or of *per capita* food production or *per capita* national income for certain nations. But other statistical trends are also of clear political interest: urbanization in underdevel-oped countries; difference in *per capita* national incomes as between northern and southern nations; rates of depletion of world natural resources; absolute economic growth of the United States and of various other states. Trend projection extends into the future the recent graphs of these statistics, or carries through the logical devel-opment of such less easily graphed trends as nuclear diffusion or increased cultural-economic unification of various regions and of the world. To project a trend into the immediate future (where a quanti-tative projection is least unreliable) is generally the first step in the analysis of what is taken to be a present problem. Long-term projec-tions, if less likely to be accurate, are generally more useful in their shock value: by demonstrating the incredible magnitude of a prob-lem in 30 years, they suggest the rationality of considering it as a problem today.

The third great assumption, the assumption of *probable re-currence*, declares that the future will be like the past and unlike the present; that events[15] that have occurred again and again in the past

---

[15] There may also be recurrent sequences: cycles of war and peace, of unipolar-ity and multipolarity in the world system; stages of economic, social, or political development of nations.

are to be anticipated in the future. A historically oriented theorist might then go on to contend that we must logically anticipate as highly probable futuribles such events as the decay and collapse as a great power of each of the great states of today; revolutions, in major powers and in small states, whose leaders threaten or intend to export such revolutions throughout a region or throughout the globe; sustained and intense efforts, on the part of one or another challenger-state, for world dominance; even more frequent struggles to dominate a regional subsystem by a rising power that will also struggle for subsystemic "independence," that is, for the isolation of its chosen sphere of dominance from the influence of external great powers; recurrent local wars, war crises, civil wars, and internal turbulence with external intervention; occasional general and unlimited war; and the possible end of the multistate political system entirely, through either cultural disintegration or global empire. The anticipator of problems would then leaf through this gloomy pile of prospects to see what symptoms of the occurrence of each could be found in the present and to conjecture about which actors are most likely to play which rolls. Those prospects with the strongest current indications he would pick out for close study. For example, he might write one or more scenarios of a future challenge by China for world dominance, based on examinations of China's present and potential ideology and capabilities and of the structure of previous challenges by other states. The anticipator would then consider these contingencies as future problems for certain states. At last he would return to his own state in the present, and ask what sort of policy might seek to prevent (or provoke), prepare against (or write off) these contingencies. He would then have moved from anticipatory analysis to problems analysis.

The fourth great assumption, the assumption of *historical surprise*, will require much more creative effort to carry it through. A sharp eye for ignored, minute trends or neglected and unobserved recurrences may inspire or substitute for creative imagination in this respect; even so, a certain originality of talent not demanded of the tillers of other fields is needed here. To assume historical surprise is to assume the probability of novelty in history; to predict a surprise, or, less demandingly, to anticipate types of surprise, is to predict some innovation that is likely to seem unexpected when it occurs. Perhaps the largest arena of modern innovation, and of politically relevant surprises, has been in science and technology, particularly as these have been applied to weapon systems and to national economies. To assume that surprising things will happen in these fields, and to attempt to reduce the confusing impact of innovation by anticipating it, is quite plausible though far from easy. Thus, analysis of the consequences of antiballistic missile systems was well under way in a period when the common opinion was that such systems were implausible. Similarly, the "fantasies" or dreams of scientists and strategists can provide some of the novelties whose political effects problems analysts work out in order to forestall or to utilize them. In a sense, only those surprises that would astonish the man in the street, but that are expected or even sought after by some groups of research workers, are proper raw material for a contingency analysis; a total surprise would be so improbable that no one would be likely to take an interest in analyzing its problematic aspects (except perhaps in science-fiction form). Limited surprises are, however, amenable to the analyses of those political specialists who have enough of a scientific or technological sense to see them as probabilities.

These four assumptions are, when each is relentlessly and exclusively pursued, all false. But they are all partially "true": if we were to take any period in the past we would certainly find that, over that period, some conditions had remained substantially as they were while others had continued changing in the direction in which they had been changing. We would surely find that some contingencies or crises that were novel for the period but precedented in history had arisen, side by side with others that were without close precedent, though similar in broad shape to prior surprises in history. If to follow one and only one of these assumptions while inspecting the future is simpler, it is also less likely to be fruitful than to make a projection that bears all four assumptions in mind, each as certain to be partially true and none wholly true of the future.

Nevertheless, the serious would-be forecaster may well constrain himself by only one such assumption as a training exercise. He may properly, in other words, use the assumption(s) least in tune with his temperament as a learning device, to limber his mind, to flex it until it loses its characteristic rigidity. But when he seriously examines the future, he will assume that there are "structural certainties," structural features of the present that can be transferred to the future as they stand, and he will examine the structure of the present and try to reason out what they are. He will assume that there are "foreknowns" or "dominating processes," strong and powerful tendencies, manifest in the present and out of human control, and he will examine the trends of today, try to reason out which show the greatest vigor and least masterability, and project these. His possible futures will have alternatives, they will branch at certain points, they will have room for contingencies, for possible crises foreseen less surely than certain structure and dominant process. Some of these possible crises he will make up from his knowledge of history and an assumption of recurrence, others from his knowledge of technology and an assumption of surprise, yet others from his inspection of current events and his intuition of the specific crises they suggest, foreshadow, and conceal.

Many will not have the flexibility of imagination needed to proceed on all four assumptions at once. This is one of the areas where group research into the future can provide semiautomatic correcting facilities for individual biases. For even if each member of such a group is only self-conscious enough to know which of the assumptions best fits his own character, he can pursue his speculations directed by that assumption alone; then if there are members reflecting each temperament and pursuing each of the four courses on the same topic, and then using their own speculations to converse with and to criticize those of contrary-minded others, and to order and to complete the whole work of the group, that group may in its output approximate the work of an individual more talented in this respect than any of its members, and will surely as a group excel the separated work of any or of all those members.

The scope of group research into future problems

Although a very large future-research team might actually try to follow out all these assumptions exhaustively, limited groups are probably best advised to restrict their speculations to the most likely and/or most consequential contingent futures, as seen from the viewpoint of a single state. The analysis might focus on a definite time (5 or 10 years in the future), or on a span of time (from the present to 10 years in the future), or on no definite period. The analysts would judge the most probable and consequential fixed relations, continuing trends, recurrent events, and novelties. They might try to turn these into one consistent most probable future, or several different but internally consistent contingent futures, or a mass of separate contingencies. They would then define the problems facing the state in question in this future or set of futures or contingencies, and subject them to problems analyses. From these studies of future problems they would at last refer back to the present, in order to consider what measures might be taken to forestall, prepare for, or precipitate such futures.

Simplicity would suggest that groups construct multiple contingencies (at least in their first attempt at systematic anticipation), and that these contingencies should be specific events rather than general conditions, even though most specific contingent events will be intended to illustrate a general condition. The specifics may be simple (for example, a sequence of internal troubles leading to revolt, civil war, and foreign intervention in a strategically vital state). A complex contingent sequence is generally called a *scenario,* and is presented in the form of a short narrative summary of fictional events, in which the whole sequence is possible and significant, while each event in the sequence plausibly follows from the ones before it. Again, it is no doubt simpler for analytic groups to begin with single contingencies and work up to more complex scenarios.

Some proposals of Saul Friedländer[16] about the appropriate scope of prediction of two-state or world-systemic relations of conflict

[16] "Forecasting in International Relations," in Bertrand de Jouvenel, ed., *Futuribles,* II (Geneva: Droz, 1965), pp. 1–112.

and coalition, and some other proposals of Feliks Gross[17] about prediction of foreign policy problems, may be useful guides to methods as well as to scope.

Friedländer contrasts short-term forecasting (up to 2 years) with long-term (10 to 15 years). For short-term forecasts, he proposes that analysts assume that power relations will remain constant, and concentrate their predictive attempts upon the actors' probable decisions (and interacting chains of decisions) about a given problem. We may infer from Friedländer's paper that the forecaster should then try to follow four instructions, in order:

1. Observe the situation, not as it "really" is, but through the eyes of each actor under observation.
2. Identify the aims of each actor, that is, the changes he wants to make in the international situation. Concentrate not on ultimate aims (semimythical desires) but on strategic aims (a limited number of relatively stable, often explicit, broad practical objectives).
3. Identify any distracting motives (personal and sectional interests) that may divert the actor's behavior from the channels of national interest as he sees them.
4. Identify the tactical aims of the actor, in the light of the means he sees available and the aspects of the situation which he believes subject to manipulation.

Friedländer would then have us decide what sorts of policy lines would be likely to emanate from a rational actor who feels that he faces *this* problem, who seeks *that* objective, and who thinks that he can choose from among *these* capabilities.

Gross's proposal is best considered in the light of Friedländer's. Gross proposes that the time-scope of forecasting foreign policy lines and decisions be very short term: this month, this year. For very short-term forecasting we need a working hypothesis about what the strategic objectives of a state are. (See steps 2 and 3 above.) Next, the immediate body of data available to us is examined, in the light of the hypothesis of objectives; we seek preparations, we seek a trend or general tendency of the acts of the state. We ask, given the stated strategic objectives: What already-made (but concealed) choices of tactical objectives do the preparations and actions suggest? In turn, examining a set of alternative tactical objectives inferred from strategic objectives and actual commitments, we ask for each one: When the preparations are finished, when the actions generate their logical next step, when the actor moves to satisfy his tactical objective, what kind of situation could be presented to us (to the state from whose viewpoint we observe these developments) as a challenge, threat, or opportunity—as a problem?

Returning from Gross's very short-term forecasts to Friedländer: the latter declares that long-term forecasts (10 to 15 years) should not consider the particular decisions of policymakers as lying

---

[17] *Foreign Policy Analysis* (New York: Philosophical Library, 1954), pp. 161–65.

within their scope. Long-term forecasting should restrict itself to anticipating changes in power relations. Furthermore, such forecasting should be avoided at times or in areas where the international system is judged "unstable," that is, subject to specific sudden chain reactions that will surprisingly and irreversibly alter the pattern of power (for example, nuclear wars). In stable areas, it is sufficient (1) to identify the probable independent and dominating processes (if any) that are altering the world distribution of power; (2) to assess the probable development of power relations as the result of the movements of those forces, and then (3), having identified the actors' strategic aims, to judge whether changing power relations will let them achieve these aims.

Both of Friedländer's methods (unlike Gross's) are somewhat constricted by his bias toward correct (therefore single) *prediction*. If one is satisfied with the anticipation of *alternative* futures, and of *contingent* crises, they may be more satisfactorily employed. It is clear that any attempts to write up alternative futures must center upon forecasts of capabilities and of the international power structure and its evolution, in just the manner of Friedländer's long-term forecasts. It is also clear that, to select the most plausible contingencies and scenarios, the short-term procedures of Friedländer and Gross ought to be employed as rigorously and concientiously as data and intuition will permit.

But we have already suggested that simple single-event contingencies are easiest to conceive. Consequently, a group is best advised to begin its work by seeking to create a list of relatively probable short-term contingencies, significant or critical, resulting from possible deliberate decisions by major actors. This list could be selected from a larger list, proposed offhand, if that list were then shortened in and by critical arguments, attacks, and defenses that adhere to Gross's and Friedländer's short-run criteria. The surviving contingencies would then be meat for problem analyses.

Organization and general procedure of research

The organization of groups speculating about the future ought to be loose, the responsibilities individual, the procedures dialectical, the sources broad and suggestive, and the products multiple and alternative. This is to say that, once the scope of the inquiry has been defined for the group, each member ought to go off on his own, and imaginatively and in solitude construct as much as he can of the contingent futures in question. He must spread the whole fan of possible futures, all that are conceivable, omitting none, until he has logically exhausted all prospects; then, assigning a subjective probability to each future, giving reasons why one is more likely and another less so, he must choose the most likely from the many possibles. He will construct these futures by processes of probabilistic reasoning from the given starting point and within the given limits, as if he were writing a piece of fiction, but fiction intended to give the impression that it is fact. If he is writing a complex sequential scenario, he should fill the gaps in his narratives of events by asking, "What is the most probable next event?" or even by treating his fiction as if it were fact and asking "What must have happened here? What *did* happen?"[18]

Let each researcher then return to the group with a single future or a set of futures, in reasonable detail, to distribute, expound, and defend. The proper procedure for resolving these many futures into one or a few alternatives is dialectical, a discussion. One member will present a future; others will criticize that future on the grounds that it is vague, improbable as a whole or in its connections. A vague projection has too little concreteness, specificity, and detail to convince its critics that they know what the author is trying to say; he must clarify by painting the picture further. A future attacked as improbable must be defended, or replaced by one that convinces the critics that it is probable; argument here requires the defender to show, by a concrete chain of events and decisions, each of which his hearers must admit to be probable in itself, that this future can be directly and economically constructed from an agreed description of the present. An attack on specific events and connections as improbable can be met by a similar reconstruction of the chain from here to there, or by showing present trends that point in that very direction or frequent past events of the same genre.

All this reasoning is probabilistic, and the opposite of mathematically rigorous (though it may display a rigor of its own). It is therefore more appropriate that the research group construct a number of alternative futures, all admittedly possible, than that it attempt to forecast one and only one most probable future. Each of the possible futures may then be subjected to a problem analysis of the type described in the preceding chapter.

Conclusion

It is important for foreign policy analysts anticipating the future to prepare forecasts that can be inputs to a problem analysis. Since a problem must be analyzed from a state's point of view, it is important for the analysts to choose a viewpoint, American or foreign, and a scope, dyadic or world-wide, very short-run, short-run, or long-run. They will find models and sources for their labors in very current work. They can speed their analysis by operating on certain broad assumptions about the contents of the future, and improve it by organizing loosely as a mutually correcting research group. And they

[18] When the immediate resources of his own imagination are exhausted, he ought to turn to the limited but intriguing literature on the subject; see the references to this chapter.

must know that there is no time like the present to analyze the future.

References

Bell, Daniel, "Twelve Modes of Prediction." *Daedalus*, 93, no. 3 (1964), pp. 845–880. An essay on method.

Daedalus, 96, no. 3 (1967), "Toward the Year 2000." Working papers of the Commission on the year 2000; contains, among others, speculations on the future of the international system by Herman Kahn and Anthony J. Wiener, Eugene V. Rostow, Samuel P. Huntington, and Ithiel de Sola Pool.

Friedländer, Saul, "Forecasting in International Relations," in *Futuribles*, II (1965), pp. 1–112. An essential essay.

Futuribles, ed. Bertrand de Jouvenel. Geneva: Droz, vol. I, 1963; vol. II, 1965. Contain projections of the future domestic politics of Britain, Pakistan, Black Africa, Burma.

Futuribles. French-language serial supplements to the Bulletin SEDEIS (205 Boulevard Saint-Germain, Paris 7°).

The Futurist. Newsletter of the World Future Society (5501 Lincoln St., Bethesda, Maryland).

Gross, Feliks, *Foreign Policy Analysis*. New York: Philosophical Library, 1954.

de Jouvenel, Bertrand, *The Art of Conjecture*. New York: Basic Books, 1967. A handbook on method: see especially parts II and III and chapter 18.

Kahn, Herman, "The Alternative World Futures Approach," in Morton A. Kaplan, ed., *New Approaches to International Relations*. New York: St. Martin's, 1968, pp. 83–136.

———, *Thinking About the Unthinkable*. New York: Avon, 1962, chapter 8.

——— and Anthony J. Wiener, *The Year 2000*. New York: Macmillan, 1967.

Organski, A. F. K., *World Politics*. 2d ed., New York: Knopf, 1968.

The student in pursuit of an understanding of United States foreign policy already has more source material than he wants and is faced with the problem of data organization; the student of the foreign policy of other states probably has too little, and is faced with the problem of data collection. The following is a guide to the most methodical and rational procedure evident to the author for assembling in order the data relevant to (1) describing the foreign policy of any state; (2) isolating and analyzing the problems of its foreign policy; (3) surveying its capabilities and domestic structure to explain its past and present policy. This procedural guide precedes and is keyed to a list of sources intended to be of use to students of comparative foreign relations who intend to set about research on their own.

The list of sources is arranged into twelve categories.

  I. Guides to source materials
  II. Bibliographies
  III. Periodical indices and abstracts
  IV. General periodicals
  V. Area and specialized periodicals
  VI. Newspapers and mass media
  VII. Periodic descriptive surveys
  VIII. Economic and social statistics
  IX. Military capabilities
  X. Official emanations of national policy

XI. China
XII. Certain technical materials

Procedures

The following schedule of procedures might well be followed by researchers engaged in data-gleaning.

1. Describing foreign policy
   a. Procure official statements. [IVA, B, C; XA, B, C (China: XIA)]
   b. Acquire hostile and third-party official descriptions. [Same sources as 1a above]
   c. Secure recent and current academic and unofficial descriptions.
      (1) *Books.* [IIA, then IIB; then if necessary IIC, D, E; and IA, B, C, D]
      (2) *Older, indexed articles.* [IIIA, B, C (China: XIB)]
      (3) *Newer, not yet indexed articles.* [IVD; relevant section of V]
   d. Gather journalistic and polemic descriptions. [IVF, G]
   e. Seek to clarify and/or settle arguments among the above sources by obtaining information on the actual physical behavior, the acts or operations or performances of the state from:
      (1) *News media of global coverage.* [IVE; VIA, B, C]
      (2) *Locally active media.* [VID, E, F, G]
      (3) *Briefer post facto surveys.* [VIIA, B]
   f. Judge and synthesize description, as in Chapter 1.
2. Isolating and analyzing problems of foreign policy.
   a. Collect problem analyses and policy proposals from the nation's domestic press. [VIG. (United States IIIA; IVA, E, F, G; VIA, B, C)]
   b. If this material is too thin or too biased, collect background material, problem analyses, and reported policy proposals from:
      (1) *The Western press.* [IIIA; IVE, F, G; VIA, B, C]
      (2) *Academic and other analysts.* [Same as 1c above]
   c. Structure the problem analysis, as in Chapter 8.
3. Explaining foreign policy.
   a. From capabilities. [Economic, VIII (China: XID); military, IX, also IIID and VA]. Use this information, and the procedures presented at the end of Chapter 3.
   b. From will/prescription. [IIA, B, C, D for histories of policy; same plus IIIA, IVE, F, G, relevant section of V, and VIA, B, C for special qualities of current leadership, biographies (for which see XIIC also), and so on; IVA, B, C, XA, B, XIA for material for content analyses. Also XIIB for methods of psy-

chometry, XIIA for methods of content analysis (both requiring substantial further development)].

c. From political culture. Refer to Chapter 5 for relevant material (mostly in need of creation through field research in political socialization, attitudes and opinions, and so forth).

d. From political institutions and processes. Refer to Chapters 6 and 7 for relevant material. [Update from VIIA, B, C, and VIIIA, B; more recently from IIIA, B, C, IVD, F, and relevant V; yet more recently from IVE, G, and VIA, B, C].

Note that these procedures merely provide an ordered set of references to be consulted and contemplated. The preceding chapters supply questions to be asked of these sources. No procedure is available, regrettably, for the attainment of inspiration and insight and their synthesis into a logically coherent vision.

Sources

I. Guides to source materials

A. Boehm, Eric H., ed., *Bibliographies on International Relations and World Affairs: An Annotated Directory.* Santa Barbara: Clio Press, 1965.

B. Zawodny, J. K., *Guide to the Study of International Relations.* San Francisco: Chandler, 1966.

C. Mason, John Brown, *International Relations and Recent History: Indexes, Abstracts and Periodicals.* (Vol. 1 of *Research Resources: Annotated Guide to the Social Sciences.*) Santa Barbara: Clio Press, 1968.

D. U.S. Library of Congress, General Reference and Bibliography Division, *A Guide to Bibliographic Tools for Research in Foreign Affairs.* 2d ed., 1958.

II. Bibliographies

A. *The Statesman's Year Book* (annual). Contains lists of the most recent reference works concerning each country, and is a most useful starting point for the student about to begin putting a country bibliography together.

Subject Guide to Books in Print, U.S.A. Contains recent books, under headings (for example, "China-Foreign Relations").

B. Roberts, Henry L., *et al., Foreign Affairs Bibliography: A Selected and Annotated List of Books on International Relations, 1952–1962.* New York: Bowker, 1964. Fourth in a series of selective bibliographies that together span the years 1919–62. More recent material is to be found in the quarterly journal *Foreign Affairs.* Both the bound volumes and the periodicals have useful notes on each of the books listed.

C. **Bibliographical sections of periodicals**
International Organization.
American Political Science Review.

D. *Bulletin Analytique de Documentation Politique, Economique et Sociale Contemporaire.*
International Bibliography of Political Science.
Select Bibliography—Asia, Africa, Eastern Europe, Latin America.

E. *A London Bibliography of the Social Sciences.*

III. Periodical indices and abstracts

A. **General periodicals**
Readers' Guide to Periodical Literature.
IBZ, International Bibliography of Periodical Literature (Internationale Bibliographie der Zeitschriften Literatur).

B. **Scholarly periodicals:** *Social Sciences and Humanities Index.*

C. **Political science periodicals and articles:** *International Political Science Abstracts.*

D. **Military periodicals and materials**
Air University Index to Military Periodicals.
Bulletin of the Public Affairs Information Service.
Index to Selected Publications of the RAND Corporation.
Selected RAND Abstracts.

IV. General periodicals (of fact, opinion, opinion presented as fact, and so on)

Students of the policy of a country may wish to secure news and other reports more current than those presented in the delayed periodical indices. General periodicals are generally most relevant for this purpose, though scarcely reliable. (See also current issues of the newspapers and so forth mentioned in section VI below.) The following are useful enough once their manifest biases are discounted.

A. **U.S. official**
Department of State Bulletin. Statement of U.S. policy lines.
Vital Speeches. Important U.S. rhetoric.

B. **U.S.S.R. official**
New Times. Moscow.
International Affairs. Moscow.
The Current Digest of the Soviet Press.

C. **China official**
Peking Review.

D. **U.S. and foreign academic to semiofficial-semiacademic**
Foreign Affairs. Close to U.S. government.

Current History.

Orbis.

The World Today. London.

International Affairs. London.

International Journal. Toronto.

Review of International Affairs. Belgrade.

Aussenpolitik. Stuttgart.

E. **Newsmagazines, U.S. and foreign**

The Economist. London. Astute, brief.

Newsweek. U.S., moderate-to-liberal.

Time. Close to U.S. political figures. Much anonymous opinion.

U.S. News and World Report. U.S., moderate-to-conservative; many extensive and useful interviews.

L'Express. Paris.

Manchester Guardian Weekly.

F. **U.S. and British journals of comment**

Atlantic.

Commentary.

Encounter.

Harper's.

New Statesman. London.

Spectator. London.

New York Times Magazine.

New Yorker.

G. **U.S. political journals**

National Review. Various shades of "right."

New Leader. Right socialist.

Bulletin of the Atomic Scientists.

Nation. One measured pace to the left of middle.

New Republic. Ditto.

I. F. Stone's Weekly.

Ramparts.

The Minority of One.

Monthly Review. Astute but Marxist-Leninist country analyses.

V. Area and specialized periodicals, scholarly and otherwise

The following contain occasional to frequent articles, analyses, information, documentation, and so on relevant to foreign relations.

A. **Military**

Institute for Strategic Studies, London, *Adelphi Papers.*

————, *The Military Balance*. Indispensable.

————, *Strategic Survey*. Indispensable.

————, *Survival*. Excellent.

Journal of the Royal United Services Institution. London. Very good.

Revue de Defense nationale. Paris. Very good.

Wehrwissenschaftliche Rundschau. Frankfurt.

Soviet Military Review. Moscow.

Proceedings of the U.S. Naval Institute. Useful.

Military Review. Fort Leavenworth. Useful.

Infantry. Fort Benning. Tactics.

Armor.

Army.

Navy.

Air Force and Space Digest.

Air University Quarterly. Perhaps the least parochial of the very narrow U.S. Air Force publications.

Air Power.

Aviation Weekly.

See also: *Bulletin of the Atomic Scientists; Political Quarterly* (articles by Michael Howard especially); *Foreign Affairs; International Organization; Journal of Conflict Resolution; Orbis.*

B. Western Hemisphere

Inter-American Economic Affairs.

Journal of Inter-American Studies.

United Nations, Economic Commission for Latin America; various publications: annual *Report; Economic Survey of Latin America; Economic Bulletin for Latin America; Statistical Bulletin;* series on coffee, textiles, livestock, hydrology, machine building, and so on.

Pan American Union, Alliance for Progress, Committee of Nine; various evaluation studies of economic development plans.

————, *Alliance for Progress Weekly Newsletter.*

————, *Catalog of Publications of the Pan American Union.*

Hispanic-American Historical Review.

The Economist. London. (Latin American edition, in Spanish.)

Politica. Caracas.

Combate. Instituto Internacional de Estudios Politico-Sociales, San Jose, Costa Rica.

Cuadernos. Paris.

Cuadernos Americanos. Mexico.

Dados. Rio de Janeiro.

Granma. Havana.

Panorama economico latinoamericano. Havana.

Politica internacional. Havana.
Monthly Review.

C. **Atlantic area**
The Atlantic Community Quarterly.
Interplay.
Foreign Affairs.
Survey.
Orbis.
The World Today. London.
International Affairs. London.
Agenor. Brussels.
Chronique de politique étrangère. Brussels.
Revue du marche commun. Paris.
Aussenpolitik. Stuttgart.
Europa Archiv. Bonn.
Relazioni internazionali. Rome.
Lo spettatore internazionale. Rome. English supplement.
Revista de politica internacional. Madrid.

D. **Russia and East Europe**
Survey.
Problems of Communism.
East Europe.
Slavic Review.
Communist Affairs.
Foreign Affairs.
Orbis.
Est et Ouest. Paris.
Ost-Europa.
Europa-Archiv.

E. **Asia**
Journal of Asian Studies. Annual comprehensive bibliography.
Asian Survey.
Pacific Affairs. University of British Columbia.
Far Eastern Economic Review. Hong Kong.
Eastern World. London.
Asian Recorder.
Asia.
Australian Outlook. Sydney-Melbourne.
The Australian Quarterly. Sydney.
Australia, Department of External Affairs, *Current Notes on International Affairs.*

World Review. Queensland.
1. Japan
   Japan Quarterly. Tokyo.
   Contemporary Japan. Tokyo.
   Japanese Consulate, *Japan Report*. New York.
2. China: see XI below.
3. Southeast Asia
   Journal of Southeast Asian History.
   Viet-Report.
   Vietnam Perspectives.
4. South Asia
   Indian Embassy, *Weekly India News*. Washington, D.C.
   The Hindu Weekly Review. Madras.
   International Studies. New Delhi.
   India Quarterly. New Delhi.
   Pakistan Horizon. Karachi.
   Southern Asia Social Science Bibliography.

F. Middle East
   Middle East Journal. Contains bibliography.
   Middle Eastern Studies. London.
   New Outlook. Tel Aviv.
   U.S. Joint Publications Research Service, *Translations on the Middle East*.
   Maghreb Digest.
   Orient. Paris.
   Oriente moderno. Rome.

G. Africa
   Africa Report.
   Africa Today.
   African Forum.
   African Recorder.
   U.S. Joint Publications Research Service, *Translations on Africa*.
   West Africa. London
   Africa. Paris. English-language.
   African Digest. London.
   Journal of Modern African Studies.
   The New African. London.
   Africa Quarterly. New Delhi.
   Le mois en Afrique. Paris.
   Perspective Africaine. Paris.
   Problèmes Africaines. Brussels.

Transition. Kampala.

Africa Diary. New Delhi.

VI. Newspapers and mass media:
indices; translations

A. *The New York Times* and *Le Monde* (Paris) are the most comprehensive sources available on the day-to-day, month-to-month evolution of foreign affairs, and of the foreign relations of their own
countries and the states to which they give special coverage at any
time. *The Christian Science Monitor,* and less frequently *The Wall
Street Journal* and *The Times* (London), have excellent analytical
articles.

B. All the above newspapers are, fortunately, indexed, under the following heads.
   The New York Times Index. This is in itself a major reference
   work and summary of (among other things) international political transactions, organized by country and by subject, because the
   major news items are abstracted herein.
   Index Analytique. Le Monde. Paris.
   The Christian Science Monitor Index. Corvallis. Oregon.
   The Wall Street Journal Index. New York. "General News" section
   only.
   Index to the Times. London.

C. Other major newspapers—for example (U.S.), *The Baltimore Sun,
The Washington Post, The Los Angeles Times;* (foreign) *The
Guardian* (London), *The Observer* (London), *The Sunday Times*
(London), *The Times of India* (Bombay), *Le Figaro* (Paris), *Die
Zeit* (Hamburg), *Neue Zürcher Zeitung* (Zurich), *Frankfurter
Allgemeine Zeitung* (Frankfurt am Main), *Dagens Nyheter*
(Stockholm), *Aftonbladet* (Oslo), *Politiken* (Copenhagen), *Borba*
(Belgrade), *ABC* (Madrid), *L'osservatore Romano* (Vatican City),
Asahi Shimbun (Tokyo), *La Prensa* (Buenos Aires)—are un-
fortunately not indexed, but may be scanned currently with profit.

D. The Russian newspapers *Pravda* and *Izvestia* are indexed weekly,
and some articles abstracted or translated, in *The Current Digest
of the Soviet Press* (New York).

E. Major items for foreign consumption are presented in an official
English-language organ of the (Communist) Chinese government: *Peking Review.* See also XIA.

F. A voluminous collection of current perspectives (reflecting policy)
in the state-controlled mass media of the Communist countries is
published by the United States Central Intelligence Agency, *Daily
report, foreign radio broadcasts.* This may be supplemented by the
translations of foreign periodicals presented in United States Joint
Publications Research Service, *JPRS Series* (mostly Communist-
bloc; extensive) and in *Atlas* (worldwide coverage, but very selective).

G. The domestic press of a country is usually of use in determining what are seen to be the policy problems of the day, and what the alternatives under debate are. Data on the worldwide press may be compiled from the following sources:

Editor and Publisher International Yearbook. Names of newspapers.

Merrill, John C., *The Elite Press.* New York: Putnam, 1968. The most important newspapers.

Merrill, John C., *et al., The Foreign Press.* Baton Rouge: Louisiana State University Press, 1964. Political leanings of and influences upon the foreign press.

Newspapers on Microfilm. 1963. Information regarding circa 4000 microfilmed foreign newspapers.

Political Handbook of the World. Names and political leanings.

Willing's Press Guide. Names and addresses.

VII. Periodic descriptive surveys of events and countries

A. **Weeklies**

Keesing's Contemporary Archives. London. Well-indexed weekly survey of world events.

Facts on File. Weekly news digest.

B. **Annual surveys of events**

The United States in World Affairs. New York. Review of world events and U.S. foreign policy, with bibliography.

The Annual Register of World Events. Very useful for succinct summary of each country's foreign relations.

The New International Yearbook.

C. **Annual country descriptions**

Statesman's Year Book. London. Indispensable annual descriptive summary of conditions in each country.

Europa Yearbook. London. Names and offices of governmental personnel.

VIII. Economic and social statistics

A. *The International Yearbook and Statesman's Who's Who.*

Europa Yearbook. Statistical summary, country by country.

Statesman's Year Book. Extensive statistical survey, country by country.

B. United Nations Statistical office, *Monthly Bulletin of Statistics.*

———, *Statistical Year Book.* Demographic, economic, social, and cultural statistics presented in comparative tables. Many of the most interesting are withheld by Communist countries: see D below, and XID.

C. *Bulletin of the Public Affairs Information Service.* A periodical index. Entries under "Economic conditions," "Production," "Government appropriations."

D. United States Congress, Joint Economic Committee, frequent statistics for the Soviet economy (missing from U.N. *Statistical Year Book*). Titles and frequency of issue vary; for example:
Comparisons of the U.S. and Soviet Economies. 1960.
Dimensions of Soviet Economic Power. 1962.
Annual Economic Indicators for the USSR. 1964.
Current Economic Indicators for the USSR. 1965.
Starting in 1966, these statistics have come from the joint committee's subcommittee on foreign economic policy:
New Directions in the Soviet Economy. 1966.
Soviet Economic Performance: 1966–67. 1968.

IX. Military capabilities

A. *Statesman's Year Book.* Good summaries and estimates.

B. Institute for Strategic Studies (London), *Strategic Survey.* Annual description and analysis of strategic policy, doctrine, and weapons in the main powers and world regions.
———, *The Military Balance.* Annual quantitative comparison of military forces and expenditures of major, secondary, and tertiary military powers.

C. *Bulletin of the Public Affairs Information Service.* Entries under "Armaments," "Armed Forces."

D. Statements of U.S. Department of Defense witnesses before the House and Senate Armed Services and Appropriations committees.

X. Official emanations of national policy

A. Official statements of the current policy of each country are normally best obtained by mail. Address the nation's embassy in Washington; if the United States has no diplomatic relations, address the Mission to the United Nations, New York; if the country is not a U.N. member, address the nation's embassy, consulate, mission, "trade mission," or such like, in some country with which it has relations, for example, Britain, France, India, the USSR.; or the Foreign Office of the country itself. Addresses in *Europa Yearbook, International Yearbook,* or *Statesman's Year Book.*

B. Annual statements of general attitudes are provided (appropriately) in the General Debate at the U.N. General Assembly; and the postures of states in specific controversies are frequently illuminated by their talk and voting in U.N. organs. See especially:
United Nations General Assembly, *Official Records.*
United Nations Library, *Index to Proceedings of the General Assembly.* Annual. Contains a country-index to speeches.

C. See also government-published testimony, debates, and reports of the national legislature and its committees, e.g., U.S. Senate Foreign Relations Committee Hearings, including executive statements.

XI. China

Communist China presents a special problem to American students (among others) due to (1) lack of U.S. diplomatic relations; (2) abscence from the United Nations; (3) state-controlled press; (4) more than usual secretiveness and/or boastfulness in regard to capability data; (5) multiple controls over resident foreign observers; (6) cultural gap; (7) ideological peculiarities; (8) conflicts of policy with most foreign states; (9) Aesopian language; (10) internal chaos and confusion of Great Proletarian Cultural Revolution; (11) larger than usual difference between talk and action. Nonetheless, some sources are available.

A. **Primary material**

Peking Review. Officially selected English-language articles for external consumption.

Hsinhua News Agency, *Selected Hsinhua news items*. Weekly official selections.

———, *Daily news release*. Daily, less selective.

U.S. Central Intelligence Agency, *Daily report, foreign radio broadcasts*.

U.S. Embassy, Taipei, *Translations from the Chinese Press*.

U.S. Joint Publications Research Service, *JPRS-CA: China and Asia*. Selected translations.

U.S. Consulate General, Hong Kong, *Survey of China Mainland Press*.

———, *Selections from China Mainland Magazines*.

B. **Secondary material, and indices to the last three above**

U.S. Consulate General, Hong Kong, *Current Background*.

———, *Index to Survey of China Mainland Press, Extracts from China Mainland Magazines, and Current Background*.

U.S. Information Service, Hong Kong, *Current Scene*.

U.S. Joint Publications Research Service, *China and Asian Developments: a bibliography*.

Contemporary China. Hong Kong.

China News Analysis. Hong Kong.

Union Research Institute, Kowloon, Hong Kong, *Union Research Service*.

———, *Communist China*.

C. **See VE above for periodicals on Asia as a whole, including China; also:**

The China Quarterly. London.

Asian Survey.

Problems of Communism.

The China Mainland Review. Hong Kong.

Issues and Studies. Taipei.

D. **The Chinese economy**

U.S. Congress, Joint Economic Committee, *An Economic Profile of Mainland China.* 2 vols., 1967.

Eckstein, Alexander, *Communist China's Economic Growth and Foreign Trade.* New York: McGraw-Hill, 1966.

XII. Certain technical materials

A. North, Robert C., *et al.*, *Content Analysis.* Evanston, Ill.: Northwestern University Press, 1963. Bibliography.

"Content Analysis," *International Encyclopedia of the Social Sciences.* Includes bibliography.

Material on content analysis in IIIB, C above.

B. Cattell, Raymond B., *The Scientific Analysis of Personality.* Baltimore: Penguin, 1966. Chapter bibliographies.

"Personality measurement" and "Psychometrics," *International Encyclopedia of the Social Sciences.* Includes bibliographies.

Material on psychometry in IIIB above.

C. *Current Biography.* Short biographies of leading persons.

Biography Index. Index to biographical material in books and magazines.

Index

DUE DATE

MAR 1 2 '93			
MAY 1 5 1996			
	201-6503		Printed in USA